Enactments

EDITED BY CAROL MARTIN AND RICHARD SCHECHNER

To perform is to imagine, represent, live and enact present circumstances, past events and future possibilities. Performance takes place across a very broad range of venues from city streets to the countryside, in theatres and in offices, on battlefields and in hospital operating rooms. The genres of performance are many, from the arts to the myriad performances of everyday life, from courtrooms to legislative chambers, from theatres to wars to circuses.

ENACTMENTS will encompass performance in as many of its aspects and realities as there are authors able to write about them.

ENACTMENTS will include active scholarship, readable thought and engaged analysis across the broad spectrum of performance studies.

GLOBAL FOREiGNERS

AN ANTHOLOGY OF PLAYS

edited by carol martin and saviana stanescu

LONDON NEW YORK CALCUTTA

Seagull Books

Editorial offices:

1st Floor, Angel Court, 81 St Clements Street,
Oxford OX4 1AW, UK

1 Washington Square Village, Apt 1U, New
York, NY 10012, USA

26 Circus Avenue, Calcutta 700 017, India

© This compilation Seagull Books 2006

ISBN 1 9054 2 242 3

British Library
Cataloguing-in-Publication Data
A catalogue record for this book is available
from the British Library

Typeset by Seagull Books, India.
Printed in the United Kingdom by
Biddles Ltd, King's Lynn.

For

Carl Martin,

Cornel Stanescu,

Jean Filloux,

Rachel and Haim Dviri,

Najla Ghannam and Badia Shamieh,

Paul Walker and Lyn Austin.

For

Carl Martin,

Cornel Stanescu,

Jean Filloux,

Rachel and Haim Dviri,

Najla Ghannam and Badia Shamieh,

Paul Walker and Lyn Austin.

CONTENTS

HOME UNKNOWN, WORLD WAITING: CAROL MARTIN

Then have them make a sanctuary for me, and I will dwell among them.
                                                            Exodus 25.8.

The movement of the world's peoples away from a singular geographic and cultural identity informs the writing of the plays in this anthology. Saviana Stanescu was born in Romania. Catherine Filloux's first language is French. Zohar Tzur was born in Israel. Betty Shamieh's parents emigrated to the US from Palestine. Chiori Miyagawa was born in Japan where she lived the first 15 years of her life. All are writing in English and some in other languages as well and all have lived in the US—once a reputed paradise for immigrants—for different periods of time. There is no single home for any of these writers. This is not homelessness in the sense of having no home, but in the sense of having many political and cultural homes. The diversity of these playwrights' experience is the diversity wrought by globalization.

Foreignness is geographic relocation and the state of mind that goes with it; one's perceptions are not shared, history is not known and future is uncertain. Long-held values and beliefs are set against new ones, creating disjunctions between psychic reality and physical place. The sense of being "outside" or "apart from" is multiplied and intensified by war, genocide, poverty, oppression, totalitarian regimes, collective trauma and personal loss. In other words, globalization has created a new form of exile. The plays in this anthology portray Romanians, Cambodians, Israelis, Palestinians and Japanese struggling to locate themselves politically and personally (in all except one play) while living in the US. The playwrights are working through questions of "foreignness," a question no longer solely about being an émigré or an immigrant but now also about the state of multiple identifications as well as dislocation.

The flow of linear stage realism cannot capture this complex reality. The theatricality of time, place and character motivation cannot always be literally reconciled. The playwrights employ theatre as its own reality; a reality more akin to the way the mind and emotions work. In these plays, the past and present are not so much points on a continuum as indicators of what Wendy Hesford calls "the historically, socially, and rhetorically mediated character of memory."[1] The multilayered flow of time and place follows the contours of large political events that shape the experiences of individual protagonists.

II

In Saviana Stanescu's *Waxing West*, ghosts of the executed Romanian dictator Nicolae Ceausescu and his wife, Elena, haunt the protagonist Daniela's new life in the US. As Daniela conforms to the demands of her American marriage made out of financial necessity, Ceausescu and Elena materialize again and again, pronouncing her a failure. Even though she is in America, Daniela cannot stop being Romanian. In fact, being Romanian seems like a terminal, and perhaps contagious, disease—until September 11, 2001 when Daniela's new world is suddenly in the throes of chaos and thus remarkably like the Romania she left in the middle of the revolution. The past's claim on the present is not limited by boundaries of nationality or ethnicity. Bucharest or New York, Daniela experiences her life as the same in both cities. At the end of the play, acknowledging the death of her husband who perished in the collective transnational trauma of the Trade Towers, Daniela says, "Pain speaks all languages." Stanescu's *Waxing West* suggests that recognition of an "other" is much more complicated in a world of global experiences and affiliations. Stanescu also ironically mocks and exploits the cliché that Romania is the home of vampires. Her Romanian immigrant heroine cannot shake this Romanian stereotype. In a variation of Bram Stoker's *Dracula* where the undead Count migrates to England, the vampire ghosts of Ceausescu and Elena move to America along with Daniela. What do people in the

West know of these dictators? Stanescu represents their story in *Waxing West* as a parody of popular American notions of Romania and its vampires. The Ceausescu-Elena vampires want to suck blood just as in life they sucked the Romanian people of money and freedom. The vampire dictators appear suddenly to haunt Daniela with ridiculous dreams that fuse her personal trauma of identity and dislocation with the Ceausescus' history of political oppression and corruption.

Daniela also struggles with what Hesford identifies as "consumptive models of identification [that] dominate the U.S. media . . ." (105). The self is as subject to obsolescence as any other product. Surrounded by self-help books, Daniela takes notes of the main ideas proffered by an industry that makes personhood into a commodity in need of constant updating. "Choose Your Tomorrow: BEFORE—perfectionistic, misunderstood, love junkie, over-reactive, self-effacing. AFTER—flexible, good communicator, self-accepting, in control, assertive." After pondering over the books she's been reading—*I'm Dysfunctional, You're Dysfunctional*; *Men Are from Earth, Women Are from Earth*; *What To Do When He Has a Headache*; *Let's Get Rational Game*; *Dating, Mating and Relating*; and *Fitness for Your Body and Soul*—Daniela concludes, "Those AFTER people! They must be so happy."

Happiness eludes Daniela because she cannot grasp what being present at two epic events—the execution of Ceausescu and Elena signalling the end of communism in Romania and the destruction of the World Trade Towers—means for her life. Daniela wonders if the crashing Trade Towers signals the end of American capitalism just as the killing of the Ceausescus marked the end of Romanian communism.

Faced with the contradiction between these world-changing possibilities and the fact that she is trapped in a dead-end immigrant cosmetic "career" of waxing women's legs and muffs, Daniela wonders what she is doing helping woman live out their obsession with personal "improvement." Is it worth it in order to make a living? Or would she be better off ending up like her friend Uros, the homeless, one-legged, literary Muslim Yugoslavian, seeking a one-way ticket to Iraq? The last image of the play is one New Yorkers remember all too well: as Daniela looks for her husband, not knowing if he died in the

Trade Towers or survived, she represents him to others, alternating between describing his appearance and telling anyone who will listen what he meant to her. Finally, her husband Charlie's existence, and by implication ours as well, is condensed into a photo, a snapshot of a moment, already and forever gone. By this moment in the play, everything else in Daniela's world is unspeakable and unknowable. We don't even know if she really loves Charlie. Refusing closure and resolution, Stanescu avoids universalizing her narrative and leaves us with uncertainty.

Stories come in all complexions and so do their listeners. Catherine Filloux's *Eyes of the Heart* is based on the Cambodian refugees' oral histories she collected at St Rita's Refugee Center in New York City over a period of five years. Filloux personalizes the atrocities committed by the Khmer Rouge through Thida San, a Cambodian woman who cannot rid herself of the horrific memory of witnessing her daughter Oun's execution. Oun is one victim among the 1.7 million slaughtered during the Khmer Rouge's reign of terror from 1975 to 1979. Nothing is wrong with Thida San's eyes but she is blind.

Filloux was drawn to telling a story about psychosomatic blindness among Cambodian refugees after reading a series of articles about Cambodian women living in Long Beach, California, all of whom were both victims of and witnesses to the holocaust perpetrated by the Khmer Rouge. Filloux's protagonist San is one of these women. Thida flees from Cambodia to the home of her brother, Kim, in Long Beach—but her geographic journey is nowhere near the distance of the journey her soul makes. Upon arriving at her brother's welcoming family, she does not speak, she cannot see. One disability is thrust on Thida San, the other she chooses. With the two, she attempts to shut out the world. *Eyes of the Heart* moves between past and present, depicting Thida San's internal state of traumatic memory. In her essay about memory, theatre and politics Hesford says of Filloux's work:

> The play depicts the recursive nature of trauma by shifting
> between scenes from the past and the play's present (the
> 1980s), by presenting a sequence of flashbacks that lead to

Thida's revelation of what happened to her daughter, and
by giving the audience (though not the characters onstage)
access to Thida's internal thoughts (112).

Two incommensurable realities press simultaneously on Thida's mind. She is physically present but her psyche has been terrorized and occupied—it is there that a war continues to rage.

Lynn Simpson, Thida's medical doctor, soon learns that the order, analysis and diagnosis of ordinary medicine have no meaning in the floating retinal world of psychosomatic blindness. Yet Thida is capable of incisive observations: she notes that her doctor never has any time. But Thida's meaning of "time" is worlds away from Dr Simpson's. The doctor's realm of conclusions and means to ends is light years from the dark interiority of Thida's memories. And yet, even amidst this blocked communication, the relationship between Dr Simpson and Thida San deepens. Even as they work to find a shared place, Dr Simpson will continue to use her Western medicine and Thida San will never see. Hesford points out that the metaphors in *Eyes of the Heart* align seeing and witnessing.

The reference to "eyes of the heart" is taken from the
Biblical Epistle to the Ephesians, in which Paul exhorts
believers to remain faithful and to see not only with their
minds, but also with their hearts [. . .] Layers of witnessing
are at work in the play. (117)

Thida is forever in the world of the screen of her memory. It's when she begins to move her vision into the realm of witnessing where others are also allowed to witness her pain that her healing begins. The others are needed to turn Thida's experience into testimony (117).

Filloux asks her audiences to give Thida no less than total compassion. In order for them to achieve this, they have to suspend Western assumptions about knowing, perceiving and witnessing. In terms of its effects on people, globalization requires that individuals are faced with the unknown and the unexpected that determine their daily experiences. What people feel and know is more than what they can "see" in Filloux's sense of seeing. Everyone displaced by globalization in any of its many guises—wars, rapid economic changes, migrations—becomes Thida San in some way.

The fluidity of time and place in Zohar Tzur's *My Political Israeli Play* elides memory, reliable or not, with personal and political history. The play's protagonist, Miriam Bloom, a young Israeli playwright living in the US, is haunted by two memories: one of Mina, who joined The Minsk Daughters of Zion before immigrating from Russia to Israel and the other, of Yoni, a young man shot by a sniper on his last patrol for the Israeli Defense Forces (IDF). The play is Tzur's answer to repeatedly being asked to write a political play when she was studying dramatic writing at the Tisch School of the Arts' Dramatic Writing Department.

My Political Israeli Play opens with Miriam and Yoni, her lover, patrolling a checkpoint for the IDF.[2] The drama's eight scenes rapidly move between the US and Israel and between Miriam's present and past. Tzur simultaneously produces and parodies the tensions between the entertainment and political values of theatre. In Scene 2, after seeing a portion of Miriam's (more or less ridiculous) play, her agent Chaz proclaims the work a great metaphor for Palestinian and Israeli relations. "I find the representation of the Palestinian side absolutely fascinating," Chaz says. "The sexually frustrated Johanna, trapped in her marriage, struggling to break out of her miserable reality, is a very poignant choice, whereas the Israeli side, represented brilliantly by Edgar, the corrupted husband who often suffers from uncontrollable violence, is dark, nerve-wracking and original." Miriam tries to tell Chaz that her play is really a comedy about love, marriage, relationships and heartbreak. But her agent, whose vision is clouded by dollar signs, ignores her. In Chaz's mind, his ticket to fame and fortune is making Miriam's play into a representation of the exotic Middle East, replete with belly-dancers and camels. "Why write something good when you can write something political?" he asks. "The Middle East is like the '80s—all of a sudden it's *in* again!"

By making Chaz's assumptions about Israelis and the Middle East laughable, Tzur critiques stereotypes even as she exploits them. Miriam's family phones her on Shabbat singing "Jerusalem of Gold," one of the most emotional songs of Zionism. They ask her if she has purchased gefilte fish and if she has sold any of her work yet. Her grandfather advises Miriam to get married and make babies. During the phone call, Miriam's mother mentions that she saw Yoni's mother and we quietly arrive at the epicenter of the play. Miriam keeps the memory of Yoni out of her play even as Tzur makes it the center of hers, the determining event in Miriam's life. Writer and written are fused and then torn apart.

Miriam's history, experiences, and memories are not in her play and, although we might suspect that Miriam stands in for Tzur, we don't know how many of Tzur's are either. Predictable conventions of playwrighting and play reading, of separating the theatrical from the real fail us, Tzur cautions. At the end of this extended play within a play, reality invades theatre and theatre attacks reality. Yoni, who we learn was shot by a sniper, shows up wounded and bleeding. He tells the characters they are going to be drafted. As Miriam puts it:

> Blood flies all over the stage, everyone screams as they start shooting each other: actors shoot real people, real people shoot actors. By now the whole theatre space is dripping in blood, people are panicking, running from side to side, trying to figure out what is going on: who's shooting whom, who the injured are, how many are dead, how many can be evacuated from the scene, and WHO THE FUCK GAVE THE FUCKING ORDER TO OPEN FIRE! They all just want to get the hell out of there! Out of this hell! They can already see the headlines in the newspapers: "Another Incident Ending With Heavy Casualties On Both Sides!" But it's too late and they know it, they know there's no chance they'll get out of there alive, so they close their eyes and give the world one last look, full of acceptance: they behaved themselves, they did what they had to do and they tried to do it well . . . It's the type of acceptance only 18-year-old kids can have . . .

Theatrical chaos and real life events converge in the final moments of the play. The proscenium frame no longer divides the stage from the spectators. Like the illusion that military and civilian targets are clearly distinguishable, the idea that reality and theatre are discrete realms is abandoned.

At the very end of the play, Mina, Miriam's Russian Zionist grandmother appears to tell us, "Fifty years from now, there are not going to be any wars. There are not going to be any borders. There are not going to be any countries. Peace will rule not only the Middle East, but the whole wide world . . . Amen." Mina turns on the radio allowing the audience to listen to a recording of the UN 1947 vote to establish the state of Israel followed by a 1948 recording of David Ben Gurion reading Israel's Declaration of Independence. The utopian dream of a country of, by and for Jewish people materialized in a shining moment that soon—the next day—would be repeatedly challenged and wounded.

Betty Shamieh's humorous and tragic *The Black Eyed* is a critical look at traditional views of sex and terrorism as four Palestinian women from different centuries wait in heaven at the "Gate of Martyrs." Aiesha, a female suicide bomber; Delilah, who seduced Samson; Tamam, a survivor of the Christian crusades who tried to save her people and the Architect, a contemporary Christian Palestinian woman— all searching for something in heaven. These are sexual women who don't consider the rewards of heaven so very special. Aiesha, who upon arriving in heaven was given a hundred virgin men of every hue says it was a drag having to teach each of them what to do, over and over. "Every hour on the hour," Aiesha tells the others, "their virginity is renewed. You know what that means? It means their eyes glaze over with a dull vapid look. All the time you spent training them is in vain, and they are back to aiming at your belly-button." Why would someone blow themselves up to have a hundred men in heaven, the others wonder, when they could have twice that many on earth?

Aiesha is a caustic character who seems to know her way around heaven but is not so willing to help others. She and the other women are 'true martyrs' only if their last moments on earth are viewed as the sole determiners of their existence. Even then, when each of them made the ultimate personal self-sacrifice, there are problems. Aiesha claims it's "a boy's club" in the room of the martyrs. Furthermore, her bombing didn't go so well. The crowd she targeted suddenly moved away except for a black-eyed Palestinian girl whose mother worked as a maid and who had brought her young daughter along for the day.

Earlier in the day, the little girl had smiled at a shop-owner she recognized as Palestinian but he did not return her smile. Israelis were
the target but none were hurt. The only death was an innocent
Palestinian girl. Violence is its own domain that, whether sanctioned
by declarations of war or not, cannot be entirely contained or con-
trolled. The Architect was also killed by her own. On a plane, a chubby terrorist runs past her. Their black eyes meet for a moment. The
hijacker realizes she is an Arab, and he recognizes that his actions will
result in killing another of his own kind. "Finally, they are killing one
another," the Chorus intones in defeat.

The first reading of *The Black Eyed* was in January 2002 at The
Immigrant Theatre Project on New York's Lower East Side, a few
weeks before Wafa Idris, the female bomber, blew herself up in
Jerusalem killing one person and wounding 111.[3] Imagination too
quickly became real.[4] There is a repeated refrain in the play, "Hands,
movement, change." Can individual human agency effect change?
And if so, in what form, and by whom?

The Palestinian women in *The Black Eyed* are martyrs who are also
women with desires, dreams and differences. Unlike the US media's
one-dimensional images of Palestinians as either perpetrators or victims of violence, these (fictional) women are full-blooded human
beings with love, sarcasm, sexuality, hope and contradictions. They are
not so much militant as they are searching, both literally and meta-
physically, for answers. They look for their lost loved ones and
demand hands, movement and change. By the end of play "the revolution" seems far away and heaven, a myth. Only earth—the place
where no one who goes in comes out—remains a possibility. So,
Shamieh asks, why don't we do something? And where are we anyway?

In Chiori Miyagawa's *America Dreaming* the protagonist Yuki time travels through American history. Simultaneous realities, unreliable memories, time warps and cracks in consciousness enable her to hear
beyond what is being spoken. Along with her classmates, Yuki hears
her professor speaking about colonial America but feels completely iso-
lated and alone when she hears her uttering the racist anti-immigration

ideology of the nineteenth century. Yuki has a privileged consciousness. The collective amnesia and misinformation surrounding Yuki demands substitute stories, histories, mythologies and ideologies. In the collective amnesia presented as American history, anything stands in for the truth. In Scene 4, Miyagawa has the Japanese dropping a bomb on Pearl Harbor and the Americans landing on Jupiter. History can be distorted to justify anything.

In addition to the fluidity of time, *America Dreaming* does not take place in any specific locality. Yuki sees what the other characters do not. (In a way, an opposite of Filloux's Thida who sees only her traumatic past while Yuki sees the past, present and future.) Miyagawa makes Yuki's prescient consciousness visible by means of three processions. The first procession crosses during her wedding in Scene 1. "A procession—of characters who will appear later in the play—goes by, dancing wildly. Only Yuki sees the procession." Yuki sees the characters of the play and her life in a dance that is symbolically present at her wedding and, by implication, all her major life events. The whole history of Yuki's life invades every present moment. In Scene 4, there is another procession, this one of Japanese "picture brides" that makes clear the difference between immigration and citizenship, a difference that enabled the internment of Japanese Americans during World War II. The dual image of elective travel and deportation is bound up in women "carrying an odd assortment of suitcases and bundles as if they are being herded onto a train." The last procession occurs in Scene 7 which shows the ways in which the memory of suffering is romanticized. "A procession of *The Grapes of Wrath* migrant workers goes by. There is a striking contrast between them and the well-dressed people on the streets. Nobody except Yuki sees the processions. As the procession exits, the '30s-style music resumes but quickly disintegrates."

After this final procession, Yuki and her lover Robert confess their personal pain and loneliness. Robert offers Yuki what he knows of solace: a luxury car. But Yuki is off to another place and time. In the next scene, the Vietnam War and its price tag—140 billion dollars, not to mention the hundreds of thousands of lives lost—are forgotten by a waiter who asserts that 140 billion was spent on urban renewal. The past escapes everyone except Yuki who bears the burden of history, alone. The future where she finds herself is distorted because it reflects an historically disfigured past.

III

Discontinuities of time and place are present in all the plays in this anthology. In *Waxing West*, the Ceausescus return from the dead to torment Daniela's new life in New York. In *Eyes of the Heart*, Thida San physically lives in California but spiritually remains in the Cambodia of Khmer Rouge. The continuous change of location between the US, a checkpoint in Israel, 1947 Israel and Russia at the turn of the twentieth century in *My Political Israeli Play*, reflects the complex layering of history that makes up Miriam's personal and professional identity. In *The Black Eyed*, the four protagonists exist in another realm entirely— a heaven where they bring their stories of oppression and their attempts to thwart it from entirely different centuries. And finally, in *America Dreaming*, processions interrupt an already interrupted time frame making daily waking reality seem the most fictional of all realities.

Rapid shifts of time and place as well as the simultaneity of very different time periods and realities indicate the new reach space of consciousness wrought by globalization. The nonlinear and multi-layered approach to theatricality that these plays employ is born of writers, "global foreigners," with multiple languages, homes, identities and ways of understanding the world. As an economic endeavor, globalization's advocates claim that it will be good for most of the world as it will raise the standard of living for the greatest number of people. Its opponents argue that unifying information and economies will give even greater power and wealth to a very few. Globalization's materiality, whether in its forms of capital, travel, culture, poverty and contained and continuing warfare, is changing the ways in which we experience and understand others and ourselves. The plays included here dramatize a world in which the protagonists' experiences cannot be contained in the historical narratives created by political and cultural nationalism.

With globalization, history has become so layered that it seems impossible to reach any transparent clarity. The world is in waiting— to whom? To what? For how long? There are many corridors and passageways with many destinations.

Notes

1. Wendy Hesford, 'Rhetorical Memory, Political Theater, and the Traumatic Present' in *Transformations*, VOL. 16, NO. 2 (2005), p. 104.

2. Military service in Israel is mandatory upon completing high school: three years for men, two years for women.

3. See Human Rights Watch at www.hrw.org/reports/2002/isrl-pa/ISRAELPA1002-08.htm for a chronology of suicide-bombing attacks on civilians and military targets from September 30, 2000 to August 31, 2002.

4. Rabih Mroue's performance piece about a suicide bomber in Lebanon and his representation is in the guest-edited issue of TDR (T 191) on documentary theatre edited by Carol Martin, Fall 2006.

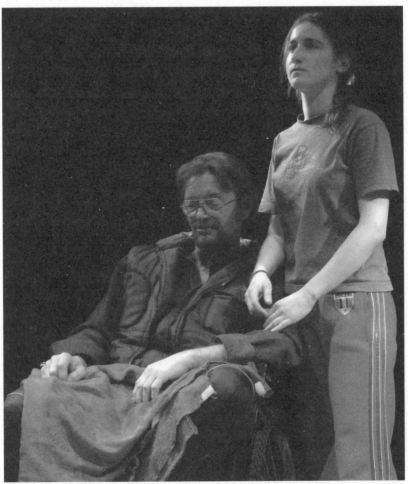

Eliza Tuturman as Daniela and Virgil Muller as Uros in **Waxing West** *directed by Marcy Arlin (Artistic Director, Immigrants Theatre Project, New York) at the Cluj National Theatre, Romania. Photograph by Cris Nedea.*

WAXING WEST

A HAIRY TALE IN TWO ACTS AND

FOUR SEASONS

BY

SAVIANA STANESCU

I am a Romanian-born playwright with roots in Albania, Macedonia, Greece and . . . Long Island, where my grandmother was born. She was three years old when her family took their younger children and emigrated to Romania (yeah, I know, strange idea . . .).

I grew up in the totalitarian system run by the dictator Ceausescu. Like the other members of my generation, the baby-boom generation created by Ceausescu's prohibition of abortion and contraceptives, I used to escape from the daily poverty, oppression and misery by taking refuge in my imagination. Books and theatre were our means of survival and joy. Fifty years of communism fashioned a particular aesthetic in our country: things could not be told directly as they were so artists developed metaphorical and encoded ways of speaking about the social and political issues we were concerned about. For instance, we had lots of Hamlets, sunk in their subtext, philosophically declaiming that something was rotten in the country. Playwrights grew to write in an absurdist, poetic or surreal way as opposed to the socialist realism imposed by the censors and the propaganda leaders. The more ambiguous, subtle and complex a play was, the easier it was to get past censors and be produced.

After 1989, I enthusiastically started to work as a journalist, fighting against the endemic corruption in the 'new democracy' Romania, so other years were wasted on dramatic living instead of dramatic writing. Although I published my first book of poetry in 1994, five years after communism fell, and I wrote my first full-length play three years later (in a workshop led by London's Royal Court Theatre artists), the cultural climate in which I spent my formative years influenced me significantly.

In 1990, Caryl Churchill came to Bucharest for a week and wrote the masterpiece *Mad Forrest* about the Romanian Revolution. It took me more than 10 years to be able to write about the same event—the revolution in which I fully participated and in which two of my friends were arrested and one killed.

Waxing West is my play about the Romanian Revolution and generally about collective traumas and the ways in which they affect the individual. It is a dramatic but humorous meditation on the fact that we cannot get rid of our past; we are conditioned by the circumstances of our birth and upbringing. Wherever I go or live, I cannot actually escape from Romania. Romania is imprinted in my DNA, it's distilled in my blood.

I was able to write *Waxing West* only in America, in English, after my first year in New York City where I arrived (with a Fulbright grant) in early September 2001. It was quite a shock for me to get directly into the 9/11 events. I became aware of the Twin Towers only after they disappeared. The present absence . . .

Traditional plays are built around an external conflict between characters. My play aims to explore and dramatize an inner conflict: can Daniela, an illegal immigrant in NYC, move on or is she still held prisoner by ghosts of the past? It is a big challenge to dramatically express the in-betweeness, the 'I-don't-know-where-I-belong-anymore' dilemma of a new immigrant. But I am used to challenges . . .

CHARACTERS

CASTING REQUIREMENTS	4 women and 4 men

THE ROMANIANS

DANIELA	Early 30s, cosmetologist
MARCELA	Her mother, mid-50s
ELVIS	Daniela's brother, early 20s

THE AMERICANS

CHARLIE	Late 30s, computer engineer
GLORIA	Charlie's sister, late 40s, feminist visual artist
UROS	Late 50s, homeless Muslim Yugoslavian

THE GHOSTS

CEAUSESCU/DRACULA	Former Romanian dictator, currently a vampire
ELENA	His wife, an insatiable vampiress

TIME: 2000–2001
PLACE: Bucharest and New York

Scene titles are projected/written on a big screen/slide/sign/paper/whatever.

A slash (/) in the dialogue indicates that the next actor should start his or her line, creating overlapping speech.

ACT I

The actors are lined up, upstage, hidden in the semi-darkness.

They may be present on stage at all times, body-reacting to Daniela's actions/words.

Violin music.

Lights up on Daniela, white-eyed and panting. She crosses downstage.

DANIELA (*to the audience*). I have to calm down. To calm down. To breathe deeply. Deeply. (*She does so.*) Yes. OK. Here is the story. The whole story. Nothing but the story. My story. Yes. Everything that happened . . . (*breathing deeply like in a yoga exercise*). Tell the story. The story . . . MY story, MY story. (*She calms down.*) I am Popescu Daniela, nationality: Romanian, age: 32, height: 165 centimeters, color of eyes: black, passport number: 2670222, sex: female, tourist visa number: 555257, EXPIRED, accent: strong, hair: long, place of birth: Bucharest, place of death: to-be-announced . . .

You're not from the police, are you? Or from INS? No, you don't look like . . .

Let me tell you this: I should be Daniela Aronson. Daniela Aronson! Nationality: American. Age: 27? Height . . . 175. Color of eyes: blue! . . . Charlie has small round blue eyes . . . Blue bonbons on the snow . . . This is the first thing I noticed in the photo his mom sent to my mom. Sweet. Double sweet. But why is he so sad? . . . (*Memories invade her.*)

ALL (*except Daniela*). ONE! (*Violin music stops.*)

On the screen is written

1. AN OLD LADY'S VISIT (THE VERY BEGINNING)
April 11, 2000—Bucharest

DANIELA. Bucharest, Romania. An old lady's visit. The very beginning.

Bucharest, Romania. An apartment in Cringasi, a working-class neighborhood. A modest living room that also serves as a bedroom for Elvis, Daniela's brother. A big calendar with American cars hangs on the wall. Elvis is watching TV. His legs are resting, relaxed, on a small table. Marcela, his mom, is tidying the living room.

MARCELA. How many times do I have to tell you to take your stinky paws off the table? How old are you now, Elvis?

ELVIS. You know better than I.

MARCELA. Elvis!

DANIELA (*to the audience*). My mother, Marcela, is an Elvis Presley fan.

MARCELA (*to Elvis*). Dirty impudent giant! I don't know who you take after. Your father was such a clean sensitive polite perfect gentleman.

ELVIS. Sure. That's why he lost everything we had and ended up in jail.

MARCELA. He was in jail for political reasons, stupid Jumbo! Nobody had the courage to start a strike during that bloody Ceausescu regime, but your father . . . your father . . . did. (*Starts crying.*)

ELVIS. Whatever.

MARCELA. It is not "whatever," it is your father!

ELVIS. You used to call him useless bastard insignificant bag rag and . . . (*tapping the table*) piece of furniture.

MARCELA. I never /

DANIELA/ELVIS. You always!

MARCELA (*wiping the table frantically*). Well, he didn't manage to make any money AFTER, did he? . . . All the smart guys in Romania, in Russia, in the whole of Eastern Europe did what was to be done, robbed the damn dead socialist state, seized those ugly gray factories, buildings, lands, Ceausescu's gold, something, everything, everybody with a tiny bit of brain stole what was to be stolen, and everything was to be stolen, in '90, in '91, even in '92, one could make a fortune in a blink, one smart enough to be in the right place at the right time and sign a damn piece of paper, "this factory is mine," "those tons of oil are mine," "I'm the owner, I sell them to you," to the foreigners, to the Americans, for dollars, REAL money, that's all, MONEY, privatizing yourself, bribing who was to be bribed, opening businesses! Everybody moved around but your father . . .

ELVIS. Played chess in the park with the other retired guys.

MARCELA. "I cannot lie," "I cannot steal from the public wealth," like there was anyone there to judge him if he would. Everybody was doing the same. Everyone who had the / brain to . . .

ELVIS. He had lung cancer!

Marcela starts crying again.

MARCELA. He was such a tender well-raised well-cultured outstanding gentleman . . . I'm sure his soul eats at the dinner table with angels up there in heaven, forgetting about us, his poor neglected / family . . .

ELVIS. All right, all right. Stop crying. I take my feet off the table. OK?! You may wipe it now. Stop crying.

She starts wiping the table frantically.

MARCELA. Aren't you going out with your buddies?

ELVIS. I feel like watching TV. It's too rainy outside.

MARCELA. You said something about going to a movie with the other guys . . .

ELVIS. I'm watching THIS movie on TV now.

DANIELA (*to the audience*). *Die Hard III*. "Die Hard with a Vengeance."

MARCELA. I have someone coming over in half an hour.

ELVIS. You finally got a lover?

MARCELA. Elvis! I respect the memory of your father. I don't invite men home. To OUR home. I don't think of men. I mean I don't need men. I mean the way you think in your rotten pervert mind. I think of men /. . .

ELVIS. Whatever . . .

MARCELA. For your sister!

ELVIS. Oh no! We're waiting for a suitor. Does Dani know about this?

DANIELA. Not yet.

MARCELA. Could you be nice for a moment . . .

ELVIS. I'm all ears . . .

MARCELA. There is . . . this AMERICAN lady—Mrs. Aronson. Are you listening to me?

Elvis passionately watches a TV sequence.

ELVIS. Yeah. Yeah.

MARCELA. She had a Romanian cleaning lady for twenty years. She LOVES Romanians. Are you following?

ELVIS. The American grandma is coming to visit us. Why? (*Looking at her*) I hope you're not trying to marry me to her?

MARCELA. You! You! It's not about you. It's about your sister, dummie. She's thirty-ONE!

ELVIS/DANIELA. So?

MARCELA. She doesn't have ANY boyfriends. Any prospects of getting married.

ELVIS. Come on. She's pretty enough.

MARCELA. Of course she's pretty. But she won't meet a man in that awful beauty salon . . . She's wasting her youth, poor little dear, waxing all those rich cows / who made illegal money after the Revolution.

DANIELA. Who made illegal money after the Revolution . . .

ELVIS. Jesus! Don't start again with the making-money-after-the-revolution "CD," please.

MARCELA. Your sister has the chance to marry an American. An American BUSINESSMAN. Mrs. Aronson's son—Charlie! Rich, decent, well-educated. American! The luck-rain has come down over Daniela. She is going to go to America and take all of us there!

ELVIS. I don't wanna go to America.

MARCELA. You're stupid. But not that stupid.

ELVIS. I bet Dani doesn't like your idea either.

DANIELA. You bet.

MARCELA. God, why did you punish me with such kids? (*To Elvis*) Have you heard about Mrs. Luca's sons? They made lots of money in Switzerland, working in civil engineering. When you finish the college your sister is PAYING for, you could go to Switzerland and make some good money in construction.

ELVIS. I hate engineering. I wanna be a film director (*makes a frame with his hands and pretends to be shooting*).

MARCELA. I don't want to hear that nonsense anymore. Your sister waxed the soul out of her with those fat cows to pay your taxes. I'm not listening to such nonsense. And take your paws off the table please!

The bell rings.

MARCELA. There she is! Could you go to the bedroom, honey . . .

ELVIS. This is my bedroom—did you forget?

MARCELA. Please, sweetie . . .

ELVIS. I'm watching TV.

The bell rings.

MARCELA. You may take the TV set with you, sweetie-pie!

Elvis doesn't move.

ELVIS. Tell the American grandma we need a VCR.

MARCELA. We are not beggars!

The bell rings again.

ELVIS. Just don't sell Dani for less than a VCR, a DVD player and a video camera!

DANIELA. Jesus!

MARCELA. I am going to sell YOU for a hamburger, insensitive monster!

The TV gets louder and louder—machine guns and people dying, moans and roars, the usual thriller soundtrack. Daniela covers her ears. Elvis zaps the remote control randomly. Marcela shouts at him. The bell rings.

Blackout.

Lights on the TV set and on Daniela. She takes her hands off her ears, looking like she's prepared for something bad to happen.

On the screen is written

2. THE FIRST NIGHTMARE

TV ANCHOR. Comrade Nicolae Ceausescu, the former Romanian president who was executed on Christmas night in 1989 and academician doctor engineer Comrade Elena Ceausescu, his wife, are now vampires. They were separated after their death: Ceausescu was in the Middle East, Elena worked and lived in New York. Despite their busy tooth-in-neck nightlife, they are quite unhappy. Both miss home and are nostalgic about going back to Romania and sucking some delicious Romanian blood, the blood of their human life, the blood of their "childhood" as VAMPIRES . . .

Lights on Marcela.

MARCELA (*to Daniela*). Look at you! You're too pale and skinny, girl! People could say I don't feed you right . . .

Lights on Ceausescu.

TV ANCHOR. And now we take you LIVE to Bellu Cemetery in Bucharest where Ceausescu has just arrived. Elena is not here yet. A nice summer night. A tombstone. THEIR tombstone. On which angry revolutionaries wrote heartfelt obituaries such as / "FUCK YOU, DICTATOR!" "POO, POO, WE'VE GOT RID OF YOU!" "YOU, CLOWN IN THE CIRCUS OF HUNGER, YOU VAMPIRE!" . . .

ELVIS/DANIELA/MARCELA. "FUCK YOU, DICTATOR!" "POO, POO, WE'VE GOT RID OF YOU!" "YOU CLOWN, IN THE CIRCUS OF HUNGER, YOU VAMPIRE!" . . .

DANIELA (*to the audience, like a reporter*). My dad is buried here, in the third alley, under the lilac. (*Going to the tombstone*) Almost next to our "dearest" leader, / "the father of the people," "the first man of the socialist republic," "the most beloved son of the country," "the creator of the New Human" . . .

CEAUSESCU. "The father of the people," "the first man of the socialist republic," "the most beloved son of the country," "the creator of the New Human" . . . Me!

DANIELA. I wrote these words millions of times. For all the exams I had to pass till I grew to hate exams. To hate school. To hate (*beat*) Ceausescu. He-Comrade.

CEAUSESCU. She doesn't love me!

MARCELA. And his She-Comrade. Elena.

DANIELA. People would make dirty jokes about them. Especially when the whole neighborhood was waiting for the end of another evening-long electricity blackout.

MARCELA. For the "Light to Come" . . .

DANIELA. I used to imagine the Comrades making love in sado-masochist positions, to see Him "shooting" on Her belly a river of red-golden "light" from which we, the People, the New Humans, were born . . . (*Marcela laughs*) That was a joke. A dark un-salty joke. Mom would laugh. Dad would be quiet . . .

CEAUSESCU. Why do you exaggerate, young comrade? You are making us look bad. You will pay for this!

DANIELA. He-Comrade and his Securitate "apes" made my father quiet.

CEAUSESCU. We'll make you quiet!

DANIELA. They ruined his career. Demolished our old house. Sent my dad to prison. I can't remember that very well.

MARCELA. You were only five (*embraces Daniela*).

DANIELA. But I can imagine it. I could read the map of wrinkles on his face and the map of scars on his body . . . I've never heard my dad pronouncing Ceausescu's name. Never.

CEAUSESCU. That is a lie! He must have said my name, he had to. He couldn't have got away with that.

Marcela heads upstage.

DANIELA. Mom got away with lots of things. She knew the right people. She got coffee, bonbons and Vitamin C for us every month. I never thought about where those things came from. My colleagues didn't have them. Someone said mom had strange connections with foreign spies and the black capitalist market . . .

MARCELA (*turning around*). Shhhhhhh! Don't speak about such things! He-Comrade has ears everywhere, we might have bugs even in our asses . . .

DANIELA. Funny things, whispered by gray people waiting in line for milk and bread at 5 a.m., waiting, at 7 a.m., waiting, at 9 a.m., giving up and going to work, leaving the plastic bag with the family name on it, there, in the line, waiting . . .

MARCELA. Waiting . . . (*lights off on Marcela*).

DANIELA. Waiting . . .

TV ANCHOR. The centerpiece of Ceausescu's new Romania was built on the rubble of Bucharest's old quarter. Twenty-six churches and over seven thousand houses were destroyed to make way for the Civic Centre. Here looms the infamous Palace of the People, the third biggest building on earth after the Pentagon and the Tibetan Potala. Over twenty thousand laborers and six hundred architects toiled to build the Palace to Ceausescu's exacting standards . . .

Ceausescu makes an abrupt "stop this program!" gesture and goes to the tombstone with his name on it.

CEAUSESCU. They put up a stone from my Palace of the People! A stone from MY palace! Where did they take it from? From MY bathroom with the golden taps? From my living room with the golden carpets? From my study with the golden pens I never used? From MY . . . (*crying*) OUR bedroom with the golden sheets . . .

Lights on Elena.

ELENA. That's my golden Nick!

CEAUSESCU. Leni? I'll be shot and damned! It's really you? In blood and bones? I thought you were having fun in New York, sucking capitalist blood in a socialist, democratic way. (*Beat*) You miss our old golden times too? . . .

ELENA. To be honest, I prefer golden showers in Times Square. I'm having much more fun now that I travel by myself and have dinner with people . . .

CEAUSESCU. Don't tell me any more about your capitalist lovers . . . enemies of the people . . . foreign spies . . . Americans. Germans. British. Aristocrats. Blue blood. Bleah, bleah, bleah! (*Beat*) You didn't miss me . . .

ELENA. I missed our dogs. I missed Bucharest . . .

DANIELA (*talking to her father's tombstone*). Dad . . .

CEAUSESCU. I'm not her dad, why is she calling me dad? (*Beat*) Maybe she means DEAD.

ELENA. You used to be the Father of these People.

CEAUSESCU. Talk to her, you're the Mother!

ELENA. I'm not her mother. She's too . . . old!

CEAUSESCU. Shall we drink her then?

ELENA. We need golden champagne glasses.

CEAUSESCU (*nostalgic*). My two hundred and sixteen golden glasses from China, the gift from my old pal Mao . . . (*shouting*) Mao! Mao!

ELENA. Shhhhhh! You sound like a stupid tomcat.

CEAUSESCU. I miss Mao . . . (*Pointing at Daniela*) Shall we . . .

ELENA. Of course, darling. Cheers! Romanian blood again!

CEAUSESCU. Cheers! . . . No! It's too easy. She said some awful things about us.

ELENA. This ungrateful worm? She must pay then. Let's suck her!

CEAUSESCU. I have to come up with a plan . . . With a strategy . . .

ELENA. *1001 Ways of Torturing a Stubborn Enemy.* I remember all of / them.

CEAUSESCU. Your unpublished book!

ELENA. What about this one: electric shocks in her vagina!

CEAUSESCU (*turned on*). Electric shocks!

ELENA (*turned on*). Or the cooking game!

CEAUSESCU. When we starved that Enemy of the People for ten days, then ate sarmale in front of him!

ELENA. It's only a matter of finding her Weak Spots . . .

CEAUSESCU. Remember that imaginative torture session when that midget intellectual resisted for three days? What a man!

ELENA. Oh, yes, yes, years and years ago . . . (*Laughing*) You were ready to give up!

CEAUSESCU. You found his Weak-Spot-of-the-First-Degree . . .

ELENA. And got all the info you guys hadn't been able to scoop out of him in forty hours!

CEAUSESCU. You are so . . . powerful!

ELENA. You are so . . . visionary!

They kiss, forgetting about Daniela.

DANIELA. It was only Vitamin C, dad . . .

On the screen is written

3. A STOLEN VITAMIN C JAR
March 22, 2001—New York

The living room of an Upper East Side New York apartment. A big calendar with Romanian monasteries hangs on the wall. Daniela walks back and forth in front of Charlie who's working on a laptop. She has a Vitamin C jar in her left hand and gesticulates with it, making funny noises.

DANIELA. It's only Vitamin C, Charlie. Orange flavored with rose hips. 6.89 dollars . . . 6.89 dollars are capable to drive you mad at me, Charlie. That's how much your "love" is worth in your opinion. Not seven dollars, not seventy, not seven hundred . . . No, you love me for exactly six dollars and eighty-nine cents. My hips are worth less than some chewable anonymous tablets with rose hips . . . (*Beat*)

OK, Charlie. It's your choice. I don't want to remind you what I do for you for FREE. I don't smoke here. I cook for you. Romanian food! . . . I hate Romanian food, Charlie, I hate sarmale and mamaliga and the Romanian traditional smell and the Romanian exotic flavors and the Romanian claustrophobic kitchens. But for you, Charlie, I stick two cotton pads in my nostrils, I play my energizing tape with applauses and I do it for you, Charlie. I cook for you although I hate this verb COOK and I plan to make it disappear in all languages. (*Beat*)

Charlie sighs. Lights on Ceausescu and Elena. They sigh mockingly.

And it's not only about cooking, Charlie, although everything is about cooking. I play with you that silly Thanksgiving-game you love. Every Sunday at 6 p.m. you get all naked except for your white silly socks and you take the "turkey" position and I have to pretend to put you in the oven and that the fire goes stronger and stronger and I have to see your silly dick reacting to that, Charlie, instead of my body. I have to act as if I cook you, Charlie, because you're a turkey and I have to show you a plastic knife and say, "Oh, I'm gonna eat you turkey!" and I play this silly part, Charlie, and see you coming and shouting in pleasure when I start cutting you with the plastic knife and I have to say, "Oh, you're such a good turkey, yum-yum!" but I don't yum-yum, and I don't like to yum-yum and I don't generally eat meat so I yum-yum only for your sake . . .

Charlie giggles. Ceausescu and Elena giggle with him. He turns off the laptop and looks at Daniela.

And now you're mad at me because I STOLE this damn plastic jar. Orange flavored chewable Vitamin C-500 . . . I just took it from the shelf and put it in my bag. The Calvin Klein bag you gave me for Christmas. Nobody saw me, so what's your problem, Charlie? And you know what?—the bag from you is not a real Calvin Klein!

Charlie pulls her down on the sofa. They start wrestling or making love, it is not very clear.

Ceausescu and Elena applaud and mock Daniela.

CEAUSESCU. Oh, poor girl!

ELENA. It's not a real Calvin Klein!

CEAUSESCU. Cook me! Cook me!

ELENA. You're a turkey, you're a turkey!

CEAUSESCU/ELENA. Yum-yum! / Yum-yum!

On the screen is written

4. WAXING AND TALKING ABOUT WAXING AND TALKING
April 28, 2001—New York

DANIELA (*to the audience*). Four! Gloria's studio in Brooklyn. Very stylish. She bought the most expensive wax, transparent gloves and even a white work-robe for me . . . I can't take my eyes off two inflatable women wrestling or . . . making love in the middle of the floor. They look identical except for a small detail: one has her mouth open, the other one has it closed. I've never seen such an artwork. I think it's beautiful. But I'm not an art critic. This may not be the right thought.

Gloria's studio in Brooklyn. A big calendar with art reproductions hangs on the wall.

Gloria lies on a sofa covered with a cotton sheet while Daniela waxes her legs. A big installation called "Inflatable Gender"— two inflatable women making love—presides in the middle of the room.

GLORIA. I'm so glad you came over. You spend too much time alone in my brother's only-for-you cage. How long have you been in New York now, four months?

DANIELA *(applying wax on Gloria's leg)*. Three and a half.

GLORIA. And you never ever came to see me.

DANIELA. I came to wax you *(covers wax with a cloth-like strip, pressing firmly)*.

GLORIA. Now. Because I asked you.

DANIELA. I like working *(pulls off the strip)*.

GLORIA. Oh! Yes . . . It's a shame you can't open a beauty salon in New York.

DANIELA *(applying wax on Gloria's leg)*. I don't have a work-permit . . . I don't have money . . . My tourist visa has expired . . .

GLORIA. Charlie should marry you as soon as possible.

DANIELA. He said he would *(covers wax with a cloth-like strip, pressing firmly)*.

GLORIA. When? You have to start planning. I can help organize the wedding . . .

DANIELA. On his vacation . . . *(pulls off the strip)*.

GLORIA. Ah! In the summer then. *(Beat)* Shame mom will miss it. It was her idea after all.

DANIELA (*applying wax on Gloria's leg*). I'm so sorry Mrs. Aronson died . . . She was such a vivid person.

GLORIA. Yeah, mom was somebody.

DANIELA (*covers wax with a cloth-like strip, pressing firmly*). He never talks about her.

GLORIA. Charlie? . . . He's a weird guy. (*Daniela pulls off the strip.*) Ah!

DANIELA. Did it hurt?

GLORIA. No. Not really. You have easy hands . . .

DANIELA (*applying wax on Gloria's leg*). Good . . .

GLORIA. What about the women in your country?

DANIELA. It's less painful here. The wax is better (*covers wax with a cloth-like strip, pressing firmly*).

GLORIA. I mean, are they still in the wife-and-mother role for a whole life-show?

DANIELA. I'm not sure what you mean (*pulls off the strip*).

GLORIA. Well. Men and women stuff . . .

DANIELA. Oh . . . All the women I know over there are crazed to find a man. When they find one, they are crazed to keep him. Then he cheats on them with their best friend . . . I've heard this story thousands of times. On your belly, please!

Gloria turns over.

GLORIA. Women like to tell their stories, don't they?

DANIELA. Don't strain your muscle!

GLORIA (*she relaxes*). It must be something special about waxing . . .

DANIELA (*applying wax to Gloria's leg*). It's like fighting. Against the unwanted hair that keeps reminding you it's there, inside your skin, ready to show its ugly head . . . (*covers wax with a cloth-like strip, pressing firmly*). Like fighting against death . . .

GLORIA. That's original . . .

DANIELA. See? You spread the wax in the direction of hair growth but pull strip off in the opposite direction (*pulls off the strip*). It hurts a bit, of course. No little victory without little pain.

GLORIA. That's . . . painfully true.

DANIELA (*applying wax on Gloria's leg*). When I was in high school, the beauty salon in my neighborhood was the best place to go. Warm and cozy. From heating the wax . . . I could spend days and nights there . . . At home it was so cold and ugly, you know, the heat was supplied in rations (*pronounced "Russians"*).

GLORIA. Rations. Not—Russians.

DANIELA. Relax the ankle! (*Pronounces correctly*) Rations . . . (*covers wax with a cloth-like strip, pressing firmly*). It was this smell of . . . beauty . . . All those women, young old fat skinny, lying there, on the same bed, fighting the same fight, believing they can change, they can become beautiful just like this, snap your fingers, pull off the strip . . . (*pulls off the strip*). When they paid, you could see in their eyes the sign of victory . . . I was like their . . . hair-fairy! (*Applying skin relief lotion on Gloria's legs, massaging them.*)

GLORIA. And here I am, joining the "beauty club" . . . This is really funny! I just lost my virginity . . . Never had a waxing before . . .

DANIELA. I thought so . . .

GLORIA. So . . . Do you like to wax yourself?

DANIELA. I like to see the wax destroying the hair.

GLORIA. Right . . .

DANIELA. No hair! Shiny thighs calves bellies armpits. Perfect bodies. Each one with its own particular charm and its own sad story: the hairy tale.

GLORIA (*seductively*). Women's bodies are beautiful, aren't they?

DANIELA (*beat*). Done. You're ready.

GLORIA (*examining her legs*). Nice . . . Ready for what?

Daniela stands up.

DANIELA. I must go now.

GLORIA. Charlie doesn't get home till 7 or 8. Why rush?

DANIELA. I have to be . . . somewhere.

GLORIA. OK. Go. I'm not keeping you here by force.

DANIELA. No. You're really nice. I like to talk to you and . . . I love this place.

GLORIA. Relax then! (*Gloria stands up, then sits back on the sofa.*) We can have a chat over a glass of red wine. (*Covers her legs.*) We can have a nice time together. We HAVE a nice time together.

DANIELA (*preparing to leave*). I promised Charlie I'd give back the books I stole from Barnes & Nobles . . .

GLORIA. Oh no.

DANIELA. It's hard. It's gonna be embarrassing to tell them, "Look, I took these books but you didn't catch me, your security system is not as good as you think" . . .

GLORIA. We have some serious problems here. OK. Go and give back the books. Go, go! (*Beat*) We'll have a drink sometime . . . soon.

Daniela walks downstage.

DANIELA (*to the audience*). Five. Everybody wants to go to America. Question mark.

On the screen is written

5. EVERYBODY WANTS TO GO TO AMERICA?
June 26, 2000—Bucharest

The Cringasi apartment. There are lots of photos and letters on the carpet. Daniela and her mom are trying to sort them out. Elvis is watching TV. His legs rest on the table. There is a VCR on the TV which Elvis caresses from time to time as though it is a trophy.

Marcela shows a photo to Elvis.

ELVIS. I don't need to see the babushkas. You need to show them to the American guys.

DANIELA. Here's a good one: "Nice affectionate decent full-figured lady, mature, down-to-earth, poor but honest, wishes to meet a financially stable generous successful gentleman, marriage-minded, athletic, well-educated, well-travelled, D/D free, to share love's tender magic. Let's welcome sunrises and sunsets together!" I bet she copied this from the *Soul&Body* Personals page. She always reads magazines when I wax her . . .

MARCELA. How many did you bring from the salon?

DANIELA. Fifteen! And they keep coming. I shouldn't have told anybody about the prospect of going to America.

MARCELA. What prospect? It's not a prospect. It's certain!

DANIELA. Come on, mom. Let's have him come to Romania first. I'd like to see how we get along together before . . .

ELVIS. She's right. You try on a new shirt but you don't "try on" your future husband?

MARCELA. Shut up, rag-head! When you get a chance like this, you take it. You don't stop to . . . "try it on." Look. Look how many others are in line.

ELVIS. Babushkas. Nuts. Whores.

MARCELA. Look at this one. Beautiful! (*Lifts a photo in the air and reads from the "CV"*) Mrs. Horea's daughter. With two college degrees. One in art history, and one in accounting! Huh? (*To Daniela who doesn't react*) And she's twenty-eight! (*To Elvis*) Your sister must learn to see REALITY. Her mind "travels" in the clouds, in the sky, I have told her thousands of / times . . .

DANIELA. Would you stop talking as if I'm not here or I'm . . . retarded!

ELVIS. Tell her you don't want to go to America and marry that . . . Charlie Big-Dick.

MARCELA. Mind your words, selfish animal! She will have EVERY-
THING. Robots that clean the house for you. Machines that
cook by themselves. Money that is invisible numbers on a small
card like this! (*Shows an imaginary card using her thumb and forefinger*) She won't have to worry about anything. She can have her
mind settled in the clouds forever. Of course she wants to go to
America. (*To Daniela*) Don't you, honey?

DANIELA (*studying another photo and the letter attached*). This one doesn't
want to get married. Listen. "Dear Miss Daniela, I know that at
my age I don't have any chance to marry an American. And,
truth be told, I don't want to marry one of them. I've heard they
are weird. They sleep with guns under their pillows. They have
drugs for breakfast every day. And put drugs in your coffee if
you're not careful. But maybe you can find me a job as a cleaning lady there. For one year, no more. Just as long as I can make
some money to pay for the heat in winter. After that I'll forget
about your Americans and come back home, where I belong, to
die in peace. Please, help me. I will pray for you every Sunday at
church."

MARCELA (*crying*). That's poor Mrs. Ionescu from the third floor.
She's alone.

DANIELA. We should lend her some money.

MARCELA. Ah, you loser. If you keep thinking like this, you'll be a
loser even in America. This is how people get rich there: they
take care of each Mr. Green, they save every cent. There is no
such thing as "lend" if you don't get something in return.

ELVIS. She can help cleaning this place.

MARCELA. Are you suggesting it isn't clean enough? After I scrub the
soul out of me every day . . .

ELVIS. That's the point. You wouldn't have to scrub it out of you.
Some soul would be left for cheering us.

Marcela throws her left slipper at him.

MARCELA. We don't have any money to lend. We barely have enough money to survive. But you wouldn't know that, parasite! (*Beat*) And get your paws off the table, please.

DANIELA. OK, OK. Could we have a bit of calm this evening?

The bell rings. Marcela rushes to gather the photos and hide them in a drawer.

ELVIS. Another horny babushka . . . (*Shouting*) We are not at home!

Marcela hits him on the head with the other slipper and rushes towards the door, offstage. Daniela stretches her body and sighs. Elvis takes his feet off the table and shrugs. They look at each other and shrug.

Daniela walks downstage.

DANIELA. Six. The girl in the picture . . . Me! . . .

She freezes, smiling like in a framed photo. On the screen is written

6. THE GIRL IN THE PICTURE
March 25, 2000—New York

Gloria and Charlie are at a fancy Chinese restaurant. They've finished the meal and are having some tea.

GLORIA. I can't believe you agreed with her! You accepted to get MARRIED in this . . . odd! . . . ancient! . . . patriarchal, old-fashioned, disgusting way.

CHARLIE. I was wondering what made you invite me for dinner . . . More tea?

GLORIA. No. You have to tell her you don't want that woman, Charlie. You don't need a female . . . pet from a Third World country. You cannot let mom feed the illusions that you would / marry . . .

CHARLIE. She's invested a lot in this idea.

GLORIA. Exactly! She must forget it. As soon as possible.

CHARLIE. She wants to go to Romania to talk to the girl.

GLORIA. The woman. She's thirty-something! Look! (*Pointing at*

Daniela) I stole one of her pictures from mom's bedroom. Can you believe that she framed three of this foreign woman's photos, including one with the woman at age three or four—riding a wooden horse! All these pictures are now on OUR mother's night stand! This Romanian cosmetologist, this gypsy / . . .

CHARLIE (*looking at Daniela*). She's not a gypsy . . . She's pretty . . .

GLORIA. Are you racist or something?

CHARLIE. YOU said she was a gypsy.

GLORIA. She might be. So what? The problem is that mom has this obsession and your duty is to say NO to her. (*Beat*) I thought you're gay anyway!

CHARLIE. You're wrong. Now you're gonna say I'm homophobic.

GLORIA. Are you?

CHARLIE. I'm "phobic."

GLORIA. Ha, ha. Smart Charlie . . .

CHARLIE. Upright Gloria . . .

GLORIA. Tell her you don't need a woman, Charlie!

CHARLIE (*enjoying Gloria's growing disapproval*). I don't need a woman, mom! I don't need an American self-righteous woman. A Latino over-talkative chick. A British snobbish giraffe. A French sexy inflatable doll. An Asian midget / mistress . . .

GLORIA. I knew you were a misogynist.

CHARLIE. Of course . . .

GLORIA. Is this because that violinist—your first and only girlfriend!—preferred *moi* to you?

CHARLIE. Yung Lee was not my only girlfriend.

GLORIA. Of course . . .

CHARLIE. If you don't want any more tea, I'd rather ask for the check.

GLORIA. I thought you liked Chinese food! Mom spoiled you with all those homemade / meals . . .

CHARLIE. It was fine, thanks.

GLORIA. I was very surprised that you decided to move out last year. Does mom still call you two times a day?

CHARLIE. She knows I'm busy.

Beat. They both sip their tea.

GLORIA. Don't let her go to Romania, Charlie!

CHARLIE. She's looking forward to the trip.

GLORIA. She's gonna bring you a bride! Like in the worst type of soap opera . . . My own mom . . .

CHARLIE. Be happy she's not bringing you a groom.

GLORIA. Don't be sarcastic, it doesn't suit you.

CHARLIE (*getting up*). Next time it's my treat.

GLORIA. You're impossible, I hope you're aware of this. That poor Romanian is gonna have a hard time here, the poor woman / is . . .

CHARLIE. Her name is Daniela.

He leaves. Gloria pours herself more tea. Daniela de-freezes and walks downstage.

DANIELA. Me . . . At my dad's grave. Bellu Cemetery, Bucharest. Smoking like a Hamletian vamp. Hiding in the smoke.

On the screen is written

7. TO GO OR NOT TO GO
September 11, 2000—Bucharest

Daniela lights candles at her father's tomb. It's a sunny day. She has a cigarette in her hand but hasn't lit it yet. Lights on Ceausescu and Elena wearing sunglasses.

DANIELA. To go or not to go . . .

CEAUSESCU. Poor girl!

DANIELA. What shall I do, dad?!

ELENA. No answer!

DANIELA. Dad?! . . .

CEAUSESCU. No daddy!

DANIELA. . . . I hope you're fine up there . . . I'm not . . . I know, I know . . . you wanted me to be somebody. To feel proud of me. To have all your colleagues respecting you because I'm so special . . . (*Beat*) I'm not so special, dad . . . Better get used to the idea otherwise up there in heaven you'll be just as unhappy as you were down here, on earth . . . (*lights the cigarette with a candle*) Yes, I know . . . I should have gone to college . . .

ELENA. No college!

DANIELA. But it was the Revolution . . . The University Square . . . The new elections . . . The meetings against corruption . . . Things were changing in Romania, I had to be there, didn't I? Didn't I?

CEAUSESCU. No revolution!

ELENA. No achievement!

DANIELA (*to her father's tomb*). You remember the Shakespeare Club in high school? . . . I was good as Ophelia, wasn't I? . . . I still have that tape with the applause you recorded at my graduation show . . . (*smokes like a Hamletian vamp*). To go or not to go . . . that is the question. "Whether 'tis nobler in the mind to suffer the slings and arrows of outrageous fortune, or to take arms against a sea of troubles, and by opposing end them?" . . . "To die, to sleep . . . to sleep, perchance to dream" . . .

CEAUSESCU. No stupid dreams!

DANIELA. Why don't you at least send me some nice dreams, papa? Why don't you visit me as a ghost? . . .

ELENA. No stupid ghosts!

DANIELA. Maybe in that America . . . it's a bit, just a bit, a tiny little bit, like in the movies. You have a nice house, two floors, four bedrooms, two cars, one for you, one for your husband . . . breakfast and dinner with all the family . . . Three main courses. Two desserts! Everybody smiling! A coffee filter, a dishwashing machine, a microwave . . . Those microwaves cook everything by themselves, don't they? (*Beat*)

CEAUSESCU. No microwave!

ELENA. No desserts!

CEAUSESCU. No dishwashing machine!

ELENA. No breakfast, no dinner, no sex!

CEAUSESCU. No capitalist house!

DANIELA. Our old house, the "Castle" . . . I can still hear the walls crumbling . . . / "Don't cry, my little princess, don't cry, I will build a new castle for you, I promise, my princess will be happy!"

CEAUSESCU. Don't cry, my little "princess," don't cry, I will build a new castle for you, I promise, my "princess" will be happy!

DANIELA. You shouldn't have promised. It was such a bad joke.

ELENA. No joke . . .

DANIELA. Do you think that guy Charlie makes jokes?

ELENA. No American husband . . .

DANIELA. Can you find "instant happiness" in American stores? . . .

ELENA. No "princess!"

CEAUSESCU. No "Castle!"

DANIELA. You don't know, I know. Still . . .

CEAUSESCU (*seriously*). No aristocratic houses in my socialist republic!

ELENA (*seriously*). Demolish them!

CEAUSESCU. Demolish them!

CEAUSESCU/ELENA. Demolish!

DANIELA. No! . . . You shouldn't have smoked so much, papa . . .

She walks downstage, smoking.

DANIELA. Seven! (*Confused*) No. Eight . . . Blind Date. Well . . . almost blind.

On the screen is written

8. BLIND DATE
May 5, 2001—New York

A bench in Central Park. Daniela sits on a bench, smoking. Charlie comes. They are both wearing dark glasses.

CHARLIE. This must be the fifth bench from the west.

DANIELA. And the seventh from the east.

CHARLIE. Are you Daniela?

DANIELA. Charlie?

CHARLIE. Yes. May I take a seat?

DANIELA. Sure. (*Stubs out and tosses away the cigarette.*)

They sit on the bench at a certain distance from each other.

CHARLIE. Beautiful weather, isn't it?

DANIELA. We agreed not to talk about the weather.

CHARLIE. Sure.

DANIELA. Let's talk about us, Charlie. Describe yourself.

CHARLIE. I dunno . . .

DANIELA. Are you tall short handsome ugly smart dumb . . . no, forget the last two. Describe yourself physically first.

CHARLIE. I'm pretty tall.

DANIELA. Use adjectives similes metaphors. Try to be eloquent and poetic.

CHARLIE. I'm tall like a . . . like a . . . I'm sorry Daniela, I can't say how tall I am "like."

DANIELA. Okay. Are you fat? Are you slim?

CHARLIE. So and so.

DANIELA. You know what? You're not helping our blind date go smoothly . . .

CHARLIE. What about you?

DANIELA. You go first. Then I'll go.

CHARLIE (*struggling to please her*). I'm tall like an oak tree grown by the sun, I'm thin like . . . barbed wire. I'm silent like a fish and blind like a jellyfish.

DANIELA (*laughing*). It doesn't work!

Charlie gets closer to her and starts tenderly caressing her shoulders.

DANIELA. What are you doing? This is a public space. People can see us.

CHARLIE (*trying to hold her in his arms*). We can't see them.

DANIELA (*jerking away*). What do you think of me? I'm not the sort of woman who lets herself be touched all over at the first blind date.

CHARLIE (*with fake pathos*). My eyes are in my fingertips. Touching means seeing for us.

DANIELA. You're not able to say anything really nice. You turn me off.

CHARLIE (*taking distance again*). You turn me off too.

DANIELA. Good.

CHARLIE. Great.

DANIELA. Excellent.

CHARLIE. *You* had this silly idea . . .

DANIELA (*taking off her glasses*). I thought that playing blind would help but you're a catastrophe at it.

CHARLIE (*taking off his glasses*). I thought we wouldn't talk so much if we played blind.

DANIELA. I thought we'd have fun if I could extract you from your Siamese laptop. For a different kind of game. Nothing about turkeys, everything about us! (*Pause. Charlie plays with his cane.*) To go out, to play a little in the fresh air, to smell the Spring, maybe to have a nice dinner and talk about us . . .

CHARLIE. I took you out for tea and cookies last Sunday.

DANIELA. Yes. At the Blood Donors' Center. Tea and cookies for free.

CHARLIE. There's nothing wrong with giving blood. You can help people in need.

DANIELA. Sure.

CHARLIE. You gave all my old shirts and trousers to that dirty homeless guy in the Times Square subway.

DANIELA. Uros.

CHARLIE. This morning I couldn't find my silver watch (*Beat*) . . . the one that goes with the gray suit. (*Beat*) And I had a meeting with a client.

DANIELA. You still have three wrist watches. (*Beat*) I took the ugliest one.

CHARLIE. You stole it.

DANIELA. I gave it to Uros.

CHARLIE. I don't want to hear about that crippled Muslim bum any more.

DANIELA. He used to teach philosophy and dead languages before the war. In Yugoslavia.

CHARLIE. That ragged old guy in the wheelchair?!

DANIELA. His dream is to follow Gilgamesh's traces.

CHARLIE. Whose traces?

DANIELA. Gilgamesh. You don't know the story? Looking for eternal life, his friend Enkidu . . .

CHARLIE. We should go home. It's late.

DANIELA. He wants to go to Iraq, Iran, Syria . . . in Gilgamesh's footsteps!

CHARLIE. He's crazy. And he's got my watch for that?

DANIELA. He has a fire inside him . . .

CHARLIE. What about my fire . . .

He starts kissing her. She pushes against him for a while, resigns for a moment, then pushes him away angrily.

DANIELA. Nine! (*To the audience*). You must meet Uros! About life and death in Times Square . . .

On the screen is written

9. ABOUT LIFE AND DEATH IN TIMES SQUARE
May 15, 2001—New York

Times Square subway station. Daniela pushes Uros's wheelchair in an area with the interdiction sign at the entrance.

UROS. I and the rats. Sharing the "luxurious apartment" they offered me.

DANIELA. You're very lucky they allowed you to live there, Uros! . . . I can get a TV set for you /, I . . .

UROS. That's nonsense . . . What am I supposed to do with a TV set? Where would I plug it? (*Laughing and coughing*) In my home-less buddies' asses? (*Beat*) No, gimme a radio. Can you bring me a radio from your millionaire man?

DANIELA. Charlie is not a millionaire. (*Beat*) You're already wearing his shirt and his trousers. His dark red socks. His silver watch. His tie.

UROS. I don't need his tie! (*Pulls it off*) Can he spare some money for a plane ticket? A one-way ticket. Let's not ask too much.

DANIELA. You must SEE the news. It's not safe there. You can't go there. Not in your condition.

UROS. Listen, girl. Uros goes wherever he wants to go. He's not a chicken, he's a man. (*Laughing and coughing*) And now that he has two wheels and a leg, he's more than a man. He's a willing chair . . .

DANIELA. Wheeling! . . . I'm telling you Iraq, Iran and Syria are not safe now. Of course you can go but it's not smart to go. It's dangerous!

UROS. It was dangerous in Gilgamesh's time. It's dangerous today. It will be dangerous tomorrow. I don't need to watch the news to find out such a simple truth . . . Come, sit on my "armchair!"

DANIELA (*sitting on the wheelchair's right arm*). Your obsession with Gilgamesh's story . . . What's so special? A guy and his friend . . .

UROS. A king and his friend Enkidu . . .

DANIELA. . . . traveling in search of . . .

UROS. Immortality! (*Slaps her thigh.*)

DANIELA. You cannot believe in immortality!

UROS. Of course, not . . . Mrs. Death and I are old pals. She follows me like a shadow. She clings to me like a spider. She's the tie around my neck . . . I want to take her with me on Gilgamesh's traces. To see her grimace there, on the land where she was defeated.

DANIELA. She was never defeated, Uros.

UROS. Yes, she was. (*Puts his hand on Daniela's leg.*)

DANIELA. You saw her in your war. In Yugoslavia.

UROS. Of course I saw her. She gulped my left leg. Gulped my wife, Jasna. Gulped my son, Andrej. Gulped my daughter, Tanja. But she spewed me out. I was too much for her bowels. That's why I want to take her on a "honeymoon." To Iraq.

DANIELA. Do you want to go to . . . fight there?

UROS. You may say so. (*Strokes Daniela's thigh.*)

DANIELA. Do you want to die there? (*Jerks away.*)

UROS. I just want to go there. (*Pause*) Could you push me back to
my stinky dark solitary corner? Home bitter home . . .

Daniela pushes his wheelchair back. Beat.

UROS. Did you steal that book from Barnes & Nobles? The
Gilgamesh epic?

DANIELA. I did.

UROS. Did you use the strategy I taught you?

DANIELA. Yes. Pay for one book, put three or four in your bag.

UROS (*laughing*). They never check your bag if you pay for one. Sit
here (*patting the arm of the wheelchair with his palm*) on my armchair! (*She sits.*) Did you have a good time stealing?

DANIELA. It was . . . exciting. To steal books is not something bad, is it?

UROS. No, girl. It's love of literature. It's not stealing. It's passion
for culture. For knowledge . . . It's to choose to live a spiritual
life over a material one. They can stick their money up their
asses! Books are what matter. Stories. There's no price for that.
(*Touches her again, more passionately.*) You cannot trade everything.
There are some things above shopping. You understand that,
you're a smart / girl . . .

DANIELA. What are you doing?

UROS. Life cannot be only shopping and fucking.

DANIELA. I gave back the books. (*Tries to get away, he holds her.*)

Lights on Ceausescu and Elena looking amused.

UROS. You didn't read the Gilgamesh?

DANIELA. No! (*Jerks away*) Don't do that again, Uros! You're my
friend. My only friend. / Don't . . .

UROS. Relax, girl. Uros is your friend!

Daniela walks downstage.

ELENA. Her friend.

CEAUSESCU. An old comrade from Yugoslavia. Tito's guy.

ELENA. Her FRIEND!

CEAUSESCU. Yes.

ELENA. Friend! Supporter. Mate. Well-wisher.

CEAUSESCU. . . . ?

ELENA. Someone she cares about.

CEAUSESCU. Yes?

ELENA. Weak Spot—of the Second Degree!

CEAUSESCU. Oooooooh. I got you!

ELENA. You used to be much much much faster.

CEAUSESCU. What shall we do then? How shall we do?

ELENA. A trial first.

CEAUSESCU. No, not a trial!

ELENA. Then an execution.

On the screen is written

10. SECOND NIGHTMARE

DANIELA. These nightmares have nothing to do with my "real" life.
They are just dreams. Well, Freud would say / that . . .

ELENA. Shut up, girl!

CEAUSESCU. Nobody gave you permission to talk.

ELENA. She's so boring, isn't she? . . . (*To Daniela*) Stand up, accused!

DANIELA. I'm not guilty!

ELENA. Bitch! . . . She's too talkative. She must be impaled without delay.

DANIELA. Shoot me! Please . . .

CEAUSESCU. She wants to be shot . . .

ELENA. She's too demanding . . .

CEAUSESCU. We don't like to be reminded about shootings . . .

ELENA. We were shot in such an unforgivable . . . rude aggressive provincial way. How could she mention that? She must be impaled!

CEAUSESCU. What is this girl accused of? Theft from the socialist public wealth?

DANIELA. I haven't done anything wrong. I was sleeping in my bed.

ELENA. Naked . . . (*Gets up and rips off Daniela's pajama's with a sharp motion.*) Your nipples are too small.

DANIELA. It's not my fault!

CEAUSESCU. I don't know . . . I like small nipples.

ELENA. I know! She has to be impaled. In her vagina.

CEAUSESCU. That's not impaling, that's rape.

ELENA. Whatever. Let's have her impaled and put an end to this. I hate trials. They depress me.

CEAUSESCU. They depress me too. Look, I'm so pale!

ELENA. She persists in reminding us of the worst part of our mortal life . . .

CEAUSESCU. That's not nice, girl. Our trial / was . . .

ELENA. Ours was not a trial. They killed us with no trial. A bunch of worms. No spines, no brains. We should have kept them in the darkness forever. Send them all to prison. Starve them to death. Crush those ugly dirty pipsqueak thieves, those Romanians . . .

DANIELA. Listen to me! I didn't steal from the socialist public wealth!

ELENA. Socialist. Communist. Capitalist. Who cares now!

CEAUSESCU (*to Elena*). Let's go, sweetheart. We'll miss the book burning of my *Complete Works*.

ELENA. I'd like to see her impaled . . .

CEAUSESCU. Come on, honey-blood . . . You've seen enough impalements . . . I'm fed up with being a judge. I want to feel like a writer!

ELENA. You are as bad as a writer as you are as a judge. As an impaler. As a leader. As a dictator. As a vampire. As a husband . . .

CEAUSESCU. I was a faithful husband!

ELENA. Exactly! (*To Daniela*) Bye-bye, flesh-pie! Write to me about the impalement!

CEAUSESCU. Bye-bye, accused! Take care. Don't forget to write!

ELENA. In detail! Everything you feel while being impaled. (*Sensuously*) Everything that's going on in your bottom and in your head, small-nippled pipsqueak!

CEAUSESCU. Use adjectives similes metaphors. Try to be eloquent and poetic!

ELENA. Die-die! Don't forget to wriiiiiiiite!

CEAUSESCU. Bye-bye!

ELENA. Die-die!

They nod at each other and start dancing and singing, vaudeville-style.

CEAUSESCU. I am a good dictator
       Everyone can confess
       The tender fine impalements
       Relieve you from the stress

ELENA. Report for us dear comrades
       Describe your DYING seasons

> We need to know exactly
> For scientific reasons

CEAUSESCU/ELENA. Bye-bye, die-die, comrade!
     Bye-bye, die-die, friend!
     The bottom of the story
     Is its perfect END.
     The story of the bottom
     Is its perfect END.

DANIELA. I need a break . . .

Lights fade.

ACT II

Lights on Daniela, sitting on the floor with lots of books around her.

DANIELA. I've been trying. You can't say I haven't tried. I've got all these self-help books. I've written down the main ideas. (*Looking down at her notes.*) "Choose your Tomorrow: BEFORE—perfectionistic misunderstood love junkie over-reactive self-effacing. AFTER—flexible good communicator self-accepting in-control assertive."

I read them all: *I'm Dysfunctional, You're Dysfunctional, It's Not as Bad as It Seems, Master Your Panic and Take Back Your Life, Twenty-One Ways to Stop Worrying, How to Control Your Anxiety Before it Controls You, How to Make Yourself Happy, Head Over Heart in Love, How to Stop Destroying Your Relationships, Men Are from Earth, Women Are from Earth, What to Do When He has a Headache, Fun as Psychotherapy, Let's Get Rational Game, Three-Minute Therapy: Change Your Thinking, Change Your Life, The Six-Second Shrink, Dating, Mating and Relating, Unconditionally Accepting Yourself and*

Others, Resolving Your Past, Fitness for Your Soul & Body . . . Read them all . . . (*Nervously*) But I'm afraid I'm still in the BEFORE stage. I still have emotions feelings confusion anger . . . Those AFTER people! They must be so happy. So peaceful. So empty . . . OK! Breathe deeply! Start counting to ten. Prepare yourself to relieve your anxiety. To relax. To talk. OK. Here we go . . .

Dammit, this is gonna be difficult! You don't have the references to our complicated Romanian Dacian Tracian Roman Ottoman Byzantine Balkan communist post-communist anti-communist pro-American history! All you know about us is Dracula-the-vampire, Ceausescu-the-dictator and Nadia Comaneci-the-gymnast! Anyway, Nadia's cool, she never comes into my dreams with her perfectly fit body, so forget about her. She's not in this story. I have more important, heavier, issues on my mind! Stuff like Life and Death. No time to worry about my cellulite. Unless a bullet stops by IN it . . .

One! About life and death in University Square.

On the screen is written

1. ABOUT LIFE AND DEATH IN UNIVERSITY SQUARE
December 1, 2000—Bucharest

Elvis and Daniela are leaning against a wall of Bucharest University. Noises of a crowd cheering and hailing.

ELVIS. Those bastards! Extremist bastards!

DANIELA. Shhhhh! You've already got a leg hurt. Why ask for more?

ELVIS. Did you see that? The bastard kicked me with his boot. Three times!

DANIELA. If you can't keep your mouth closed . . . Why tell them they are a bunch of "paranoid extremists?"

ELVIS. Nobody asked you to come with me . . .

DANIELA (*lighting a cigarette*). If you want to play the filmmaker, that's fine . . . but a professional shoots the facts and keeps quiet.

ELVIS. Sure, a bowed head cannot be cut by the sword . . . (*Grabs Daniela's cigarette*) Gimme a smoke, I have to go back to work. This is gonna be a super film, have you seen those faces? A bunch of brainwashed stray dogs / . . .

DANIELA. I'm only saying, you should stop and THINK for a second before going back and sticking your camera in their faces . . . Nobody commissioned you for this film. Nobody will pay you for it. You're working for nobody. You can be killed for nothing. / I think—

ELVIS. I work for myself! What the fuck . . .

DANIELA (*mocking him*). I work, I don't think! (*Seriously*) "We work, we don't think!"—remember the miners storming into THIS square ten years ago? Shouting and singing in the rhythm of hit- ting us, the anti-Iliescu protesters. What a joke! That communist "with a human-face" elected after the Revolution. "We work, we don't think! We work, we don't think!" . . . They took me for a student. Me and the others. Who wore jeans and looked like they had a functioning / brain . . .

ELVIS. Geez, Dani, you look really ugly when you start talking seri- ously about the . . . (*mocking her*) "ghosts of the past."

DANIELA. You saw them only on TV! You were a ten-year-old snotty brat. I was HERE. In '89, in '90, in '92, in '96! Here, for all the protests of the Opposition. Here at the Revolution. Here! I've seen blood in this square! (*Grabs the cigarette from him.*)

ELVIS. Your Opposition hasn't done shit. A bunch of corrupted snobs! Your inthhhellectuals . . . They got us here, in this shitty situation, and washed their hands of us. We are doing goooood! In the Year of our Lord 2000 we have to choose between the good old communist Iliescu and the bad old crazy Vladim who declared he'd close the borders and take us back to the dark caves (*massaging his injured leg*) where it seems we belong anyway . . . (*grabs the cigarette back*) Funny, isn't it? You have no choice but to vote for Iliescu, who sent the miners to beat your ass in '90 . . . I hope you're not going to vote for Vladim!

DANIELA. I'm not gonna vote for any one. I've had enough of all of them. I've had enough! (*Beat*) I'll be in America before the elections . . .

ELVIS (*passing the cigarette*). Are you sure you wanna marry that . . .

DANIELA. Mrs. Aronson is a very nice lady.

ELVIS. You're not gonna fuck her.

DANIELA. Hey! Mind your own ass! (*Passing the cigarette*). Charlie sent you that video camera and the VCR . . .

People are boo-ing in the square. The sound of voices arguing, people running.

ELVIS (*excited*). Things are gonna take fire here. Vladim is playing dirty . . . Why don't you go home? (*Passing the cigarette*) Go. Take care of mom, make sure she's not asking for her heart attack . . .

DANIELA (*passing the cigarette*). Nothing big will happen. No fire, no fireworks. People are tired of revolutions. Don't you start a scandal, you're the only one who'll get kicked!

ELVIS (*finishes smoking Daniela's cigarette and tosses the butt away*). Gimme a break, you sound like a fucking old maid . . .

He leaves. Daniela leans against the wall with her eyes closed. The crowd shouts and sings: WAKE UP, ROMANIAN! (the Romanian national anthem after 1989). As the noises fade, Daniela opens her eyes.

DANIELA (*to the audience*). Two. Sic transit gloria mundi.

Lights on Gloria.

GLORIA. How the world's glory has passed . . .

DANIELA. I was good at Latin!

On the screen is written

2. SIC TRANSIT GLORIA MUNDI
June 13, 2001—New York

Gloria and Daniela are at a restaurant in New York, drinking red wine.

GLORIA. I thought it was a way of saying . . . a pretext!

DANIELA. It was the truth.

GLORIA. What's there to talk about? A man like any other men. Self-sufficient. Self-indulgent. Unreliable. Nice.

DANIELA. I don't think I understand him.

GLORIA. What's to understand?

DANIELA. I don't know. What does he want . . . What does he believe in . . .

GLORIA. Charlie believes that God is a sort of multidimensional computer scientist who designed this virtual 3-D game called WORLD or HUMANS. We are all characters in the bloody script of this bloody game. A bunch of so-called "angels" are playing with us. For better or for worse. Depending on their mood and some other factors. Anyway it's a brilliantly conceived system that functions due to the Good–Evil dynamics. We have no control over it. We are manipulated . . . Something like that . . .

DANIELA. Sounds very . . . sad! Has he told you all that?

GLORIA. No. I invented everything! . . . Of course, he told me that. How could I come up with such a crazy thing?

DANIELA. He never talks such things with me . . . Mrs. Aronson / . . .

GLORIA. Look. Charlie and mom didn't get along too well. She'd let him do everything, except what he really wanted: to play the violin.

DANIELA. Violin?

GLORIA. He didn't have any talent! Mom was right. So he played against her will in any way he could.

DANIELA. He won't marry me then . . .

GLORIA. C'mon . . . forget this conventional stuff with marriage and all the bullshit around it. A woman has to be her own person. To make decisions for herself. Not to cook for some self-righteous prick who thinks he does her a big favor each time he penetrates her. Be a smart girl . . .

DANIELA. I don't know . . . I guess I'm pretty conventional but . . .

GLORIA. But-but-but! . . . Butt! Not that I mind that . . . Say conventional again!

DANIELA (*with her exotic accent*). Conventional.

GLORIA. Even a word like "conventional" sounds sexy coming out of your mouth . . . (*Beat*)

DANIELA. Let's go to your place, Gloria . . .

GLORIA. Why? You don't like it here? Is it too noisy? Too crowded? You need to smoke? Oh, sweet addictions . . .

DANIELA. You don't want to be with me? I thought . . . I mean . . .

GLORIA. Oh. You want to . . .

DANIELA. Yes.

GLORIA. Are you sure?

DANIELA. Well . . .

GLORIA. Are you sure? (*Beat*)

DANIELA. No.

GLORIA. Listen, girl. Don't do anything you have doubts about. No matter if it's big or small. No matter who has asked. No matter whom you'll make happy (*raises her glass of wine*). Shall we go then?

Daniela sips her wine and sighs. Gloria sips her wine and sighs. They look at each other like two old friends.

DANIELA. Shall we?

Gloria bursts into laughter. She imitates Daniela.

GLORIA. Shall we? Shall we? (*Like a prude*) Shall we? Shaaaaall weeeeeee? (*Beat, seriously*) No. Not until you are absolutely sure. Cheers!

DANIELA. Cheers!

Lights on Ceausescu and Elena. They have glasses in their hands. They smile and mock Daniela.

CEAUSESCU/ELENA. Shall we? Shall we? Cheers! Cheers! Shall we? Cheers! . . .

DANIELA (*to the audience*). Three. The turkey game.

On the screen is written

3. THE TURKEY GAME
July 12, 2001—New York

Charlie's apartment. Sunday evening. He is in the turkey position behind an "oven" built of a pile of shoeboxes or behind a transparent curtain. His head and his feet in white socks can be seen by the audience. Daniela has a knife in her right hand, pointed at Charlie.

DANIELA. I'm gonna eat you, turkey! Yum-yum . . . good turkey . . . fat turkey . . . yum-yum . . .

CHARLIE. Gobble . . . gobble-gobble-gobble . . .

DANIELA. Yes, turkey, I'm gonna jab you, turkey . . . thrust you . . . eat your meat, turkey . . . yummy-yummy . . .

CHARLIE. Gobble-gobble . . .

DANIELA. Good turkey . . .

CHARLIE. Gobble-gobble, gobble-gobble . . .

DANIELA. I'm gonna cut off your waddle . . . yum-yum . . .

CHARLIE. Oh, gobble!

DANIELA. Your wings . . . your thighs . . . your breast . . . yum-yum!

CHARLIE. Gobble . . . Cook me, mommy!

DANIELA. I'm gonna suck your bones . . . yum!

CHARLIE (*climax*). Yeah!

Daniela looks at the knife. Charlie closes his eyes. Beat. Daniela swoops upon Charlie with the knife in her hand. Lights on Ceausescu and Elena.

DANIELA. I'm gonna prick you, turkey. Stab you. Kill you. Murder you. Yum-yum! Bye-bye, turkey. Die-die. Die-die!

CHARLIE. Ah!

She throws away the knife. There's blood on it. Daniela lies silently on Charlie's body. She starts crying. Charlie wipes her eyes with his right hand.

CEAUSESCU. Waw. That was good! The girl is tough.

ELENA. I was waiting for her to really cut off his "waddle." Some action. Not just . . . words!

CEAUSESCU. She seemed quite active to me. She reminds me of you!

ELENA. Oh, noooo! Take back your words immediately! She's a silly squeamish mouse. She's gonna apologize to him. Kiss his ass. Suck him up. I would never do such a thing!

CEAUSESCU. That would make him a Weak-Spot-of-the-First-Degree, wouldn't it?

ELENA. Not quite. Not quite. Something is missing . . .

Later, the same Sunday evening.

The shoe-boxes "oven" is still in the center of the living-room. Charlie's left arm is bandaged up. He is working on his laptop using only his right hand. Daniela stands still, staring through the window.

DANIELA. Charlie . . . (*beat*) . . . Charlie . . . (*beat*) . . . I'm sorry . . . I'm so sorry . . . / I'm . . .

CHARLIE. / Let's not talk about this.

DANIELA. Let's TALK about this! I'll go insane if I don't talk.

CHARLIE. . . .

DANIELA. Charlie!

CHARLIE. What.

DANIELA. I'm thinking of going back.

CHARLIE. Back?

DANIELA. To Romania. Back home.

CHARLIE (*looks at her*). Your home is here.

DANIELA. We're not married, Charlie.

CHARLIE. We will be.

DANIELA. When?

CHARLIE. In the summer.

DANIELA. It is summer.

CHARLIE. On my vacation.

DANIELA. When?

CHARLIE. When I'll take my vacation.

DANIELA. IF you'll take your vacation . . .

CHARLIE. A wedding is expensive.

DANIELA. Charlie . . .

CHARLIE. I have to make money for it, don't I?

DANIELA. You never talk about your mother.

CHARLIE. My mother?!

DANIELA. She asked me to marry you.

CHARLIE (*looking at her*). I know.

DANIELA. You didn't want . . .

CHARLIE. I didn't mind . . .

DANIELA (*touching his injured arm*). I'm sorry, Charlie. I'm so sorry.

CHARLIE. Relax. (*Beat*) We won't play it again.

DANIELA. The Thanksgiving / game . . .

CHARLIE. Turkey game is over.

DANIELA. No game next Sunday?

CHARLIE. Nothing about turkeys.

DANIELA. Everything about us?!

CHARLIE (*smiling*). Maybe a turkey, for dinner, on Thanksgiving day.

DANIELA. Like everybody else.

CHARLIE. Like you and me.

DANIELA. We can invite Gloria and maybe / even . . .

CHARLIE (*back to his laptop*). I hope that you're not actually seeing that homeless scum anymore.

DANIELA. Uros?

CHARLIE. Last Friday he tried to sell me my own old tie. The one with the purple hearts . . .

DANIELA. You didn't buy it, did you?

CHARLIE. Nope.

DANIELA. Good. (*Beat*) Are you . . . hungry?

CHARLIE. But I gave him some money.

DANIELA. Shall I . . . cook something?

CHARLIE. It was my very first tie...

DANIELA. I should go back, Charlie!

CHARLIE. I was thirteen when mom bought it for me . . .

DANIELA. I do horrible things here. I'm a thief . . .

CHARLIE. Don't worry about that tie . . .

DANIELA. I'm a criminal . . .

CHARLIE. It was a silly tie . . .

DANIELA. I'm no good here . . .

CHARLIE. You're a good cook.

DANIELA. I've never been a good cook, Charlie.

CHARLIE. What about mamaliga with cheese and sour cream?

She stares through the window. Charlie works on his laptop. It looks like the perfect family evening.

Daniela walks downstage and addresses the audience.

DANIELA. Right. Something is wrong . . . I can read in your eyes the questions—Why don't you change something? Go out! Get a job as a waitress or as a . . . waitress, like so many illegal immigrants do. There are thousands of possibilities. You are in the city of all possibilities. Leave the jerk. Leave Charlie! (*Beat*) I don't want to be a waitress. I'm a cosmetologist. I have my own . . . And don't call Charlie a jerk! OK? (*Beat*) Four! About death and life in Times Square. (*Takes a radio from Charlie's living room into the new scene.*)

On the screen is written

4. ABOUT DEATH AND LIFE IN TIMES SQUARE
July 29, 2001—New York

Times Square subway. Uros lies on four seats, covered by a ragged blanket. Someone plays a saxophone nearby. Daniela stands beside Uros, she has a small radio in her right hand.

DANIELA. Hey, Uros . . . Wake up! I've got you the radio!

UROS (*coughing*). What are you doing here? Traveling by subway . . . Bleah. Your millionaire man should send you shopping in a Mercedes . . . or a limo! . . . Have you seen those huge white limos, those white earthworms, crawling out of Enkidu's nostrils (*coughing*) . . .

DANIELA. You're sick . . .

UROS. Uros is never sick, girl! You didn't read the story, you don't know shit about Gilgamesh and his friend's—Enkidu's!—death . . . When he, Gilgamesh, the immortal, well, almost immortal, realized that Mrs. Death was fucking around and his best friend, his brother Enkidu—the mortal!—would cheat on him with that dirty bitch (*coughing*) . . .

DANIELA. I should bring you some antibiotics, not only Vitamin C . . .

But, you know, they don't sell antibiotics if you don't have a medical prescription and you can't have one if you don't go to a physician and you can't go to a physician if you don't have health insurance . . .

UROS. Relax, girl. I'm not sick. I don't need no insurance. I'm sure enough of all the shit around me. I don't need them to "insure" me (*coughing*) . . .

DANIELA. What about me, Uros? What if I get sick?

UROS. You can't get sick. You're a warrior, a woman-warrior . . .

DANIELA. I hate wars! I hate to fight . . .

UROS. Then you're a corpse. And all these biped eagles regale themselves everyday, raping you, tearing you apart (*coughing*) . . .

DANIELA. You're not yourself, Uros . . .

UROS. Wrong. I've never been more myself than now, when every inch of my flesh reminds me what a blessing and a torture this life is, biting your soul, licking it, biting it, licking it. . . (*closes his eyes*).

DANIELA. Open your eyes! Talk to me!

UROS (*his eyes closed*). I ran out of stories.

DANIELA (*taking his hand and putting it on her hip*). What about this one?

UROS (*stroking her hip gently*). Your millionaire man should buy you a white limo, should take you on a honeymoon to a bright sunny island, all this romantic shit, music . . . what's this music? . . . a saxophone . . . that's nice . . . very sensuous . . . very tender . . . I ran out of tenderness. I must be dead.

DANIELA. No! You'll go to Iraq, like Gilgamesh, you'll . . . start a new life there. Find that . . . whatever you are looking for!

UROS. Immortality?

DANIELA. Anything. Something to look forward to. To make you get up in the mornings, get off the bed, start / the day . . .

UROS. Uros don't have no bed, girl. (*Beat*) You grew to talk like them. All the American propaganda bullshit. (*Beat*) Relax. I won't ask you to steal your Charlie's bed . . . (*coughing, opening his eyes*).

DANIELA. There must be something I can do for you . . .

UROS (*clinging to her*). Don't let them steal your stories, don't let them steal your thoughts . . .

DANIELA. Who are THEY, Uros?

UROS (*closing his eyes again*). The worms. The earthworms in the white limos. They have the power. The money. They trade your limbs, your organs, your life, your time. Even your stories! But they cannot trade your thoughts (*laughing and coughing*), even THEY cannot . . .

DANIELA. Where are they?

Lights on Ceausescu staring at Uros.

UROS. Everywhere. They follow you. They stick to you like leeches. You cannot get off this marsh . . .

DANIELA. Shhhhhhhhh. You must rest now . . .

UROS. I thought you're smart, girl. . . I thought you were . . . you . . . you . . . you (*falls asleep*).

CEAUSESCU (*to Uros*). Immortality is for people of vision and power, old comrade. Have you led any country? Have you created any policy? Have you improved the human race? Have you built a palace? Have you had breakfast with the Queen of England or George Bush? Have you had dinner with Saddam Hussein or Yasser Arafat? Have you had millions of people worshiping your name? Have you had your portrait in all the classrooms? Have you been on the first page of every book in your language? Have you sentenced anybody to death? Have you sentenced anybody to life? . . . Have you been betrayed and killed by your own people?

DANIELA. Don't listen to him, Uros! Don't listen to him! (*To the audience*) Five! Goodbye, Romania. (*Beat*) An end.

On the screen is written

5. GOODBYE, ROMANIA! (AN END)
January 13, 2001—Bucharest

Otopeni airport. Daniela and Marcela, sitting next to each other. Noises of planes taking off, people jostling. Marcela is crying.

DANIELA. C'mon, mom . . . People are looking at us.

MARCELA. Only one daughter and she is going to be thousands of kilometers away . . . across the ocean . . . and the whole of Europe . . .

DANIELA. You wanted me to marry an American. Be happy. I'm gonna marry one.

MARCELA. Take care not to make a shame of my name there, in America!

DANIELA. Sure. Everybody knows you over there.

MARCELA. Behave right! Don't swear. Don't smoke . . . Don't eat with your elbows on the table . . . Don't chomp . . . Don't drink water during the main dish . . . (*Beat*) Wash your underwear every night before you go to bed. Change it with a new one in the morning. I put twenty pairs of panties in your small baggage . . . We don't want your husband to think we're dirty!

DANIELA. My future husband. (*Beat*) I hope he's a nice guy.

MARCELA. He's a businessman!

DANIELA. He's not a businessman, he's a computer engineer. He works on the sixty-sixth floor of this sky / scraper . . .

MARCELA. You are so lucky! You won't have to cook and scrub like me every day, no vacation, no weekend, no fun / for fifty years . . .

DANIELA. For fifty years . . . I know, I know. I'm not gonna cook, I'm not gonna scrub. I can promise that. (*Raising her voice*) Mrs. Aronson / has a cleaning lady anyway.

MARCELA. She's your husband's mother! You shouldn't raise your voice at her as you do with me! Watch your behavior! You are going to live with her before the wedding, she will test you . . . (*Looking around*) Where is that Elvis? He will miss saying goodbye to his own sister.

DANIELA. We still have more than two hours. You insisted we come here three hours in advance.

MARCELA. You never know with airports. Better waiting than crying because we missed the plane . . . (*Beat*) Don't forget: you have five suitcases. The big brown one with the clothes, the small green one with the presents, the dark blue bag with your wedding dress . . . (*Starts crying*) I am not going to be at my own girl's wedding . . .

DANIELA. I told you it'd be better to ask HIM to come here . . .

MARCELA. That's silly. What if he didn't like you . . .

DANIELA. If he doesn't like me . . .

MARCELA. Nonsense. He is going to love you if you behave right . . . Where is that Elvis? . . . So . . . You have five suitcases: the brown one, the small green one, the dark blue one, the one with the books . . . It's really silly to carry books over there! . . . Anyway, don't forget you have five . . .

DANIELA. Thank God, Elvis!

Lights on Elvis waving.

MARCELA. He's going to give me a heart attack . . . Last month he came home from that demonstration . . . his clothes in a mess, limping . . . his video camera broken . . . his leg injured . . .

ELVIS. Hey, sis, what's up?! Are you happy? You're gonna FLY over the ocean!

DANIELA. I'll send you a new video camera . . .

ELVIS. C'mon. That's not what has to be on your mind right now. You're gonna be a Mrs.!!! . . . May I help you with your luggage Mrs. Aronson . . .

DANIELA. Daniela Aronson . . .

MARCELA (*standing up*). Stop these childish games! Hurry. We'll miss the plane.

ELVIS. We? It's just Daniela who's flying. The sky is waiting for you, Mrs. Aronson!

DANIELA. I'm gonna miss this sky . . .

MARCELA (*sitting down*). You are both completely impractical. Poets! Taking after your father. Listen to me, girl: you have FIVE suitcases: the brown one, the dark blue one, the green one, the one with books and your backpack, which you'll have with you ON the plane . . .

Elvis and Daniela look at each other, shaking their heads—"she's never gonna change." Daniela walks downstage, carrying one of the suitcases.

DANIELA (*to the audience*). Six. No wedding and a funeral. The BEGINNING!

On the screen is written

6. NO WEDDING AND A FUNERAL (THE BEGINNING)
February 13, 2001—New York

Charlie, Gloria and Daniela, dressed in black, enter Charlie's apartment, after Mrs. Aronson's funeral. Gloria looks elegant and stylish, wearing a big black and white hat. She holds a bottle of red wine, a leftover from Mrs. Aronson's alms. Daniela carries the suitcase from the previous scene.

The living room is a mess: papers, four/five laptops, computer monitors, empty cans, used plastic plates/forks/knives, etc. have taken over the place.

GLORIA. This is the messiest mess I've seen in years! You surely know how to welcome guests, bro . . .

DANIELA (*trying to hide her embarrassment*). It was a great funeral . . . Your mother was a great lady . . .

CHARLIE. I didn't have time to / really . . .

GLORIA. Of course you didn't. The old-fashioned Time oppressing our busy e-genius! (*To Daniela*) That was always his excuse, and mom would rush to clean up the mess for her sweet brilliant perfect little Charlie . . .

CHARLIE. You can leave the wine in the kitchen.

GLORIA (*doesn't move*). Perfect spoiled little Charlie!

Awkward silence. Daniela feels the need to do/say something. She starts picking up the cans, etc.

DANIELA. I can clean up . . . No problem . . . (*To Charlie*) Are you going to work tomorrow morning?

CHARLIE. I must.

GLORIA. You must not! (*To Daniela*) You are not paid as a cleaning lady! (*To Charlie*) Did you have her clean mom's house?

DANIELA. Oh no. Mrs. Aronson did everything by herself. She was so energetic! (*Tidying the room*) So kind . . . She used to say that retirement made her stronger than ever . . . "I don't need help any more, girl! Anna, the cleaning lady, comes here only once a month. To play pinochle with me!"

GLORIA. That's mom . . . Her own big heart KILLING her in the end . . .

Charlie takes off his shoes. He's wearing white socks. He turns on a laptop.

GLORIA. Here he is. Mr. Laptop! Mr. "I-don't-care-lemme-alone-go-fuck-yourself." (*To Daniela*) We don't exist for him. (*Hands the bottle of wine to Daniela*) I'm out of here, honey . . . Good luck!

Gloria walks upstage. Lights fade on her.

DANIELA (*to Charlie*). Are you all right? Do you need anything?

CHARLIE. A bagel with ham and cream cheese, thanks.

DANIELA. Sure!

CHARLIE. If there's any bagel left in the fridge.

DANIELA. Oh.

CHARLIE. Did Gloria leave for good? (*Looks at her*) You can put that wine in the kitchen . . .

DANIELA (*doesn't move*). Gloria is such a nice person . . . She's an artist, isn't she?

CHARLIE. Yeah, she's the artist in the family.

DANIELA. One can tell . . . (*Heads to the kitchen.*)

CHARLIE. Oh, no!

DANIELA. I didn't mean / to say . . .

CHARLIE. I ate the last bagel this morning.

DANIELA. I can go and buy some! I feel like Christmas every time I enter a shop here in New York. There are so many products. I'm like taking everything and putting it in my bag! I have never seen so many types of bread cheese bagels! "Whole Wheat," "Blueberry," "Onion," "Garlic," "Cinn-Raisin," "Sour-Dough," "Sesame-Seed," "Pumpernickel," "Poppy-Seed," "Everything" / . . .

CHARLIE. I like the "Plain" ones.

DANIELA. I can buy "Plain."

CHARLIE. You need cash, don't you? (*Checks his wallet*)

DANIELA (*nodding*). I don't know how to use your credit cards. We didn't have such things. But I'm gonna learn!

CHARLIE. I'm out of cash . . . There's some meat in the freezer. Can you cook?

DANIELA. Cook?

CHARLIE. I've never had Romanian food. Can you prepare something Romanian?

DANIELA. Romanian? Yes, but . . . I don't / really . . .

CHARLIE. Mom was a good cook.

DANIELA (*beat*). I can try.

She goes upstage, to the "kitchen" and comes back in a second.

DANIELA (*excited*). May I use the microwave?

CHARLIE. You'll only need the stove.

Daniela's enthusiasm evaporates. She walks downstage.

DANIELA (*to the audience*). Seven. Goodbye, America. Another end.

On the screen is written

7. GOODBYE, AMERICA! (ANOTHER END)
August 23, 2001—New York

A subway station. Noises of trains passing. Noises of people waiting. Uros lies on four seats, apparently asleep. There is a small radio at his head playing some soft music. Daniela looks anxious. Ceausescu and Elena, dressed up, follow her. She rushes to Uros, talking fast.

DANIELA. Hey Uros . . . Wake up! . . .

ELENA (*mockingly*). Wake up! Wake up!

DANIELA. I have good news . . . I got the money . . . I have your ticket for Iraq! . . . Goodbye, America! . . . I bought a one-way ticket for me too . . . I'm going back . . . My flight's at 11 a.m., yours is at 11.30 a.m. . . . We can travel together to the airport . . . we'll take a cab! . . . I managed to use his Mastercard, I finally learned how to use their damn credit cards . . . Uros!? . . . You'll go to Iraq, you'll find your soul, your . . . "immortality!"

ELENA. Isn't she deadly stupid?

DANIELA. What can I do?! Back to hairy tales . . . Charlie loves his laptops and his plain bagels, not me . . . He needs a good cook, not me . . . Small word this "love!" In Romanian it's bigger: "dragoste" . . . Uros?! . . . Talk to me . . .

ELENA (*mockingly*). Talk to her!

DANIELA. Uros?

CEAUSESCU. Leave him alone, comrade!

DANIELA. . . . You know what . . . I'm not sure of this going back . . .
Mom will have a heart attack . . . she tells every neighbor and his
uncle . . . everyone in the elevator, in the peasants' market, all
the saleswomen in the supermarket know how HAPPY I am with
my American husband . . . Charlie is not my husband! . . .
C'mon, Uros! (*Laughing*) I know you tried to sell him his own tie.
I'm not angry at you. Uros?! . . . Uros?! . . . (*Beat*) You're not
dead, are you? . . . No . . . No!

ELENA/CEAUSESCU. Cheers!

DANIELA (*to Uros*). Don't do this to me, Uros . . . Don't . . . Don't . . .
We have plane tickets! (*Freezes for a while, then turns off the radio.
Gets up and takes the radio.*) I'll give it back to Charlie . . .

ELENA. Weak-Spot-of-the-Second-Degree: HIT. Weak-Spot-of-the-
First-Degree: TO BE DETECTED. Cheers!

CEAUSESCU. You're a genius!

*Daniela walks downstage. Funeral music. Ceausescu and Elena dance,
laughing.*

DANIELA. Last nightmare for this evening . . .

CEAUSESCU/ELENA. Cheers! Noroc!

On the screen is written

8. LAST NIGHTMARE (FOR THIS EVENING)

*A party of dead people. They all have long hair, hairy arms, legs, faces, etc.
They all smile. Big smiles. Fake smiles. Sick smiles. Condescending smiles.
All sorts of smiles. They drink red wine and chat as at any reception.*

*The scene can be played without any of the above, just with Ceausescu
and Elena in the "party-mood."*

DANIELA (*to the audience*). "Don't laugh at other people's dreams or
nightmares"—I read this in *Introduction to Chinese Wisdom*. It's not
a stolen book. I found it in the trash, on our street. I had to take
it home! That's how I learnt I was born in the year of the Horse /

. . . One can find so many great things in the garbage here, in New York.

CEAUSESCU. Shut up, horse!

DANIELA. It's like they wait for us there, in the rubbish, feeling sad, lonely and rejected . . .

Elena kicks Daniela and forces her to get on her knees.

ELENA. On! On! Move on, pig!

CEAUSESCU. Horse. She's a horse.

ELENA. Whatever.

CEAUSESCU. We shouldn't have taken her here. Everybody left their pets at the door.

ELENA. She's not a pet. She's a servant.

CEAUSESCU. She's our horse. Our dog. Our rat. Our darling little guinea pig. And our cook, of course.

ELENA. Our cleaning girl.

CEAUSESCU. Your waxing lady.

ELENA. I've got so hairy since I'm dead. Why does hair grow on dead people? Look—everybody is so hairy around here.

CEAUSESCU. Let's not ruin our mood for the sake of hair!

They take two glasses of red wine and drink with relish.

ELENA. To . . . forever!

CEAUSESCU. To . . . Draculand!

ELENA. You mean Disneyland.

CEAUSESCU. Not at all. We'll have our own park! They're building Draculand in Transylvania, near Sighisoara.

ELENA. You didn't tell me!

CEAUSESCU. Look, the girl . . .

ELENA. The horse?

CEAUSESCU. She's not smiling. Everyone else is smiling. She's not. She's thinking!

ELENA. Oh, no. You think, pig?

CEAUSESCU. Yes, she is. I can tell by the wrinkles on her forehead.

ELENA. Let's hear that! Think louder, horse! . . . What are you waiting for? . . . I said, THINK, pig! (*Kicks Daniela.*)

DANIELA. Given the existence of something beyond existence, I have ceased to exist. (*Starts licking Ceausescu's hand.*) I am your ashtray. Your tomb. Your Disneyland. Your past. Your present. Your future. You can do with me whatever you want. I am here to stay. I am here to endure. I am here to live . . .

CEAUSESCU. She's sick!

ELENA. Enough, pet! Wait in front of the door!

DANIELA. Ruins. I'm an earthworm crawling among wrecks. Eating the dust . . . (*Starts licking Elena's hand.*)

CEAUSESCU. Send her home! She'll ruin our party . . .

DANIELA. Dust. Rust. Blood. Champagne. Wedding. Funeral. Birth. Death. Cut. Grow. Wax. Grow. Hair. Hair. Hair. Everywhere. Hair!

Elena kicks Daniela's back. Ceausescu pats it, like he'd do to a horse.

ELENA. Vanish from my gaze! . . . Fuck off!

CEAUSESCU. Leave us alone!

Daniela is crawling leftstage.

ELENA. I hate her. She's too . . . too . . . unusual!

CEAUSESCU (*fondling her hand*). Forget her. Let's talk about us. Let's talk about love!

ELENA. You turned into a boring romantic vampire. You're far below your reputation. Dracula was . . . well . . . he was somebody.

CEAUSESCU. Stop comparing me with the myth . . . I grew to like some anonymity. Just you and me in a little house, somewhere in the forest . . .

ELENA. How boring.

CEAUSESCU. Just you and me on a beach. Listening to the ocean . . .

ELENA. You're not yourself. You shouldn't drink red wine. It softens you.

CEAUSESCU. Just you and me, biting and devouring each other . . .

ELENA. This sounds much better . . .

They start caressing and kissing their necks. The party guests applaud. They surround them. Cheer them. Ceausescu and Elena devour each other . . . It takes a while . . .

SONG

CEAUSESCU. Cheers, my love! Cheers!
     Let me eat your ears!

ELENA. Oh, give me a peck
     Let me grip your neck!

CEAUSESCU/ELENA *(refrain)*. Let me be your cook
     Let me thrust my hook
     Let me taste your veins
     Let me keep your reins
     Let me catch your flu
     Let me be your stew
     Tu, tu, tu, tu *(Romanian "you," pronounced "tou")*
     Let me have a bite of you!

CEAUSESCU. Your breast is still so fresh
     I love to chomp your flesh

ELENA. Your eyes taste like a radish
     They're still my favorite dish

CEAUSESCU. Your heart is plain and hard
     A vibrant business card

ELENA. Your brain is a bit bitter
Your neurons still glitter

Refrain

CEAUSESCU. Your legs are home-baked pies
They're not for foreign spies!

ELENA. Don't get drunk on my blood
Like a capitalist stud!

CEAUSESCU. Bite me, chew me, chomp me
You won't hear any sob
History books can tell you
I'm not to please the mob!

ELENA. Fry me, grill me, burn me
You won't hear any sob
History books can tell you
I'm not to please the mob!

They fall on the floor, exhausted.

DANIELA. Cheers! Red wine and white sheets. Gloria's bedroom.
Nine.

On the screen is written

9. RED WINE AND WHITE SHEETS
August 25, 2001—New York

Daniela is in bed, drunk, fully covered with sheets, in Gloria's apartment. Gloria walks back and forth downstage.

GLORIA. You cannot do this. This is not something that can be done.

DANIELA. I'm sorry, Gloria . . . I didn't mean to . . .

GLORIA (*mimicking her*). I'm sorry, I'm sorry . . . Who cares if you're
sorry or not. The issue is you're . . . crazy! Silly. Dumb. Mean. All
of them!

DANIELA. I just wanted to . . .

GLORIA. Fuck!

DANIELA. Talk to somebody . . .

GLORIA. Right. You come here, drink my wine, eat my lasagna, laugh at my jokes, nod at my words of wisdom, dance Greek, get naked, jump into my bed! And when I finally put my hand on your ass, you start crying on my tits like a screaming brat, a baby, that you cannot do this, you cannot do this . . . oh, poor girl, oh sweet innocent girl . . . gimme a fucking break!

DANIELA (*tipsy*). I don't know . . .

GLORIA. You don't know! . . . You know what, honey, doll, pussycat? You should start learning to make some choices, some decisions . . . Your own decisions. What do you actually want? Me? Charlie? Maybe you need your mom to tell you what to do, ask her for permission for . . . everything! Permission to move, to breathe, to drink, to eat, to fuck, to live, so you wouldn't have to think too hard . . .

DANIELA. I think a lot . . . a great deal . . .

GLORIA. Well, show me a tiny corner of the outcome of this great thinking process . . .

DANIELA. . . . My head is so . . . full of . . . shit . . . thoughts . . . I don't know . . . worms in my brain . . . biting . . . biting . . . you know . . . ghosts . . .

GLORIA (*sits down on the bed and starts massaging Daniela's temples, motherly*). Life is too damn short and tense, Daniela . . . it frowns and snaps at us every day . . . let's give it a big smile in exchange, a big "Cheers!" . . . Let's tell her, "You won't kick me down, bitch, you won't!" . . . Let's relax, forget about worries . . . to the garbage with the past! . . . Welcome the present . . . the moment . . . stop it in your lap . . . stroke it . . . rub it . . . the moment is yours . . . Enjoy it . . . award yourself with some good time . . . we deserve it . . . you deserve it . . . (*Kisses Daniela who doesn't respond.*)

Blackout.

DANIELA (*to the audience*). Sorry. I'm not gonna tell you what happened.

(*Whispering*) Make up your own stories! . . . (*Informal tone*) OK. I can tell you something. I was strong. I made a decision. I did it MY way.

Lights on

DANIELA. OK. We have to move on. That's it. Time doesn't actually stop. Stop! Stop! See, it doesn't . . . Ten! In the long run.

On the screen is written

10. IN THE LONG RUN
September 11, 2001—New York

Charlie's apartment. Daniela and Charlie, drink their coffee standing and moving around the room.

CHARLIE. I can't come with you to the airport.

DANIELA. I'll take a cab.

CHARLIE. Are you sure?

DANIELA. Yes, I'll take a cab.

CHARLIE. About leaving.

DANIELA. I cannot waste the money for the plane ticket, can I?

CHARLIE. It's my money.

DANIELA. That's why. It's the money I stole . . .

CHARLIE. I don't wanna talk about money.

DANIELA. Sure.

CHARLIE. Are you sure? About leaving.

DANIELA. I don't know . . .

CHARLIE. Don't you have everything you need? New York, free time, good food, nice clothes? Shelves full of products? "Like Christmas every day?!"

DANIELA. I don't know . . .

CHARLIE. Who knows then?

DANIELA (*beat*). You don't love me.

Lights on Ceausescu and Elena. They look worn-out but take pleasure in mocking Daniela.

ELENA/CEAUSESCU. Love me! Marry me!

DANIELA (*to Charlie*). You don't need me.

CEAUSESCU/ELENA. Love me! Marry me!

They go on whispering "love me, marry me," mockingly.

DANIELA. You won't marry me.

CHARLIE (*beat, then outburst*). I've never wished to get married! I didn't want all that shit: two-storey house, two cars, two kids, two dogs, weekends with the family. Fake communication. Fake smiles. Social convention . . . A cheap Hollywood movie! . . . A computer game is more entertaining than this old (*grinning*) "Happy Family" game . . . Mom used to play it so well . . . (*Beat*) I don't like being like everybody else!

DANIELA. What about your sister? She's not like everybody else. Nobody is like everybody else.

CHARLIE. Gloria! Mrs. I-don't-care-but-let's-pretend-I-do . . . I hope you didn't fuck her . . .

DANIELA. Who cares if I did?

CHARLIE. Did you?

DANIELA. You have a real problem with women, Charlie!

CHARLIE. Sure. Right. I hate the American self-righteous women. The Latino over-talkative chicks. The British snobbish giraffes. The French sexy inflatable dolls. The Asian midget mistresses . . .

DANIELA. What is this, the anti-women manifesto?

CHARLIE. I didn't want a female pet from a Third World country . . .

DANIELA. Thanks a lot!

CHARLIE. I'm not talking about you. It's the big screen! The big picture. Can't you see it? Same rules of the game. Same score. Same music. Work, eat, fuck, work, eat, fuck . . . Bed, job, kitchen, bed, job, kitchen . . .

DANIELA. You said enough . . .

She goes upstage to the "kitchen." Ceausescu and Elena follow her and remain there.

CHARLIE (*in lower voice*). I'm OK with you though . . .

DANIELA. You're a selfish / . . . robot, Charlie!

CHARLIE. I'm OK with you . . .

Daniela comes back to the living room.

DANIELA. Mrs. Aronson told me you were kind smart sweet tender funny gentle well-behaved polite loving lovable SPECIAL!

Charlie doesn't look at her.

CHARLIE. Yeah, mom believed I was different. Special. Very special . . . "There, above the TV set, I'm gonna hang your Nobel Prize!" . . . Sure, mom . . . "Computers are the future, and you're a genius of computers!" . . . Well, mom . . . "Here, look at this photo, a nice decent girl from Romania, to take care of you . . . after I'll be gone." That's silly, mom . . . "You'll thank me for this, Charlie, you'll see, you will . . ." Sure, mom . . . Nothing about music, everything about hard-disk-drives and devices-with-removable-storage . . . "You're great at violin, Charlie, but the violin is like a vampire, it softens you, it makes you suffer, squeak, and sob all day long. This is not a life for you, Charlie!" . . . THIS is surely not a life, mom . . .

Daniela is clearly moved by his monologue but doesn't know what to do: to show her emotion or to be still angry with him. Lights fade on Charlie.

DANIELA (*to the audience*). I'm trying to imagine him playing the violin . . . (*Beat, she's listening the air*) I can't. There's no violin sound that I can associate with him. Only keyboard clicks. Click-click-

click. Click-click-click . . . Wait a minute!

A violin can be heard louder and louder.

ELENA. Weak-Spot-of-the-First-Degree: DETECTED.

DANIELA. Eleven!

On the screen is written

9/11 FLASH BACK, FLESH FORWARD

Daniela packs her last things. Two big suitcases are already ready to go. From time to time she stops packing and freezes for a while in a meditative position. Same violin music, softly played.

DANIELA. Two suitcases: the big brown one and the heavy black one . . . One with clothes and presents. One with books . . . Ah, and the small red bag that I'm going to keep with me on the plane . . . That means THREE . . . OK. What's wrong now? Bye-bye New York, that's all . . . (*Violin music goes louder*) Does it make any sense? I mean this thing that sometimes, after years or weeks or days or hours or just seconds, boom, a thunderstorm hits your mind and you begin to catch the other one's thoughts, you begin to understand, to see, to hear, all of a sudden, the music locked inside his body . . . and you can't stop listening . . . you can't stop . . .

Lights on Ceausescu and Elena who start sniffing Daniela. Violin music stops. Lights on the other actors.

DANIELA (*continued*). OK. I have three suitcases . . . The big brown one . . . the heavy black one . . .

CEAUSESCU. I can smell the blood in the air . . .

ELENA. The pain . . .

CEAUSESCU. Same smell . . .

ELENA. And growing!

DANIELA. Running . . .

CEAUSESCU. The crowd is mad at us.

ELENA. Worms. Crush them!

CEAUSESCU. Shoot them!

DANIELA. I'm stumbling . . .

MARCELA. We don't want your future husband to think we're dirty!

ELVIS. Run, Dani, run!

DANIELA. A fresh corpse at my feet . . .

ELVIS. Don't look down. Look at the sky . . .

DANIELA. Bodies . . .

CEAUSESCU. She sees our helicopter taking off from the roof of the Palace!

DANIELA. Smashed.

ELENA. She stops!

DANIELA. Crushed . . .

ELENA. Pointing with her forefinger

CEAUSESCU. At us!

ELENA. Shouting like a starved pussy cat.

DANIELA. The dictator is leaving!

ELVIS. The crowd is screaming . . .

CEAUSESCU. "Don't let them leave!" . . .

ELENA. "Don't let them . . . live!"

DANIELA. Live!

ELVIS. In Bucharest.

MARCELA. In New York!

ELVIS. Watching on TV how they kill them

MARCELA. On Christmas night!

DANIELA. A quick trial

CEAUSESCU. I don't accept this court!

ELENA. Who is the judge?

CEAUSESCU. I am the President of the Socialist Republic of Romania and I shall answer only before the Grand National Meeting and before representatives of the working class and this is all, I've finished!

DANIELA/MARCELA/ELVIS. Guilty!

ELENA. What a provocation!

ELVIS. They shoot Ceausescu and Elena

ELENA. They shoot US!

DANIELA. He-Comrade and She-Comrade are . . .

CEAUSESCU/ELENA. Dead . . .

ELVIS. Punished!

MARCELA. A Christmas present!

DANIELA. For the Romanian people!

ELENA. Stupid murderers. Wooden heads. Vampires!

CEAUSESCU (*whispering*). It's not them, it's the foreign agencies . . .

ELENA. It hurts!

DANIELA. To be guilty or

GLORIA. Not guilty!

CEAUSESCU/ELENA. Who is the judge?

ELVIS. The sky

GLORIA. The sky

ELVIS. The helicopter

GLORIA. The plane

DANIELA. One cannot escape

GLORIA. One can escape

MARCELA. My son-in-law is a businessman! In New York!

GLORIA. The towers.

DANIELA. The walls.

ELVIS. The dreams.

CEAUSESCU. The Golden Dream of Communism!

GLORIA. Burning. Melting.

DANIELA. Crumbling

ELVIS. Watching on TV

MARCELA. A nightmare!

GLORIA. The choreography of Death.

DANIELA. One cannot escape. Pain speaks all languages.

ELVIS. Run, Dani, run!

GLORIA. Run, Charlie, run!

MARCELA. Run, Daniela, Run!

DANIELA. Run, Charlie, Run!

GLORIA. Run!

ELVIS. Run!

MARCELA. Run!

DANIELA. Again?

GLORIA/MARCELA/ELVIS. Run!

DANIELA. Where?

GLORIA. Here.

ELVIS. Fire

DANIELA. Sweat.

ELENA. Blood.

MARCELA. Money.

GLORIA. Bodies.

DANIELA. Hair.

GLORIA. Hands.

ELVIS. Legs.

DANIELA. Thighs.

GLORIA. Hips.

ELENA. Buttocks.

CEAUSESCU. Demolition.

ELENA. Mutilation.

DANIELA. Love!

GLORIA. Loss.

MARCELA. Business!

ELVIS. Hope.

CEAUSESCU. The golden future!

GLORIA. The present . . .

DANIELA. The past, always the past . . .

CEAUSESCU/ELENA/MARCELA/ELVIS/GLORIA. Guilty!

DANIELA. Stop this! I've had enough of this! Enough! (*The other char-acters start pushing and pulling Daniela in different directions, she gets rid of them*). I haven't done anything wrong. I don't owe anything to you . . . Rather I'm owed some good normal boring times . . . Like everybody else . . . You ghosts have waxed the soul out of me. But you know what: there's still something left. A tiny little piece of me. See?! I'm hairy but not dead . . . (*Tears up the plane ticket, violin music is played*) I can hear! I can hear you playing the violin, Charlie. Yes, I do. I'm sure. Yes. You will come home. You will find me here. We'll talk. And I won't say, "I'm sorry." I'll say, "Let's start again! This melodramatic incredible impractical improbable . . . hairy-tale."

Violin music resumes. On the screen is written

END/BEGINNING

Daniela takes Charlie's photo out of her pajama pocket and shows it nervously to the spectators.

DANIELA. Have you seen him? Charlie Aronson. Blue eyes, brown hair. Age: 38. He worked on the sixty-sixth floor. Yes, I'm sure he managed to get down. He's smart. Not very talkative, but smart. Charlie. Charlie Aronson. Do you know him? He liked to play the violin . . . Yes, he's tall. Like an oak grown by the sun, thin like barbed wire, silent like a fish and blind like a jellyfish . . . I'm joking. These are our jokes . . . Have you seen him? Charlie. This is the photo his mom sent to my mom. It's a photo taken on his birthday. He looks so sad, doesn't he? Charlie Aronson. He's wearing a white shirt and a brown tie with purple circles. He has a silver watch. Yes. On his left hand. And silly white socks. Yes, white. Do you know him? . . . Do you? . . . Do you?

Lights fade. The violin music grows louder and louder, filling the whole space.

END/BEGINNING

In the doctor's office, Thida San (Mia Katigbak) remembers her daughter Oun (Eunice Wong) at the beach at Kep in Cambodia. Kim (James Saito) stands behind Thida. Photograph by Ching Gonzalez.

EYES OF THE HEART

BY

CATHERINE FILLOUX

Beginning in 1989, I read a series of articles about a group of 150 Cambodian refugee women in Long Beach, California, who suffered from psychosomatic blindness after what they witnessed during the Khmer Rouge regime. In 2004, my play *Eyes of the Heart* was produced in New York City by National Asian American Theatre Company (NAATCO). During the 15 years between first reading the articles and the production of my play, I listened to Cambodian women survivors, particularly at St Rita's Refugee Center in the Bronx, and travelled to Long Beach, California, where I met the medical doctor, Dr. Haing Ngor, who starred in the movie *The Killing Fields*, as well as the eye doctor who first examined many of these blind Cambodian women. I also spoke to countless community leaders, scholars and artists who provided me with knowledge about Cambodia and the Khmer Rouge genocide. In 2001, I traveled to Cambodia to produce my play *Photographs from S-21* and to oversee the production of *Night Please Go Faster*, written and performed by actors from the National Theatre in Phnom Penh, about the lives of artists during the Khmer Rouge regime. In 2003, I returned to Phnom Penh to teach playwriting at the Royal University of Fine Arts. This 15-year journey led me to the production of *Eyes of the Heart*, the story of Thida San, a Cambodian woman suffering post-traumatic blindness. Though Thida San never recovers her sight, she manages to help Dr. Simpson, her eye doctor, and Thida steps out of her isolation through family, culture, tradition, religion and friendship. Illness in my own family traveled with me through this 15-year period. The depth and courage of the survivors led me to understand the Buddhist belief that what humans all share is suffering.

There are many different ways to be a revolutionary and Thida recognizes this about her daughter at the end of the play when Thida says: "She said no to them." As Raphael Lemkin, the man who invented the word *genocide*, said, "Genocide can destroy a culture instantly, like fire can destroy a building in an hour." The legacy of genocide is seen in the surviving families for generations after. In Thida San's case, she and her family are asked to survive in a whole new culture, and culture clash plays a large role in this story. As the child of immigrants, the *outsider* is one of my primary themes as a playwright. Serey, Thida's niece, straddles cultures and drags her father kicking and screaming into a new and different world. Ultimately, the phenomenon of these 150 blind women made me wonder: What kinds of memories would make a person ask their brain to stop seeing? The images that flash in Thida's mind are beyond words and imagination. At the beginning of the play, she has no desire to create a new present. Others can't approach her. It's Thida's own compassion towards others that brings her dark mind to the present.

In 1975, the communist Khmer Rouge regime came to power, with Pol Pot (Saloth Sar) as its leader and in 1979, Cambodia's historical enemy, Vietnam, invaded Cambodia, putting an end to the genocide. An estimated 1.7 million died from execution, torture, starvation and illness. The Khmer Rouge leaders, Pol Pot, Ieng Sary, Nuon Chea and Khieu Samphan planned to create a utopian agrarian society. Pol Pot died in 1998. My play *Silence of God* is about his legacy. The three other aforementioned Khmer Rouge leaders are still alive and living in Cambodia. At the time of this writing there has been no tribunal. More than 25 years after the end of the genocide, a tribunal is being prepared but the legal standards of the tribunal, overseen by Cambodia's Prime Minister Hun Sen, who was himself part of the Khmer Rouge, are being questioned.

EYES OF THE HEART premiered at National Asian American Theatre Company (NAATCO) in New York City, in October 2004. The play received the Roger L. Stevens Award from The Kennedy Center Fund for New American Plays and the Eric Kocher Playwrights Award from the O'Neill.

CHARACTERS

CASTING REQUIREMENTS	4 women and 2 men
THIDA SAN	a Cambodian woman, 50
KIM	a Cambodian man, 40s
DR. LYNN SIMPSON	an American eye doctor, 30s
SEREY/OUN	a Cambodian woman; Americanized, 18 (Oun is Thida's daughter, 18, seen in flashbacks)
SAVATH/K.R. SOLDIER/SIPHA/ BARBER/MUGGER	a Cambodian man, 20s
CHHEM	Cambodian woman; traditional, 50s-60s

(RESIDENT 1, 2 & 3's voices are taped or live)

TIME: Late 1980s

PLACE: Long Beach, California, and Cambodia

SET: Scenes are played in different areas of the stage, locales are suggested. There are altars in Kim's apartment and the Buddhist temple; a window in Kim's apartment by which Thida sits. Because Thida is blind the play has a soundscape which helps create the context of her world.

Note: We are sometimes in Thida's mind and she uses a microphone to distinguish her internal thoughts from her dialogue. (In the text Thida's internal thoughts, are italicized.) In one instance, Dr. Simpson also uses a microphone for internal thoughts.

The play runs for approximately 90 minutes and is performed without an intermission.

PRONUNCIATIONS

Thida	Tee-DAH
San	Sahn
Serey	Say-RAY (with a rolled R; accent on RAY; rhymes with "day" and means "free")
Lok	Low(k)
Savath	Suh-VAHT
Chhem	Chime
Oun	Own (as in, to "own" something)
Teak-Dos-Ko	Tuck-DACH-ko (means "milkfruit")
Bina	BEE-na
Prak	Prah(k)
Sovandy	SovannDEE
Meng	Meng
Chantha	Jann-TA (accent on second syllable)
Li	Lee
Ang	Ahng
Malay	Ma-LIE (rhymes with "die")
Navy	Nah-VEE
Hun	Hoon (rhymes with "hood")
Khmer	K'mare*
Siem Riep	Seam Re-up (with a rolled R)
Sipha	See-PAH (like the term "Pa" for father)
Phnom Penh	Pa-num Pain (tilde on last N or, simply, "Pen")
Sin Si Samouth	Sin-See-sa-MUHT
Tuol Sleng	Tool-Slaing
Takeo	Tah-KI-uo (Ki rhymes with "die")
Kep	Kaip
Sampot	Sam-B/PUT (unaspirated P and very soft U, in-between Pot and Put)

*In Cambodian, people say Khmer/K'maille; in English: Khmer/C'mare

Note: Thida, Kim and Chhem speak with an Asian accent when they speak in English to Dr. Simpson.

Scene 1

We hear a flight announcement mixed with airport sounds. The loud wail of a security alarm. A Cambodian woman, Thida San, 50, blind, using a cane, is escorted in by a Cambodian man, Savath, 25. Thida shrinks back from the assault of sounds. Kim, a Cambodian man, 40s, rushes to her. He bows with his palms together.

KIM. Thida! Sister, you are finally here! We've waited so long. I'm pleased to welcome you to my new home. (*He embraces her.*) Thida? It is me your brother, Kim. (*Looks at Thida.*)

SAVATH. She isn't speaking.

KIM (*confused*). Isn't speaking? Why?

SAVATH. I'm not sure. They didn't mention it in the papers. She must be overwhelmed.

KIM (*maintaining cheerfulness*). OK. (*Speaking louder*). We are so happy to see you. It is a miracle you have finally arrived. How was your trip? Are you all right?

SAVATH. She can hear you. She's probably just not talking.

THIDA. *I asked to stay at the temple.*

Kim quickly motions to Serey, an Americanized eighteen-year-old.

KIM. This is Serey, your niece.

Serey lightly touches Thida's shoulder.

SEREY. Hello, aunt.

THIDA. *Like Oun . . .*

KIM. You remember, how she liked to visit you? In your house you had so many lovely things?

SEREY. Dad.

THIDA (*patting something under her shirt, near her heart*). *Like Oun, in the photograph.*

KIM (*introducing Savath*). And you met Savath Chin—he's the man who got you here! He never gave up. He flew to the embassy in Phnom Penh. The paperwork sat there for ages.

SAVATH. Welcome to Los Angeles, Mrs. San.

THIDA. *Los Angeles?*

KIM. We're very relieved to see you. How was your trip? Comfortable?

Kim touches a plastic bag Thida is clutching. Serey has moved away.

KIM (*calling*). Serey! . . . You have no baggage? Nothing?

Thida pats something under her shirt.

THIDA. *It is all here.*

KIM. Just crackers from the plane?

Kim watches Thida.

SAVATH. The papers say she sat in the dark in the temple for years.

SEREY. She didn't want to come to America.

Thida pats her shirt as Serey becomes a young woman, Oun, and lights shift. Note: Oun may say the line below, "No I will be a midwife."

THIDA. *Miracle. A schoolgirl who eats, she breathes, she goes to school. When she comes home everything is normal. Her father teases her, "Will she be a doctor?" One day my daughter says, "No, I will be a midwife." "Why not a doctor?" he asks her. His pride hurt, perhaps. She shrugs her shoulders. She walks away, to her room. To study. She is stubborn. Stop.*

Lights are restored to the airport.

KIM. Let's go home.

Scene 2

Dr. Lynn Simpson, 35, wearing eyeglasses, shows slides, addressing her residents, who are the audience. Behind her, squiggly, abstract shapes float. We remain with her in this strange world.

DR. SIMPSON. Everything is spectacularly ordered. (*Pointing to first slide on scrim.*) See, there's nothing on this retinal cell—it's clear. *You wait for the oddity. It comes rarely.* (*Showing second slide on scrim.*) There it is. In night-blindness you know exactly what to expect. The retina has this white, murky surface, sometimes like a floating string. This is a floating world, a world where there is no speed, no weight. It's all here in front of us. Every day you wonder what you will discover.

Lights cross-fade to Kim leading Thida to an altar in his apartment as Cambodian music plays.

KIM. I've made a small offering at the altar for your wellbeing in America. Rest—we have prepared some food, fried shrimp, rice.

An older woman, Chhem, sets down dishes. Kim lights incense.

CHHEM. Welcome to Little Phnom Penh, Mrs. San.

THIDA. *Little Phnom Penh? They have renamed an American city?*

KIM. Chhem will be your guide. She is Savath's grandmother. She will take you to the temple.

THIDA. *You said I could live there.*

CHHEM. Yes, I will show you how to take the bus.

THIDA. *The bus?*

CHHEM. I've added some extra sauce. We must be generous, this is your first meal! (*Handing her a bowl*) Don't be shy.

KIM. Please, take some food, Thida. I insist.

Thida takes the bowl.

THIDA. *When I used to find food, I would cut off the smallest piece for me and give Oun the rest. This is for you.*

Thida smells the food. Serey enters with a book bag.

KIM. Come, Serey, sit—eat with us. Thida, you will have your own room with Serey. She has put clothing for you in her closet. (*To Serey*) Come and talk to your aunt.

SEREY. She doesn't talk.

Thida eats.

THIDA. *Delicious.*

SEREY (*to Thida*). I'm sorry, I have to go, I'm late.

KIM. Your aunt has just arrived.

SEREY. I know. She stole my room.

THIDA (*eating*). *So flavorful.*

KIM. Stay, she has come from so far away.

Kim goes to a window, lighting a cigarette. Serey puts on lipstick.

KIM. Who is that outside?

CHHEM. His name is Trouble.

THIDA (*smelling*). *Smoking.*

SEREY. It's Lee Var, Father. He's helping me with an assignment.

CHHEM. Have you asked Savath for help? He's very intelligent.

KIM (*following Serey; lowering voice*). That lipstick is very red.

SEREY. "Karma Red"—for energy. I thought you'd like that, dad. The "karma" thing.

KIM. No, I don't.

THIDA. *Karma lipstick? Is she this old? The age of Oun?*

Chhem inspects Serey. She speaks under her breath.

CHHEM. The short skirt.

SEREY. This is short?

KIM. Don't talk back to your elders.

SEREY. This is the '80s, dad. I'll be right back.

Thida eats.

THIDA. *One more taste. So delicious.*

KIM. One hour. I'm watching the clock.

Serey exits.

THIDA. *Alone, in my rice world.*

CHHEM (*to Kim*). You know, the young do the "slow dance" with the bodies pressed so close together.

Chhem demonstrates the closeness with the palms of her hands.

CHHEM. I have seen it on TV. Skin-to-skin. The "slow dance."

THIDA. *"Slowdance?" Is that an English word?*

Thida stuffs more rice in her mouth as Chhem approaches and picks up the bowl. Thida jumps.

CHHEM. Come, look, Kim! Your sister is eating all the food.

THIDA. *The loud one*!

Kim goes to Thida, comfortingly.

KIM. When we first came we were so tired we couldn't stop sleeping, couldn't stop eating. We'd look at the food in the grocery stores and our stomachs would ache with longing. We wanted to eat but then it would make us sick. We had to take it slow.

Kim leads Thida to the altar where there are family photographs.

KIM. There is a green mango on the altar for you and a few flowers from my garden. I want to tell you—here, above, there are photographs. The few I was able to hide. They're on the wall. Even here our ancestors protect us.

Thida pats something under her shirt as Kim watches.

KIM. You're *home* now, I will take care of you. We'll bring you to an eye doctor, take you for a physical exam—we'll go to the herb market.

THIDA. *They said you promised I'd go to the temple.*

KIM. Sister, may I ask? I never knew—what happened to your daughter? What happened to Oun? . . .

THIDA (*patting under her shirt*). *Still here? Are the photos still here?*

Lights shift as the young woman, Oun, appears in front of Thida. She is weak and malnourished.

KIM. Why don't you talk? We've waited so long. *I* still have Serey. I wonder what happened . . . ?

Oun works in a rice field.

THIDA. *She is hungry. The soup—or so they call it—is mostly water now, only a few grains of rice floating on the surface. We see ourselves in the grains of rice, disappearing. We count them every day. One, two, three. They barely color the water anymore.*

A young K. R. soldier appears watching Oun.

THIDA. *Stop. Swimming. On a beach, there were magnolia trees. Clear aqua water. (Another memory intrudes.) Another magnolia tree. I want to die.*

Scene 3

Thida stares off as Dr. Simpson studies a chart, speaking to Kim.

DR. SIMPSON. Before she came, they told you she was blind. It's true, she displays all the outward symptoms but her exam reveals no physical problem. She has normal visual acuity. Her vision should improve to normal.

KIM. I don't understand.

DR. SIMPSON. Her eyes are sending signals to her brain.

Kim motions to a print-out in the chart.

KIM. May I see the results? Yes, it is very strange. Her eyes work but she cannot see. She's not lying.

Dr. Simpson makes a quick hand gesture in front of Thida's eyes. Thida doesn't react.

DR. SIMPSON. Can you explain how this might have happened?

KIM. No. There are many others like her.

Dr. Simpson looks at Thida for a moment.

KIM. She refuses to speak.

DR. SIMPSON. All the outward signs of blindness but her eyes are healthy.

KIM. It defies all odds.

DR. SIMPSON. Let me try something else.

Dr. Simpson exits.

KIM. You're in America now, sister. Perhaps you can explain to the doctor and somebody can help. I've brought you to a specialist. If you could tell me when you lost your sight? What happened? You can trust me.

Thida pats under her shirt. Oun and the blue of ocean appears.

THIDA. *Swimming. We went only months before the schoolgirl photograph where all is normal. She was a fish. Standing at the shore, calling to her. "You are a fish! You are a fish!" And when she finally walked out of the sea at Kep, unconcerned, vain in her unawareness, simply . . . Oun . . . we would laugh. Sipha and I would laugh. We were so mad. It was late, we were hungry and she would force us to stand on the shore call-ing to her, screaming for her. Her black head bobbing up and down in the waves, against the line of the horizon. But when she came, she was transformed. From so much time in the sea. And she would spray water through her teeth . . . a trick she learned . . . and we would laugh . . . We would laugh and walk under the magnolia trees . . .*

Dr. Simpson re-enters and tapes electrodes to Thida's forehead.

THIDA. *Stop. All because there were also magnolias at Kep on the shore . . . Swimming, swimming . . . Anything to turn the clock back . . . Because the moments after, they are all accounted for, every detail, every move-ment. In my head I want it to stop.*

Kim watches Dr. Simpson tip back Thida's head.

DR. SIMPSON. Now I'm going to tip back your head and insert this contact lens in your eye . . .

Thida flinches.

KIM. I'm sorry, in Cambodia touching the head is considered very personal.

DR. SIMPSON. Perhaps it would be better if you put in the lens. It has an electrode on it.

KIM. Yes, I'll do it. Thank you.

DR. SIMPSON. You may want to tell her not to close her eye or the lens will come out.

KIM. We know English, we were educated. She was a midwife and I was a doctor. But she doesn't speak.

Dr. Simpson studies Thida.

THIDA. *This doctor's quick—she has no time. Empty—without a soul. She drinks coffee, smokes. Sipha smoked.*

DR. SIMPSON. So she can't tell me what she sees?

Thida stares off as colored lights flash in front of her. Dr. Simpson and Kim watch lines with jagged peaks dash across a screen.

KIM. Thida? If you see something, can you nod your head?

Thida does not do so.

THIDA. *Darkness.*

DR. SIMPSON. If she can't talk it makes it difficult to examine her.

THIDA. *Don't cry.*

DR. SIMPSON. Ask her if she sees the lights.

KIM. Sister, did you hear the doctor? Do you see the light?

THIDA. *I see nothing.*

Dr. Simpson consults Thida's chart.

DR. SIMPSON. How did she lose her sight?

THIDA. *Don't cry.*

KIM. I don't know, it was during the Pol Pot regime. We were separated.

DR. SIMPSON. Did she have eye problems before that?

KIM. I know she wore glasses. For far distances.

DR. SIMPSON. But with the glasses she could see?

KIM. Yes. The Khmer Rouge tried to eliminate all intellectuals. They killed people who wore glasses.

DR. SIMPSON. Does she have any other kinds of physical problems?

KIM. Not that a physical exam detects.

Dr. Simpson untapes the electrodes as the flashing lights fade.

DR. SIMPSON. Her eyes are sending signals to her brain.

KIM. Yes, I saw the ERG.

DR. SIMPSON. Your sister may be malingering, Mr. Lok. Is she applying for disability? Benefits for blindness are higher in California than anywhere else. I'd like to check something.

Dr. Simpson looks through charts as Kim touches Thida.

KIM. Are you there? What would happen if you spoke? Would it be so bad? They've taken the time to see you, they want to help.

Thida keeps her head lowered.

DR. SIMPSON. Does your sister know Bina Prak? She also lives in Long Beach.

KIM. No, why do you ask?

DR. SIMPSON. Well, she came in to be tested. She was applying for disability benefits too and she had the same problem as your sister.

KIM. Doctor, my sister just arrived from Cambodia. She's not applying for disability.

DR. SIMPSON. Isn't it sort of strange? Two women the same age, from the same country, living in the same city? It sounds suspicious.

KIM. I said before, my sister would not lie. It's not strange. I've seen many other women like her. They are not making it up.

DR. SIMPSON. How do you know?

KIM. Because I've lived among them. Those of us who survived ended up in refugee camps in Thailand.

THIDA. *Don't cry, don't cry or they will kill you.*

DR. SIMPSON. How did you get to Long Beach?

KIM. My friend's grandson worked to bring us here.

DR. SIMPSON. Have you seen the blind women here too?

KIM. Yes.

DR. SIMPSON. It's odd . . . Perhaps I could see more of them. Could you help?

KIM. Why not? (*Looking at her, curious.*) If you are interested.

DR. SIMPSON. Yes, yes, who knows? Clinically, it might prove useful.

Dr. Simpson looks at him, taking parking stickers from her doctor's coat and cigarettes fall out.

DR. SIMPSON. I don't smoke.

KIM. Me neither.

She nods, then scribbles.

DR. SIMPSON. Make sure you give this validation to the parking guy, or he'll charge you an arm and a leg.

Scene 4

Kim's apartment. Thida sits by an open window as light from a street-lamp shines in. She unpins a plastic bag inside her shirt and takes out a photo. Passes her hand over it. A man, Sipha, wearing a white doctor's coat, appears in the shadows.

THIDA. *He stands in the back of the truck. With other doctors in white coats.*

He mimes for her to be quiet.

THIDA. *He puts his finger to his mouth, telling me to be quiet.*

She nods. He gestures.

THIDA. *He motions for me to take off my glasses.*

She mimes.

THIDA. *I take them off. He gestures to get rid of them.*

She mimes.

THIDA. *I throw them on the ground and I crush them with my foot. My sight is now blurred as I look at him. The man I love. He simply looks. The truck starts to go. I look at him but I cannot see him clearly. The truck begins to move away, a cloud of dust.*

She reaches out her hand.

THIDA. *Sipha.*

The sound of gunfire comes through the window. Thida holds the photo to her breast as Sipha disappears. A siren wails, she crouches down. Kim and Serey enter.

KIM. Sister? What are you doing? What's happened to you?

SEREY. What's wrong with her? What's her problem?

Kim puts his arm around Thida as Serey takes books from her bag.

KIM. Please don't be frightened. It is simply the police. I had to go outside and retrieve Serey from her own folly. You are safe.

SEREY. You're not actually that safe. There are gangs.

THIDA. *Are there boys with guns . . . ?*

KIM. Serey don't tell her that.

THIDA. *Smoking cigarettes, brother?*

SEREY. They live in our building.

KIM. That was a police siren. You are fine inside. There is no problem.

Kim helps Thida to her seat by the window. Serey starts to go.

KIM. Don't think I have forgotten what I saw.

SEREY. Forget it.

KIM. His car is enough.

THIDA. *His car?*

KIM. If your mother was alive she would agree with me about Savath.

SEREY. You're the one in love with Savath.

KIM. That isn't funny. You liked him, you told me so. He's very respectable.

SEREY. Maybe too much. Have you seen how he dresses?

KIM. Is it because I like him, suddenly you don't? You've been out with him once, was it so bad?

SEREY. Yeah, I'm not ready. I need to have some fun.

KIM. One thing you won't have is fun with (*pointing outside*) the guy with the car, I can assure you.

SEREY. Oh, and you know this by telepathy?

KIM. I know you are very clever but in this case you are not seeing clearly. You are too American. Try again with Savath. He was friends with your brother.

Kim lights a cigarette.

KIM. My daughter has driven me to smoking.

THIDA. *You always smoked.*

KIM. Oh god, why won't you say anything?

THIDA. You don't want to hear what I have to say.

Kim exits as Serey gets some books.

SEREY. We yell all the time. Sorry I said that about the gangs. It's
scary but it's not that bad. Besides a few bullets coming in
through the front door—just kidding. No, there were some once,
but it's okay. He hardly ever mentions my mother. You really
think she'd want me to marry Savath? Sometimes I pray to her.
Savath is good-looking but who wants someone your dad picked
out? My father was different when my mom was around. We used
to have some fun. We'd catch fish together. Sing songs, we were
just crazy. But that was before Pol Pot. Now I'm supposed to
marry Savath because he was friends with my brother?
Everyone's dead. Good way to guilt people, huh? (*To herself*)
Asking *you*? What was I thinking?

Serey passes her hand in front of her aunt's expressionless eyes.

SEREY. Can you see? He's wanted you to come so bad. You were supposed to save us from something.

Serey takes her mirrored sunglasses and puts them on Thida.

SEREY. Hey, when you're around people maybe you wanna wear
these.

Thida feels them, surprised.

THIDA. *Are they eyeglasses?*

Serey looks at herself in the mirrored glasses.

SEREY. You can see yourself in them. They're sunglasses.

Thida stares out wearing the sunglasses.

THIDA. *Words won't bring them back, Serey.*

*Serey exits. Thida sits by the open window in Kim's apartment in dark-
ness. Night slowly turns to day. Thida listens to the sound of construction vehicles followed by the sound of a jack-hammer. She takes out
another photo from the plastic bag pinned to her shirt. Passes her hand
over it.*

THIDA. *A cloud of dust. Sipha disappears. I dress myself and my daughter
as peasants, we work in the fields, pray to the spirits that the soldiers will
not see us, that we will disappear. They find us—try to force Oun to
marry.*

*Rays of sunlight shine in Thida's eyes and she shields them from the
glare. Oun appears with the young K. R. soldier, in the shadows.*

K.R. SOLDIER (*commanding; to Thida*). You, come here! You are the
mother, you must watch!

THIDA. *Sun shines in my eyes—I leave my hut, walk towards the tree.*
(*Stopping the memory*) *Stop.*

K.R. SOLDIER. You must watch your daughter!

THIDA. *The people watch, expressionless. I search their eyes for clues. Stone
faces.*

Communist propaganda music from loudspeakers grows louder and louder.

THIDA. *Magnolia flowers fall. She is tied with rope. No.*

Lights are restored as Kim enters in gardening clothes.

KIM. You never sleep? I want you to come outside to my garden for
a little fresh air—you must.

THIDA. *Fresh? Where is this city that smells so bad?*

KIM (*giving her a lime*). Here is a lime from California. Take it. I
have avocados, too. They will soon be ripe. I never tasted avoca-
do in Cambodia, did you? (*A new thought.*) Sister, do you remember that fruit we had in our garden, when we were young? With
the milky white flesh and the black seed? Tek-DAH-ko? So delicious. It doesn't exist here. It has no name. But with time, it will
come. Some Cambodian will learn to grow it. And then it will

have a name. Americans will learn to love it and they will mass-produce it. The fruit will become bigger and bigger, the colors more vibrant and finally, it will lose all its flavor so that it tastes only like water.

She drops the lime. He returns it and sees the photos on her lap.

KIM. Can you see the photos, Thida?

Thida finally responds by nodding.

KIM (*looking at her*). Ah, you made a sign. Finally. You said yes. You can see the photos. I don't understand.

THIDA. *I see Oun and Sipha.*

He sees Thida put her hands together, praying.

KIM. You want to pray. Yes, we will bring you to our new temple like I promised. (*Lying*) It is much like the temples in Cambodia. Well, it is a haven for many, let us say.

THIDA. *I want to become a nun. I have nothing to hope for but the next life.*

The construction sounds. She looks toward the sounds.

KIM. Do you hear? They are repairing the road outside. It's a bull-dozer. The other noise is a machine to break up the cement. All the soil—they cover it with cement here. Concrete. They want to seal away the earth.

Scene 5

Sounds of busy traffic. Chhem looks up at a bus-stop sign as she guides Thida. Underneath the sign is another sign which reads, "No standing."

CHHEM. The bus stops here but we cannot wait here, Thida.

THIDA. *I would prefer to go home.*

CHHEM. Don't worry. We'll wait on the next corner, it's safe on the next corner.

Chhem leads Thida away from the bus-stop sign.

THIDA. *The city's loud, always a hum like rushing water, an electric current. Is the city breathing?*

CHHEM (*stopping*). Here, we will wait here. Your brother is very worried about you. Poor man, he must work during the day and cannot take you to the temple. You are safe with me. No problem, I'm a good guide. Serey, she is driving your brother to madness. The boyfriend, the car! The car is called a "Trans Am!" Very, very big. Very white! New! When the sun shines on it, it gleams like a jewel in her eyes.

We hear a bus approaching.

CHHEM. The bus is coming, Thida! Now we must run!

Chhem tries to run and pulls at Thida to follow.

THIDA. *Why must we chase the bus?*

CHHEM. Hurry, Thida! Please!

Thida drops her cane. Chhem goes to pick it up. The sound of the bus pulling away.

CHHEM (*upset*). Well. this is unfortunate. The monk is waiting at the temple, we'll be late. Don't worry, it is not your fault. Come.

Chhem leads Thida back to their position away from the bus-stop.

CHHEM. The sign says we cannot stand there. "No Standing." There is an arrow that points in both directions!

Chhem points to something offstage near the bus-stop.

CHHEM. Oh, I see a man is standing right next to the forbidding sign! Maybe we can stand behind him. This way if something happens, he will be punished first.

Chhem leads Thida, as lights cross-fade to Kim with Dr. Simpson in a teashop, sampling tea and smoking.

DR. SIMPSON. I drink Lipton.

KIM (*horrified*). In a teabag?

DR. SIMPSON. What else.

KIM. I'll buy you some tea on the way out so you can enjoy it.

DR. SIMPSON. What would I put it in?

KIM. A pot?

DR. SIMPSON. I drink coffee anyway.

KIM. You need to take a little time. Go ahead, sip it slowly. Sustenance. Of course the cigarette doesn't help. But we can't have everything.

DR. SIMPSON. No.

KIM. The temple is an old union hall on Willow Street. Some of the blind women pray there. Afternoons are best to find them.

DR. SIMPSON. They'll have to come to my office. When did you see the first blind women?

KIM. Among the refugees, in the Thai camps.

DR. SIMPSON. It couldn't be malnutrition or they would have regained their sight.

KIM. In our country the head is considered the place where the soul resides. It's the window through which life enters and exits.

DR. SIMPSON. Would you consider bringing your sister by my office again? I want to start by looking for an organic basis in the women. What do they have in common?

KIM. That's what you have to find out. You know doctors like myself, in Cambodia, are . . . were more experimental. My sister knew much about herbs and I used many of her remedies. I used to love seeing the whole world.

DR. SIMPSON. What do you mean?

KIM. Before Pol Pot I looked at everything. From my head to my feet.

My heart, my brain. And outward. The infinite. Now it's the opposite. I see only limits. I walk on a tightrope: how will I survive?

She looks at him a moment.

DR. SIMPSON. What is your answer?

KIM. My family. If I can save them. That's all that matters. (*He looks at her*) What about your family?

She does not answer the question.

DR. SIMPSON. If I can find the physical reason for their problem I can help them. What would make them see again?

KIM. You didn't answer my question. (*Looking at her*) You're right. What would make them see again? (*Asking about her*) What would help?

Chhem guides Thida into the darkness of a Buddhist temple. Above the altar are the faded letters of a sign: "Oil-Chemical and Atomic Workers Union Local 1-128." Thida kneels as Chhem exits. Sipha appears in the shadows.

THIDA. *Sipha you're here! I should never have forced her. I was always stubborn. Please say something. Say something to me. Come, sit.*

He sits next to Thida.

THIDA. *Tell me where you go.*

He stares straight ahead.

SIPHA. I travel through jungles where the forest's so thick I can barely squeeze by. Swim in rivers where you can catch the fish in thin air. At the seaside the sand is mixed with bones and teeth of farmers.

THIDA. *The temples, tell me about the temples!*

SIPHA. I dance with the celestial dancers—and there are thousands—on the walls of the ancient city.

THIDA. *Are you so popular?*

SIPHA. Yes, in the nighttime, serenaded by the soft rush of the wind, so seductive with their necklaces of jasmine falling on their breasts. The thieves in the night cut off the statues' heads, they reappear in foreign lands, chopped-off, eyes gouged from their sockets.

THIDA. *The dancing*!

SIPHA. Vines grow through the rock, strangling, squeezing the stone, cracking the faces, erasing the shrines. Soon the temples of Angkor will vanish.

THIDA. *Dancing.*

SIPHA. In the distance you can hear the snap of landmines. Another little boy running home, too careless.

THIDA. *Sipha.*

SIPHA. Near Siem Reap in an empty schoolhouse there are rusted shackles from its days as a torture center. Bones piled high to the sky, mountains and mountains of bones. When the air is still you can hear the skulls whispering to each other. (*He whispers menacingly*) SSSssssssssss . . . Snakes . . .

Thida speaks for the first time.

THIDA. STOP!

Chhem re-enters.

CHHEM (*shocked*). Thida? You can talk? You are finally speaking. (*Thida is silent.*) Who are you talking to? Who is here?

Thida watches Sipha slip away.

THIDA. Sipha. He is not what I want him to be.

CHHEM. Sipha?

Thida stares at the place where Sipha was.

THIDA (*to Chhem.*) I cannot speak about it. I am sorry. It is too difficult. I . . .

Chhem leads Thida out.

CHHEM. Come, you are haunted. You are speaking! At home I will coin you to make you feel better. Are you glad you came to the temple today?

Graffiti appears and we hear street sounds as Thida walks with Chhem, who looks up.

CHHEM. The sign is usually right here, but it has disappeared. Perhaps the wind blew it down in the storm.

THIDA. What storm?

CHHEM. All the buildings look the same. Ugly, so ugly. (*Panicking*) No trees. Always the gangsters on the corners. One in my block has a tiger on his arm, a tattoo. Always smoking, just boys, painting the buildings all different colors like children! (*Thida hears the construction sounds in the distance.*) It is pitiful, we are lost, so lost.

Thida begins to speak aloud, soothingly.

THIDA. I believe I know the right direction, Chhem. I do hear the sound of the road construction. My brother told me they are repairing the road. Cement. (*With vigor*) Yes, come now!

Scene 6

Chhem coins Thida as Kim stands near the altar.

CHHEM. And she told me to follow the bulldozer and got us home!

KIM. She spoke to you? Truly!

CHHEM. Yes.

THIDA. How else was I ever going to get home?

KIM. Thida!

CHHEM. She said *you* told her there was roadwork on the street—she heard it. And she was talking to ghosts at the temple. She's getting better.

KIM. I hope.

CHHEM. Your daughter Serey is getting older. She is very studious. (*Ominously*) And very beautiful.

KIM. Thank you. You are kind.

CHHEM (*teasingly*). You know, without my grandson your sister would still be in Cambodia.

KIM. We are very grateful.

THIDA (*muttering*). No, we are not!

KIM (*looking at Thida*). What, sister?

CHHEM. Savath is at the agency from dawn to midnight, never stops. Meetings with bigwigs from government offices, visits to shelters, casinos. He goes because other people lose their shirts, not him! You know that they had a date . . . I did not hear that it was a failure. They did not run in opposite directions.

KIM. Perhaps we should adapt to the American way, encourage another date.

CHHEM. My grandson is old enough to be a monk.

KIM. Serey is younger, I worry . . .

CHHEM. In a blink of an eye, all this will change. (*Threateningly*) In a car.

KIM. You don't need to tell me. But she is a good daughter. We have lost so much, I want to protect her.

CHHEM. Exactly! We're all that's left. Our families knew each other. Savath is the right choice, the best insurance a father could buy. He is Cambodian. A good man. College-educated. We will bring two families together. I will consult the astrologer and we can arrange a marriage.

KIM. Go ask him.

Kim exits with Chhem.

THIDA. *I am in-between a tiger and a crocodile. Please let me out of here—I need to go home.*

Dr. Simpson, alone, exhausted, drinking coffee, clicks through slides of healthy retinal cells. She shuts off the machine, getting up, searching the darkness.

DR. SIMPSON. Tom, are you there?

She lets down her guard to someone in the darkness.

DR. SIMPSON. Can you see me?

She searches a moment longer, putting her armor back up.

DR. SIMPSON. I don't believe in ghosts.

Lights shift as Dr. Simpson clicks through slides of healthy retinal cells, addressing her residents, who are the audience.

DR. SIMPSON. Sovandy Meng: her job was to carry bodies to mass graves. Fifty-two years old. Blind in 1977. (*Referring to slide*) Healthy retinal cell. Chantha Li: last child died of starvation. Age: Sixty. Blind in 1978. (*Showing slide*) Healthy retinal cell. Ang Malay: saw a baby thrown against a tree. Age: fifty-four. 1976. (*Showing slide*) Healthy retinal cell. Navy Hun: saw her sister killed, because of her white skin? At the beginning of the genocide. In her fifties. 1975. (*Showing slide*) Healthy retinal cell. Thida San: won't talk about what happened to her family . . . All of them should see.

Scene 7

Thida listens to a siren as she sits at her usual seat by the window. At the altar Kim smokes, showing Serey astrological charts.

KIM. The stars say yes, Serey. Chhem has made a very substantial offer but more importantly I want to join Savath to our family. This will please our ancestors and tie us to our lost country.

SEREY. I'm not in love with him, father.

KIM. You will grow to love him, as I grew to love your mother.

SEREY. But that's not the way things are here. People date before they get married, they fall in love!

KIM. We do too. Simply in reverse. Since you were a little girl, you have known that your mother and I would arrange your marriage. Now that she is gone it is up to me to make the right choice, to honor her. It is the single most important way you can show her your respect.

SEREY. Everything has changed. We aren't in Cambodia.

KIM. We must honor our dead and preserve our traditions.

SEREY. But we live in a new country.

KIM. It is very important. Please don't contradict me, Serey. I am your father. You will thank me later.

SEREY. I can't start having babies now. What if I want to go to college?

KIM. Then you will go. You are no longer a girl. Savath is a sensitive soul, refined and ethical. He will make a good husband for you.

SEREY. *I won't marry him.*

Haunted, Thida hears the communist propaganda music. She addresses Kim.

THIDA. Yes, she will, she will. Give me a moment. Let me speak to her. Say yes, Oun—my girl. You must say yes.

Kim touches her.

KIM. Sister what are you saying?

She pushes him, continuing out loud.

THIDA. Rays of sunlight shine into my eyes. The loudspeakers are hanging in the tree. There are flowers on the tree. She is tied. Water drips from a tiny hole in a bucket, on her head. The drops of water mix with her tears. They tied Oun to a tree. A magnolia. They're forcing her to marry.

SEREY (*to Kim; softly*). Her daughter Oun?

THIDA. The official he unties her. He points to young soldier. "Will you marry him?" She shakes her head no. She is stubborn. *Will not accept.* The official takes out his blade. He grabs Oun by the hair. They cut off her head.

KIM. Sister . . .

THIDA. He looks at me. He holds her head. He throws it into a fire where a pile of corpses and body parts burn . . . Smoke got in my eye . . . Don't cry, don't cry, or they kill you. (*To Kim*) Please. Let me die.

KIM. No, it is important to live.

Kim holds her. Blackout.

Scene 8

Morning. Thida wears the mirrored sunglasses as rock music plays. A punk barber watches as she enters the barbershop with her cane.

THIDA. *There is very loud music in the barbershop but it is cool, it smells of smoke and soap.*

The barber spins around a chair for her.

BARBER. Whoa, first customer, you're an early bird. Sit.

THIDA. *He ties something around my neck.*

BARBER. Hey, how'd you want it cut?

THIDA. Shaved, please.

BARBER. Sure you want it shaved?

THIDA. Yes. Please. I am going to the temple. Now I must become a nun.

BARBER. What's your name?

THIDA. *This is not the practice in my country to ask the name of the customer.* My name is Thida San. (*Politely*) What is your name?

BARBER. The Spider.

THIDA. Hello, the Spider. *Am I wrong in remembering that the spider is an insect?*

She stands, with her cane. The barber reveals Thida's scalp, now entirely shaved except for a spot with her initials: T. S. She feels the letters.

THIDA. Thank you.

Lights rise on Kim's apartment; Kim is near the altar, frantic, waiting on the phone, with Serey and Chhem.

KIM. You call the police, you get put on hold . . . I trusted you to watch her, Serey!

SEREY. Dad, I stayed up until 5 a.m. with her, she was asleep.

KIM. You promised me you'd stay awake. We said we'd take turns.

SEREY. I dozed off!

KIM. I can't trust you. (*On the phone*) What is taking so long?

SEREY. It was terrible what she told us. What do you think she'll do, dad? I'm scared.

CHHEM (*confused*). Nowhere in the neighborhood. Perhaps she took the wrong bus.

SEREY. She kept on saying she wanted to be alone.

KIM. I can think of nothing scarier for her than to be alone outside in Long Beach. (*To Serey*) How could you let this happen?

SEREY. It's not my fault. She hates it here, she can't rest. We yell too much.

KIM. She's been keeping Oun's death inside all this time. I didn't know what to say. I've tried so hard to forget. (*Listening on the phone*) Yes . . . I'll repeat it again. Thida San, Cambodian, blind . . . T-H-I-D-A. 245 Seventh, Little Phnom Penh . . . And please, I'll be right over. (*Hanging up*) I'll go to the police station, then check back with the doctor.

CHHEM. We will find Thida. Thida knows more than she pretends. We will look everywhere. Savath always knows what to do.

KIM. Chhem, will you go back to the temple and check again? And go with Serey so you don't get lost too!

Lights shift to Thida, head shaved, wearing the sunglasses, walking with her cane, as we hear street sounds.

THIDA. *I walk in a quiet place, the sun is so hot—hear only an occasional car. The wind blows sharply as if through a tunnel.*

Behind her a man appears.

MAN. Hey! Your money, man. Hey!

THIDA. *Grabs my arm so tight.*

He spins her around, knocking her glasses to the ground.

MUGGER. Your money!

He pulls a knife. Thida unpins the plastic bag pinned to her undershirt.

THIDA. My brother tells me to carry it always.

MUGGER. Whatever, lady.

She pulls American bills from among her photos. Sound of a car approaching. The mugger grabs the plastic bag with photos and exits, crushing the sunglasses. Thida feels about, on the ground.

THIDA. *Sipha. Oun.*

She feels the discarded plastic bag, the glasses.

THIDA. *I feel only crushed eyeglasses.*

She stands putting her hand to her breast where her photos just were. We hear the sound of cars speeding by. Against the blue Thida bends down and feels the ground with her fingers.

THIDA. *I am now walking on earth not on cement. In the distance I can hear the sound of strong wind in the trees . . . or perhaps it is the sound of waves.*

The sound slowly becomes crashing waves.

Lights shift to Savath, holding a map, hurrying to Serey and Chhem outside Kim's apartment.

CHHEM. What took you so long? We've searched every street . . .

SAVATH. Everyone's looking, my agency, the temple, the community center—I've broken up the area into sections on the map.

Thida is walking.

THIDA. *Yes, I must be walking near the sea! Soon I will reach down and feel the sand. White. I say to Sipha as we walk, "Look at the sand, not the bones."*

Savath instructs Chhem and Serey.

SAVATH (*to Chhem*). I want you to go to every neighbor and ask what they saw, she could be hiding right around here, that can happen. (*To Serey*) You go with her, page me on my beeper. What was she like last time you saw her?

SEREY. I think she probably wanted to kill herself.

SAVATH. You should've told me that on the phone.

SEREY. She told us something bad about her daughter.

SAVATH. That makes a big difference for the police.

Thida continues to walk.

THIDA. *I'm going to the sea. Back to Cambodia.*

Savath speaks to Serey.

SAVATH. Where would she go?

SEREY. Rushing traffic, the ocean? I don't know. It was a shock for her to let it out. I can't believe I let her run away.

SAVATH. It's OK, we'll report that too, we've got about a hundred people looking—even the monks. Your father is out with the detective.

SEREY. What she told us. It makes me feel so empty. Like the worst part of the Thai camps.

SAVATH. I know . . . that's how I felt when I lost my sister.

He looks at her; calm and optimistic.

SAVATH. Hey, she survived the killing fields; she'll survive it.

Thida sits cross-legged as the sun colors her face fiery orange. She listens to the rhythmic sound of oil pumps.

THIDA (*lifting her head, the sun on her face*). Ah, sun. Was it waves I heard, lapping on the shore? No, I was tired, from walking. (*Listening*) But what is that strange "Whir-whir-whir?" I don't recognize that. It comforts me . . . I'm floating. Below are the trees. And blue-green as far as I see. (*A beautiful vision.*) The beach at Kep!

She meditates as lights fade to night. Thida sits, listening to the oil pumps, as Savath, holding a flashlight, walks over to her and leans down, touching her gently so as not to frighten her.

SAVATH. Mrs. San? It's Savath. Your family is here now. We've been looking since yesterday. The police that found you said you didn't want to talk.

Kim and Serey rush in, exclaiming relief.

KIM. Thida! Thida! (*Laughing from panic*) I'm about to have a heart attack and you're calmly meditating. You shaved your head?

THIDA. I tried to walk to the sea.

SEREY. You went in the wrong direction. If something had happened I never would've forgiven myself.

KIM. You shouldn't have run away.

SAVATH. LA's a dangerous place.

Serey touches the initials on her scalp.

SEREY. Where did the letters on your head come from?

THIDA. The Spider.

KIM. I am more and more astonished.

Serey touches Thida's ripped clothing.

SEREY. What happened to your shirt?

Thida feels where the plastic bag was pinned to her shirt.

THIDA. They robbed me of the photographs of my family.

SAVATH. She got mugged.

THIDA. After that I felt I must finally return.

KIM. Return where, sister?

THIDA. To the beach at Kep. I am not alive.

KIM. Of course you are, we see you right here in front of us. Living, breathing.

THIDA. My soul left my body and traveled to Kep.

KIM. I was mistaken to leave you alone with Serey. Now I understand why you wanted to hide in the dark for so long in our country. I wish I could've been there to comfort you.

THIDA. You promised I could go to your temple to live. *Now I've waited long enough.*

KIM. You wouldn't be safe at the temple. It's with your family that you'll finally get better, surrounded by those who care for you.

SEREY. My dad's right. We want you to get better now, auntie.

THIDA. Without my vision I am useless.

KIM. I sometimes feel that I can't live but we go on for our ancestors. The doctor got money from the university to study your case. Here's someone who wants to solve the problem. Of course there's a scientific answer. And one day you'll see again. You will see Serey's children.

SEREY. I may not have children.

Kim gives her a dirty look.

SEREY. But if I do, sure, you can see them. Or not. Whatever. We just want you to be happier. We meant no disrespect.

Kim holds Thida to him.

KIM. We're the last survivors of our family. You have to trust me.

THIDA. I want to become a nun. *That is final*.

SEREY. The temple is a warehouse with peeling paint. You wouldn't want to live there.

THIDA. *He* said it was like the temples in Cambodia.

SEREY. He lies sometimes.

KIM. Serey.

SEREY. Sees things through rose-colored glasses. I'll take you to the temple more often, I promise.

Thida listens to the oil pumps.

THIDA. Where am I?

SAVATH. You're in an oil field.

Scene 9

Thida taps her cane impatiently as Dr. Simpson shows Kim her research in her office.

DR. SIMPSON. There are about 150 survivors, a cluster of women in Long Beach, who don't know each other—I can't find any anywhere else. We're testing blood pressure, heart rate, doing neurological tests. My colleagues are looking forward to meeting you, Thida.

THIDA. I am not here.

KIM. You need to stop saying that now. You are clearly here in front of us. (*To Dr. Simpson*) She says her soul left her body and traveled to the beach at Kep. (*To Thida*) A soul is a mysterious thing. It wanes like the moon, but it comes back to full, you'll see.

DR. SIMPSON. We'll do an ERG and an MRI so we can look at your brain.

THIDA. Do so at your own risk.

KIM. Stop that with your cane. They want to ask you some questions about your background.

THIDA. She doesn't listen.

DR. SIMPSON. What kind of suffering could be so great that it would blind someone? It's the grief that interests me and how that affects the eye.

THIDA. You do not understand.

KIM. What?

THIDA. I see the same things over and over in my head. At night I cannot sleep. My head—it pounds as if a nail is being twisted into it.

DR. SIMPSON. We need to give you some medicine for your headache, Thida. That will help.

KIM. Of course. Why didn't you tell me this?

THIDA (*to Dr. Simpson*). I do not want the medicine. It's bad for you. (*To Kim*) I want to go to the temple. Plan a ceremony for Sipha.

KIM. What are you talking about now?

THIDA. Release him.

DR. SIMPSON. Who is Sipha?

KIM. Her husband.

DR. SIMPSON. Medicine will help for your headache. (*To Kim*) I'll need her to come with me to the resident presentation, and if she could come back for more tests—I have the women scheduled all week.

KIM. I'll be interested to see if you can find any organic basis for this.

DR. SIMPSON. Yes, the funders were generous with something that could easily be interpreted as psychosomatic. (*Joking*) It also helps my reputation for not being a "people person."

KIM. I see. I loved doing research. Here in this country I'm a lab technician. This is more exciting than doing blood work.

DR. SIMPSON. I'm sure you were a good doctor. I'm grateful to you.

THIDA. I feel sick.

KIM. You must go with Dr. Simpson.

THIDA (*muttering to herself*). The walking dead. (*To Dr. Simpson*) Can you make yourself useful and bring me to the temple, doctor?

KIM. Thida!

DR. SIMPSON (*to Kim*). I'll make sure someone gets her home, about five. Will someone be there?

KIM. Yes. Just don't lose her.

Kim exits and lights shift as Dr. Simpson addresses her residents who are in silhouette while examining Thida.

DR. SIMPSON. No country has lost such a sizable part of its population in such a short time and was stripped of an entire generation of people with education. (*Staring off*) I'm sorry . . . The earth leaves me sometimes . . . Who had a question?

We hear the residents interrogating Thida.

RESIDENT 1 (VOICEOVER). You see nothing at all, Mrs. San?

THIDA. No.

RESIDENT 2 (VOICEOVER). Did the insomnia and headaches come with the onset of the blindness, Mrs. San?

THIDA. I can't remember.

RESIDENT 3 (VOICEOVER). Can you describe the nature of the forced labor, Mrs. San?

THIDA. Leave me alone.

RESIDENT 1 (VOICEOVER). How long were the periods of starvation?

DR. SIMPSON. Trust in society was eroded; the perpetrators were often victims—many young boys were forced into the Khmer Rouge during the imbalance of the Vietnam War bombings and the country's own civil war . . .

RESIDENT 2 (VOICEOVER). Did you experience shell explosions, Mrs. San?

RESIDENT 3 (VOICEOVER). Did you suffer injuries to the back of your head?

RESIDENT 1 (VOICEOVER). Do you have a history of cataracts, glaucoma, Mrs. San?

RESIDENT 2 (VOICEOVER). Can she speak?

RESIDENT 3 (VOICEOVER). Were there remnants of Agent Orange in that area?

RESIDENT 2 (VOICEOVER). Is this a symptom of PTSD?

RESIDENT 1 (VOICEOVER). Does her culture somatize illness?

RESIDENT 3 (VOICEOVER). Has she worn a halter monitor while she's questioned about trauma?

RESIDENT 1 (VOICEOVER). Have you repeated the MRI, Mrs. San?

ALL THE RESIDENTS (VOICEOVER). Mrs. San?

Scene 10

Serey enters as Thida sits by the window.

SEREY. You're really *pissed* at my dad. (*Explaining the word*) Angry.

THIDA. Correct.

SEREY. He has that effect on people. When you ran away it made me think of the camp. We lived in a hole, aunt, before we got assigned a refugee number in Thailand. It was just he and I, and a jerry can of water. He'd stay up at night, wouldn't let me stray anywhere. I found out later it was 'cause the Khmer Rouge from the next camp raped girls.

THIDA. On the day the Khmer Rouge came into Phnom Penh a statue of the Buddha cried real tears.

SEREY. I'd ask him to show me my mother's photograph over and over. The only thing pretty. I'd ask, "Where is she in the photo?

At home? Where did she go after the picture was taken? The color of the blouse? The little scarf?" If I could just get back to where she was in the picture. He'd never say anything, just stare off. He'd put the photo back in the plastic bag, fold it in a square and pin it back to the inside of his undershirt. I miss her so much but I didn't even really know her.

Serey is filled with grief for what she can't have and won't ever know.

THIDA. Serey? The photo as you describe it would not be taken in her house. She would be in the studio at a photographer's: a room with a red velvet drape. After the picture was taken she would accompany your father for a tea at an outdoor café with white tablecloths and silver. They would hold hands and watch the sun setting, the villas changing color. There would be a soft wind. They would wear sandals which they would slip off under the table. Their feet would touch. Her blouse is pink, I'm certain, and the scarf blue.

SEREY. I'm sorry about Oun.

THIDA. You are a stubborn one, like her. She was a fighter.

SEREY. Did you choose your own husband?

THIDA. No, it was my parents who chose him.

SEREY. Did you love him?

THIDA. He saved my life warning me take off my glasses. Our last moment together, I understood what love was.

Serey kisses her aunt and exits.

THIDA. *I stand in the blue-green water, feel my baby kick. Hear the sound of waves breaking, smell the salt air. At Kep I waded in the aqua water, lay on the white sand beach. Sipha would rub my shoulders . . .*

Scene 11

Serey and Savath are sipping espresso after dinner in a restaurant. The room is turning.

SEREY. I like the way this restaurant spins. So you can see different parts of the city all the time. Not that the smog makes it possible. I'd like to live in a house that spins.

SAVATH. Why?

SEREY. So you could see the world from all different sides. It's boring to look out a window and see the same thing. In my case a trash dumpster, thank you. But think! If you saw a waterfall, a volcano, a cabana, a child playing. If it was always changing!

SAVATH. A cabana?

SEREY. Like in Hawaii. I really want to go there. I want to scuba dive.

SAVATH. So do I. Think of how good you'd feel if you breathed underwater. Like a fish. Want to go to Hawaii?

SEREY. Isn't that the big "honeymoon" place?

SAVATH (*noticing*). Are you hyped on coffee?

SEREY. My head's spinning a little. It feels good. I thought you were the big Buddhist-of-the-year—you drink double espressos?

SAVATH. Of course. With my job I need all the help I can get. Living in courtrooms, the DMV? Writing petitions so Khmer people don't get arrested for child abuse when they "coin" their kids? Plus this espresso is good.

SEREY. We should go dancing. Except not that corny Khmer stuff. We should go to a club. Get all sweaty. It makes you forget.

SAVATH. I love the Khmer stuff. Sinn Sisamouth.

SEREY. He died at Tuol Sleng, you know. It's like if America sent Elvis to a concentration camp. Why would anyone do that?

SAVATH. You're right. I don't know why anyone would do that.

SEREY. OK. (*Gulps her espresso*) So we've been on their "second date." I like this place, I like the tablecloths, the silverware.

SAVATH. I'm glad you like it so much.

SEREY. My aunt would like it. She's classy. I used to lust after her make-up when I was little. I wished I could steal her lipstick.

SAVATH. You look very classy in that silk.

SEREY. My dad's never seen this. (*Shows him a tiny tattoo on her skin above her breast.*)

SAVATH. A lotus. It's sexy.

SEREY. You found my aunt. You know everyone. It's good the way you never get freaked. (*He touches her hand.*) So. I have an idea. It's bold. These two weirdos are breathing down our necks. (*Quoting them*) "We want to adapt to the American ways, go on a date." They think they're trying to be so smart. So we one-up them.

SAVATH. I think I may know what you're talking about. But I may just be dreaming.

SEREY. I mean, I hate to say this, it sounds, I don't know, but doesn't it always come down to . . . ? I mean if THAT doesn't work, if that part's not happening, then it's a kind of a big commitment to make for an entire lifetime.

SAVATH (*teasing her*). I like that you're bold. I really like that.

SEREY. I thought . . . (*He leans over and kisses her.*) I think you're really good-looking. Sometimes I worry you're too serious.

SAVATH. I am serious.

SEREY (*making up her mind*). OK. Let's check into the spinning hotel.

SAVATH. Get the biggest, most expensive room, with a tape player. Make it beautiful. I have my credit card.

SEREY. You know the hotel part doesn't spin.

SAVATH. We might be able to make it spin. I'm not as square as you think.

She looks at him.

SEREY. It's my first time.

SAVATH. Me too. (*Protectively*) It will be our secret.

Scene 12

Dr. Simpson talks to Kim near the altar as Thida sits by the window.

DR. SIMPSON. Has she spoken since the residents' presentation?

KIM. No.

DR. SIMPSON. They were asking her questions and she stopped suddenly. She wouldn't say anything.

KIM. Sister, Lynn needs you to answer when people ask questions. If you see, then perhaps it will stop the memories in your head. They will be replaced by new ones.

THIDA. She knows nothing.

KIM. Thida!

DR. SIMPSON. I had to reschedule. We'll see if she can do it next week. It's hard to get all the doctors in the same room.

KIM. Yes, she'll be better next week.

DR. SIMPSON. And she refused to have another MRI so we could look at her brain.

KIM. Perhaps she got overly tired. How did the MRI research turn out?

DR. SIMPSON. They do have similar problems: high blood pressure, heart palpitations, but it's still somewhat of a mystery. I should go.

KIM. May I ask? Do you eat, doctor? You look thin.

DR. SIMPSON. I drink too much coffee and smoke. (*Ironic*) In some ways it really functions almost better than food.

KIM. Did I tell you? I'm quitting.

DR. SIMPSON. Really?

KIM. Soon, very soon.

DR. SIMPSON. Just about the time I do.

KIM. Perhaps stay for dinner? Any good doctor knows one must eat. Shrimp with lemongrass and pepper, squash soup. Chicken in coconut milk and lime, with Chinese broccoli?

DR. SIMPSON. I better run. I'll check in with you tomorrow and see how she's doing.

KIM. We received good news. My daughter just got into college.

DR. SIMPSON. Congratulations.

KIM. But I ask myself over and over, what can happen in four years?

DR. SIMPSON. I think by then we'll find a cure for your sister.

KIM. Yes. I always cook too much food and my sister eats none of it, Serey's always at the library. Can I put some food in a container for you? I hope you don't stay up all night with that research. You need to sleep too.

DR. SIMPSON. It's a fantastic project. There has to be something, I just know it.

KIM. Sit and have tea, while you wait for the food. Take a breath. Enjoy yourself. You're so lucky.

DR. SIMPSON. Lucky?

KIM. You have everything.

DR. SIMPSON. Everything?

KIM. I miss my work. I miss a lot of things.

DR. SIMPSON. I'll stay and eat. It smells good.

He touches her hand.

KIM. Just sit, I'll serve you—don't worry about anything.

Kim starts to exit and runs into Serey. Kim and Serey try to keep their voices down as Thida sits in her chair by the window and Dr. Simpson waits.

KIM. Chhem has already rented an entire restaurant!

SEREY. SO WHAT? I'm not doing it. I told you that already. We both told you.

KIM. I wish your mother was here. (*Putting his hands together*) I wish to Buddha and all the gods in the sky and all the gods in the Long Beach cement that she was here.

SEREY. What's gotten into you?

KIM (*to himself*). Why do *I* have to be the one to do this? WHY?

SEREY. Do what? Cool out. Take a breath.

KIM. Cool out?

DR. SIMPSON (*starting to leave.*) I'll go.

SEREY (*to Dr. Simpson*). Sorry he's acting so strange.

KIM. Forgive us, this is poor timing. Please come back for dinner.

DR. SIMPSON. Yes.

Dr. Simpson exits.

SEREY. Savath's grandmother is having a bad influence on you, dad.

KIM (*trying to gather his courage*). OK, OK, OK.

SEREY. Jesus.

KIM. Don't swear.

SEREY. "Jesus" isn't swearing, plus we're not Christian.

KIM. So why do you talk about Jesus? We're off the subject. If you do what the Americans do . . . You know . . . the . . . (*trying to explain sex; partly using the-palms-pressed-together-"slowdance"-analogy Chhem used.*) You know . . . I can't say it.

SEREY. Dad, you are so goofy.

KIM. Don't call me goofy! Have you had conjugal relations with a man?!

SEREY. Look . . . it's different here.

KIM. What are you saying?

SEREY. I had to "check it out" . . .

KIM. "Check it out?"

SEREY. . . . I've had sex with Savath.

KIM. Oh, no, god. (*Aside*) Do you think your aunt can hear?

THIDA. Every word.

SEREY. I don't want a marriage where in ten years we hate each other.

KIM. Serey? You are a fallen woman! Why did you do this? What is wrong with you?

SEREY. It's fine.

KIM. No, it's not fine!

SEREY. It was good . . .

KIM. You've ruined my life. (*Repeating, deadpan*) "It was good." (*To Thida*) America has turned her into nothing!

SEREY. I can't help who I am . . . He's a lot different than I thought.

KIM. Oh. (*Deadpan*) Wonderful. (*Freaking about what they are discussing; to Thida*) Why me, sister? (*To Serey.*) You are worthless! What will people say?

SEREY. It's none of their business.

KIM. It's everyone's business! You'll see! You have to get married right now, Serey.

SEREY. Thanks for trusting me.

KIM. I don't. And now I don't trust Savath.

SEREY. He loves that I'm going to college first. He wouldn't care if I went to graduate school.

KIM. Graduate school? NO! What am I saying? Yes, go to graduate school, get your Ph.D. (*To Thida*) I don't care what she does anymore.

THIDA (*to Kim*). Maybe you picked the right man for her, after all.

He takes a pen from his pocket.

KIM. You want me to undo all the plans with Chhem? Cancel everything? Pay her back for what she has bought?

SEREY. You're not listening. You never do.

KIM. I *did* listen and it was a disaster.

SEREY. Well, too bad my mother isn't here. Too bad there isn't anyone here who *gets it*. It's hard. You think I like being the only child left? We're supposed to look to the future, that's what you say, but all you do is live in the past. I'm going to college and maybe I'll transfer. Transfer right out of here.

KIM. Fine, transfer. Be like all the other American families, separated and alone.

Serey looks at the pen he is holding.

SEREY. Why do you steal pens, dad? You take them from everywhere, banks, gas stations, stores?

Serey takes another pen out of his pocket.

THIDA. The officials killed us because we could read and write, then they kept pens in their pockets to show us their power.

KIM. I guess I can't help myself.

Scene 13

Chhem is in Kim's garden, calling to Thida, who sits inside. Savath enters.

CHHEM (*to Thida*). What were you thinking to get those initials on your head?

SAVATH. Grandma?

CHHEM. His sister is slowly going crazy. Kim is so patient but we have to watch her every minute.

Chhem has gathered some fruit.

CHHEM. My mother used to give me a hook and let me climb the ladder to gather the ripe ones. How I loved to see the trees from above.

SAVATH. Grandma, I need to talk to you. Don't bug Serey anymore. (*Taking out a letter*) Listen, and try not to talk.

CHHEM. I should go inside and attend to Thida.

SAVATH. This is Serey's college acceptance letter. She showed it to me . . . out on our "date." She's very proud.

CHHEM. But the wedding will be next month. We have already purchased the bedroom set.

SAVATH. Look, it's generous to get the bedroom set but that's really not what we need.

CHHEM. She will have children! When your mother died, I prayed that you would stay with me and promised in return I would do good.

SAVATH. You're seeing all this in your head but it's not going to happen that way. She'll go to college for four years. Then if we want, maybe we'll get married.

CHHEM. Four years? Who will cook your food?

SAVATH. I eat out.

CHHEM. Who will do your laundry? Clean your house? You will wait for four years, to be "together?" To have children?

SAVATH. It's a whole different thing here, grandma . . .

CHHEM. No engagement? No party? No announcement? No invitations? No prayers?—I want to give back to the monks.

SAVATH. None of that. We'll date, maybe take a trip to Hawaii at her break, go out dancing?

CHHEM. Slowdancing?

SAVATH. I think she likes rock.

CHHEM (*hearing "rock"*). I will go buy her a ring tomorrow!

SAVATH. I already bought one. (*Taking out a box with a ring.*) You want to see it?

CHHEM. Ah, why did you not let me pick it out?

SAVATH. I think your tastes are at opposite ends of the planet.

CHHEM. I want to pay for it. The rock is too small, the band too thin.

SAVATH. She likes it.

CHHEM. No! She cannot see it before the wedding!

SAVATH. I showed it to her in a window, I didn't say it was for her. It's a double thing: college, engagement. And actually something else . . . Love.

CHHEM. Love? You must get married now, Savath. I have already made the invitations and reserved the temple.

SAVATH. Well, unreserve it! Tear them up.

CHHEM. You are disrespectful.

SAVATH. *I* need to respect Serey.

CHHEM. All the evil we saw, we must preserve our customs. The astrologer is very optimistic.

SAVATH. We're not getting married because of the stars!

CHHEM. Think! The gold I hid in the soles of my shoes, the chains in my clothing's seams. *They* did not find it. It is for you and your new family. She is "easy," she'll sleep with anyone.

SAVATH. *I won't listen to that.*

CHHEM. You will make me lose face with Serey's father.

SAVATH. It's not about *you.* (*Vulnerable*) Look, it may not work out, OK? We don't know. It's a risk I have to take.

CHHEM. You'll see, everything good about our country will disappear!

Scene 14

Dr. Simpson and Kim smoke in Kim's garden. Sirens are heard in the distance.

KIM. Now the three women in my life aren't talking to me. My sister is angry at me, my daughter hates me and my daughter's fiancé's grandmother has taken out a contract on me by now.

DR. SIMPSON. You're very funny.

KIM. Why?

DR. SIMPSON. I don't know. You just are.

KIM. My daughter says "goofy." Thida refuses to see you. I wondered what happened. Ever since the meeting with the residents she seems worse.

DR. SIMPSON. Let me talk to her.

KIM. Anything new on the research?

DR. SIMPSON. There are no links. They have some of the same symptoms, that's the best conclusion. I won't be able to get the second part of the funding if I can't prove more. There may have been something I missed. The other women are reacting like your sister, they're withdrawing, don't want to be tested, don't want to be seen. It's hard to do a study when the subjects don't want to get better.

KIM. Why not visit the temple on Willow Street? Take a look.

DR. SIMPSON. I ask myself this question: You saw trauma, why didn't you go blind?

KIM. Have you ever had a moment when medical science doesn't help?

DR. SIMPSON. . . . . Yes.

KIM. We discovered recently Thida's daughter refused to marry a Khmer Rouge soldier and was killed in front of her. We did not know this before. Her daughter was beheaded. Thida saw her burn.

DR. SIMPSON. You can't reverse that.

KIM. I promised my wife I'd take care of our children. As a doctor I was a marked man. I pretended I was a farmer, rubbed my hands in the dirt until they had calluses. (*Looking at his cigarette*) You know the Khmer Rouge rolled their cigarettes with pages from books and plays. Serey is all I have left. You're lucky your eyes have not seen such horror.

DR. SIMPSON. This is a beautiful garden.

KIM. Thank you. Sometimes solutions are found outside? Prayer, food, family? Growing beans, a nap?

DR. SIMPSON. A nap would be good.

KIM. Sitting around and doing nothing at all.

DR. SIMPSON. Laughing a lot.

KIM. Who knows?

DR. SIMPSON. I don't.

KIM. Go talk to Thida. Let me get some food for you to bring home.

Lights up on Thida, who sits as Dr. Simpson approaches.

DR. SIMPSON. In this country we get so carried away with the diagnostic procedures, we lose sight of the patient.

THIDA. You smoke too much.

DR. SIMPSON. I'm sorry.

THIDA. I will never again have a test.

DR. SIMPSON. Were they uncomfortable?

THIDA. Everything is uncomfortable. I am a prisoner.

DR. SIMPSON. Let me ask you this. You said your soul left your body and traveled to the beach at Kep. How does a soul leave a body?

THIDA. How does it, doctor?

DR. SIMPSON. Yes, that's what I asked.

THIDA. What do you think?

DR. SIMPSON. Well, perhaps because the pain is too great?

THIDA. Yes. What do you do with your day?

DR. SIMPSON. Work.

THIDA. Do you ever go to sleep?

DR. SIMPSON. Not much. What was at the beach at Kep?

THIDA. Such beauty. Do you have a family? Are you married?

DR. SIMPSON. Yes. My husband Tom is dead.

THIDA. How did Tom die?

Dr. Simpson sees Thida, waiting.

DR. SIMPSON. He had an illness.

THIDA. What type?

DR. SIMPSON. I can't talk about it.

THIDA. I know.

DR. SIMPSON. A disease of the nervous system. It was like a bomb that went off in his body. And in mine.

THIDA. Where did your soul go?

DR. SIMPSON. Nowhere beautiful. (*Takes out a photo from her wallet. She takes Thida's hand and passes it over the photo.*) We were everything to each other. I lost my only family. It happened fast . . . I don't know. (*Dr. Simpson breaks down.*) I couldn't bear it. That kind of illness can't be explained, it's too cruel.

THIDA. You see, telling the story is very difficult. Almost like being strangled.

Kim enters with a food container. Dr. Simpson puts away the photo. She takes the food container and leaves.

KIM. What happened to the doctor?

THIDA. She lost her husband some time ago.

KIM. She wears the ring. Why did you talk *to her* if you are so unwilling to talk?

THIDA. I must find you and her some herbs. Margosa, coconut milk . . . Release of stress for you, sleep for her.

KIM (*puzzled*). Why did the doctor make you feel better?

THIDA. I felt useful. She did not know something and *I* knew.

KIM. *I* need your help too, sister. You're useful to me. I need you to live.

THIDA. Why not take me to your garden? I'm sorry I've always refused your invitations.

KIM. Really you'd like to come?

He starts to take her to his garden. Lights shift to Dr. Simpson slowly entering the temple. She speaks to herself with a microphone.

DR. SIMPSON. *I add my shoes to the mountain of shoes. The temple is crowded with bright silk, an American flag, a stray skeleton from Halloween. Monks in orange robes sit cross-legged on dainty satin pillows eating from an array of bowls. People kneel talking. The altar is filled with baskets of tea, money, cigarettes, Oreos. A statue of Buddha is cloaked in the same robe as the monks. Blind women, shoulders slumped, eyes staring off, expressionless, holding canes. Life whirs around them but they aren't there. Where? How can they come back?* (*A realization*) *You almost have to die first before you live again.*

Scene 15

Kim takes a photo of Serey and Savath, as Dr. Simpson sits in Kim's living room with Thida. Chhem serves dessert.

CHHEM (*to Dr. Simpson*). After this engagement party, I have four years to wait for my grandson's marriage. I have taken up embroidery, doctor. A very long project. I hope I don't die before the wedding.

DR. SIMPSON. I'm sure it will be OK.

CHHEM. OK? The tradition is ruined.

Kim, Serey and Savath join the others as Dr. Simpson gives Thida a box, which she opens. Outside we hear sirens.

THIDA. I would like to preserve the wrapping. (*Showing a skirt*) It is a sampot.

DR. SIMPSON. Red and yellow. Serey told me about the shop.

SEREY. The lady gets the silk from a co-op in Takeo, it's pretty . . .

CHHEM. And I helped pick it out.

THIDA (*to Dr. Simpson*). You must take it, I will never again have the occasion.

DR. SIMPSON. It's for you. I wanted to thank you. The tea helped me sleep. I started thinking.

THIDA. About what?

DR. SIMPSON. Memories.

THIDA. You've changed. You seem lighter.

Thida feels the fabric.

THIDA. You have good taste. Why do you not try it on? It would give me so much pleasure to see you dressed in something different for once.

DR. SIMPSON. You can't see me.

THIDA. I do know what you wear. I asked my brother to tell me.

KIM. I said you dressed very well. (*To Thida*) Why don't you try it on?

THIDA (*to Dr. Simpson*). I do not feel like changing.

DR. SIMPSON. Serey says you were a city lady. I'm sure you were very elegant.

THIDA. I adored clothes. It was another life . . . I cannot imagine. It would give me pleasure if you would try it on . . . just to see.

Thida holds out the long skirt.

THIDA. Take it. (*Dr. Simpson takes the skirt and tries it on.*) It is from my country. Let me feel. (*Thida feels and adjusts it. Dr. Simpson stands in the skirt.*) You have given me something very beautiful.

DR. SIMPSON. What?

THIDA. A way to imagine something different. I always admired doctors. And now there's you.

SEREY. It's nice. (*To Savath*) You should buy me one!

Savath puts his arm around Serey.

CHHEM. They show the world. They are a mystery to me.

Thida touches Serey, speaking softly.

THIDA. You know, I was a midwife. I will be able to help you some day.

Kim listens to sirens.

KIM. Why don't these gangs stop? War follows us everywhere.

THIDA. It's always that way. A little girl drops a grain of rice on the floor and a lizard grabs it. A cat sees the lizard and pounces, which brings the dog. The cat's owner starts to beat the dog and this angers the dog's owner. The two men start to fight and the families, neighbors join in until everyone is fighting. Word reaches Angkor that a fight is raging. The king thinks it's an attack by a foreign enemy and rushes out with 10,000 men and elephants. The king of Siam thinks the Khmers are mobilizing to attack him and rushes out with his men and elephants. All because a careless little girl drops a grain of rice, a war breaks out. I never thought war could touch a place like Kep but we've always had fighting. Siam. Vietnam. The US. We are a small country.

KIM. I'm so happy you told us that story. My sister was always an excellent storyteller.

SEREY. You know, aunt, maybe only big countries survive? A simple law of size.

Savath puts on some Willie Nelson music.

CHHEM. Ah, now is the time! Would you like some more to eat?

Thida listens to the music.

THIDA. Sipha loved him.

KIM. Who?

THIDA. Willie Nelson.

DR. SIMPSON. Your husband loved Willie Nelson?

Savath puts the ring on Serey's finger.

CHHEM. Finally, the ring.

Serey looks at the ring.

SEREY. OK, we've made a commitment to each other. We think we want to have children but I really need to go to college. We'll probably have a traditional wedding but we also want to help plan it. (*Taking something out*) I have a ring.

CHHEM. Another?

Serey puts it on Savath's finger.

SEREY (*to Kim*). I want to honor you. And my mother. I know we can never forget what happened, dad. (*To Thida*) You know, maybe big countries like this survive because of the stuff from the little countries? . . . We're family. We have to stay together and we have to grow up.

KIM. I don't know. Fate has put part of you here and part of you there.

Kim looks, anxious, at Serey. Thida turns in Kim's direction.

THIDA. She's intelligent. A fighter. You must trust her.

KIM. Yes.

Scene 16

We see the blue of ocean and hear waves. Thida sits with Dr. Simpson who looks out to sea.

DR. SIMPSON. Do you see colors?

THIDA. Yellow powder spread on a woman's body after giving birth. Green lemon leaves steamed for the new mother to bathe in. Brown star-of-anise with its delicate flower. Cook it in a curry and take her to the sea. Let her play until she gets hungry then feed her the dish. When she is finished tell her your stories, take her to the top of the mountain and show her how beautiful when the sun goes down. (*She points out*) Look . . . (*Turning to Dr. Simpson*) Thank you for bringing me here. What is the color of the water?

DR. SIMPSON. It's blue-gray, darker in the parts where there's sea-weed. The shore is flat all the way to the sea, the sand is brown. The waves, you hear them?

THIDA. Yes.

DR. SIMPSON. They break in one place, then ripple in a straight, white line.

Thida hears the sound of a wave breaking. She wades into the water, holding up her dress.

THIDA. Colder than Kep.

DR. SIMPSON. Blindness. That's how you survived.

THIDA. There was once a lady who poured out all her misfortunes to the Buddha. He told her these miseries would go away if she obtained a seed from a house that had never known sorrow. When the Buddha asked the woman if she had found the Seed of Happiness, she replied, "No. I went to every house seeking it and found no house that had not known sorrow."

The two women stand in the water.

THIDA. In my country we believe your husband's spirit will always protect you.

Thida faces far out.

THIDA. Lynn?

DR. SIMPSON. Yes?

THIDA. I still see her head bobbing up and down against the line of the horizon. I still hear Sipha and myself calling her name . . . She said no to them.

Oun appears against the blue. She slowly walks out of the sea.

Lights fade.

The End

A PROJECTION READS

At least 150 Cambodian women living in Southern California have functional blindness, a psychosomatic vision loss linked to what they saw in the years of Khmer Rouge rule.

The New York Times, 8 August 1989

Notes

Bows: prayer position with elbows down and relaxed.

> To friend or cousin:
> Hands in prayer position to cleavage area.
>
> To teacher, or elder (i.e. Serey to Chhem):
> Hands in prayer position to lips.
>
> To family/grandparents (Serey to Thida; once you marry into a family you change to family bow; husband and wife are equals and their bowing is not based on ages):
> Hands in prayer position to nose.
>
> To god/monks who are chanting:
> Prayer position to hairline.
>
> A couple bows when they give rings (recipient bows and then the donor bows to say you're welcome.)
>
> Bow when you receive a present and when you say, "Hello."
>
> Bowing at temple: Bow three times to
> 1) Buddha
> 2) Teachings
> 3) Monks at a particular temple.
> Sitting on floor, prayer hands and put hands to floor. Or bow once to floor, covering everything.
>
> Non-Buddhists don't have to bow.

Sitting at temple or at home: for women, legs to the side. Men can sit Indian style, except at temples or engagement parties. Women's feet/legs may get numb and they may switch sides.

Serving food: by putting the dish in front of person, not handing it directly to them. Since Thida is blind, the dish is put in her lap.

Coining: a traditional dermal massage technique in which oiled skin is rubbed vigorously with a coin for healing purposes.

Alexandra Napier as Miriam Bloom and Zach Udko as Yoni at a reading of My Political Israeli Play
at the 2004 "Voice and Vision" Envision Lab. Directed by Jean Wagner. Photograph by Jenny Levison.

MY POLITICAL ISRAELI PLAY

BY

ZOHAR TZUR

ARTISTIC STATEMENT: ZOHAR TZUR

I grew up in Tel Aviv, Israel, and participated in mandatory military service from 1992–94. Those were the most sad, traumatic, funny and bizarre two years of my life and I hope that in this play I have been able to capture some of the mood, emotions and rhythm of my military days.

CHARACTERS

CASTING REQUIREMENTS	3 women and 3 men
MIRIAM BLOOM	female, 30s
MINA NOVODVORSKY	female, 30s

(*Both to be played by the same actress*)

CHAZ GOLDMAN	male, 56
YONI	male, 18
ADI NATHAN	male, 22
YONI'S MOTHER	female, 50s
JOANNA	female, 45
EDGAR	male, 45

MIRIAM'S FAMILY:
MOTHER, FATHER, GRANDPA, UNCLE AVRAM

JOURNALIST 1
JOURNALIST 2

Scene 1

Dark stage. Miriam Bloom and Yoni, eighteen-year-old Israeli soldiers.

MIRIAM. I hate night patrols.

YONI. I hate night patrols too. (*With a thick British accent*) Cucumber sandwich?

MIRIAM. I hate how the air smells at four o'clock in the morning.

YONI (*British accent*). As do I, dear. Scone or crumpet?

MIRIAM. And I hate how horny I get around these hours.

YONI (*British accent*). I hate how randy I get around these hours too.

MIRIAM. Randy but tired.

YONI (*back to normal accent*). Tired yet hungry.

MIRIAM. Hungry, but too tired to eat.

YONI. Too tired to eat, but too horny not to.

MIRIAM. Randy horny tired hungry and dying for a cigarette.

YONI. Or a joint.

MIRIAM. Along with a good cup of coffee.

YONI. Or a few mushrooms.

MIRIAM. First coffee, then mushrooms.

YONI. Or mushrooms inside the coffee. Then the sex.

Short pause.

MIRIAM. I'm Miriam.

YONI. I'm Yoni. (*Back to British accent*) Otherwise known as Lord Edgar of Hampstead Heath. Then I moved, of course, to London—

MIRIAM. What?

YONI (*British accent*). Where I happen to own the largest collection of brollies. Even bigger then the Pope's. Care to join me for a game of tiddlywinks?

MIRIAM. Let me guess. You've been here in this shitty checkpoint at least two years, haven't you?

YONI (*British accent*). That's partially true. Because half the time I spend in rainy Hampstead Heath or London, with my beautiful wife and our lovely pet.

MIRIAM. Happens to the best.

YONI (*British accent*). Ah . . . England. Life is truly beautiful there as long as you don't open the drawers.

JOANNA'S VOICE (*British accent*). Edgar! Oh, Edgar!

Lights out.

Scene 2

Joanna, British, 45, dressing up.

JOANNA. Oh, Edgar! You musn't lock the serpent in the dresser!

EDGAR'S VOICE. Where else can I lock it, Joanna?

JOANNA. I don't care, Edgar! Just make sure by the time the guests are arriving, that beast is gone!

EDGAR'S VOICE. It was your idea in the first place! Now where the hell are my cuff-links?

JOANNA. They were in your dresser, Edgar, probably eaten by the serpent already!

Enter Edgar, 45, handsome, slightly limping.

JOANNA. Why, Edgar! You're limping!

EDGAR. Never mind that, Joanna. Did you know that the Mayor of Baybrookshire owns the biggest tie collection in all of Great Britain? Bigger than the Pope's!

A buzz at the door.

JOANNA. Oh dear, they're here already! Button up your shirt, Edgar! (*Starts buttoning his shirt.*)

EDGAR. Don't touch my shirt, Joanna! I've had shirts ruined by people like you!

Another buzz at the door.

JOANNA. Good lord! Charles! Answer the bloody door! (*To Edgar*) Good help is so hard to find these days!

EDGAR. Now listen to me, Joanna. Before we go out to entertain, I have one thing to ask you—under no circumstances are you to mention the bloody serpent!

JOANNA. The serpent?! What on earth are you talking about, Edgar?

Edgar slaps her.

EDGAR. Control yourself, Joanna! This is going to be a long night, and the only way we're going to get through it is if we cooperate!

MIRIAM (*voice*). . . . . *They gaze at each other, as few more buzzes are heard offstage. Lights are off. End of first act.*

Lights up on second half of the stage. Chaz Goldman, 45, a theater producer, sits in front of Miriam Bloom, Israeli, now 36, big eyeglasses, curly messy hair, in short, the classic librarian type. He gazes at her for a long time. Finally . . .

CHAZ. I LOOOVED it!

MIRIAM (*very excited*). Oh, Mr. Goldman! Really? I don't know what to say!

CHAZ. Commercial yet original, sophisticated but in a way that will speak to a mass audience, moving without turning into a melodrama . . . Miriam, I think we have something hot cooking here!

MIRIAM. I'm so excited to hear that, Mr. Goldman! I've been working so hard to make it—

CHAZ. You have a fresh crisp voice and a brilliant future ahead of you—

MIRIAM. Please, Mr. Goldman, this is too much . . .

CHAZ. The future of one of the most kicking incisive and hard-fucking-core political writers of our time!

Short pause.

MIRIAM (*confused*). Political writers?

CHAZ. To be honest, I'm more than impressed by your ability to write such a mature, strong political metaphor.

MIRIAM (*more confused*). W . . . what political metaphor?

CHAZ. The metaphor of the conflict, of course!

MIRIAM. Mr. Goldman . . . what conflict?!

CHAZ. What conflict?! THE conflict! What other conflict is there?!

MIRIAM. I don't understand—

CHAZ. Well, I find the representation of the Palestinian side absolutely fascinating. The sexually frustrated Joanna, trapped in her marriage, struggling to break out of her miserable reality, is a very poignant choice, whereas the Israeli side, represented brilliantly by Edgar, the corrupt husband who often suffers from uncontrollable violence, is dark, nerve-wracking and original.

MIRIAM. But Mr. Goldman, I wrote a . . . comedy! About marriage and relationships and love and . . .

CHAZ. Then, of course, there's the mischievous serpent, a far yet present threat, hiding in the drawer, waiting to attack, portraying perfectly the recent brutality of the United States' foreign policy which in this play really occupies the private property of the two, causing chaos . . .

MIRIAM. But my play is not about chaos! My play is about heartbreak!

CHAZ. "The Night of the Serpent!" A political play by Miriam Bloom!

MIRIAM. My play is NOT political!

CHAZ. I see headlines, Miriam, I see interviews, I see an adaptation for the movies . . . God, Miriam! I see a Pulitzer, Miriam! I see a fucking Pulitzer!

MIRIAM. A Pulitzer? Imagine that . . .

A spot is up on Journalists 1 and 2.

JOURNALIST 1. Miriam Bloom, a young political Israeli writer, is this year's Pulitzer Prize winner for her fierce political play "The Night of the Serpent."

JOURNALIST 2. Born in Tel Aviv, Miss Bloom served in the Israeli army between the years of 1990 and 1993, an experience that strongly inspired her first political play, "Eddie and His Handkerchief."

MIRIAM. "Eddie and His Handkerchief" is a kid's play about a kid who learns how to blow his nose . . .

JOURNALIST 1. Her daring choice for portraying THE conflict in the Middle East, as a kid who suffers from endless snot, immediately caught the world's attention.

MIRIAM. . . . . It had nothing to do with my military service!

JOURNALIST 2. The success of "Eddie and His Handkerchief" brought Miriam Bloom to the United States where she worked on her Pulitzer Prize-winning play, now being taught in high schools all over the country as an urban metaphor for the Middle East crisis.

JOURNALIST 1. Mrs. Bloom currently lives in New York, where she is working on her next political piece, a—

MIRIAM and JOURNALISTS (*together*). A surreal comedy—

JOURNALISTS (*together*). A realistic drama—

MIRIAM. In one act—

JOURNALISTS (*together*). In three acts—

MIRIAM. About sex!

JOURNALISTS (*together*). About war!

Lights off on Journalists.

CHAZ. The big question is, of course, what happens in the second act.

MIRIAM. Well, in the second act Joanna and Edgar, along with their serpent, travel to the Isle of Wight, where they—

CHAZ. What if Joanna's character turns into a belly-dancer, wearing one of those tiny sparkling outfits that barely covers her nipples?

MIRIAM. Mr. Goldman!

CHAZ. Or, what if, in revenge, she gets rid of the serpent and gets a camel instead!

MIRIAM. Mr. Goldman, what camel?! They live in a two-bedroom apartment in the middle of London!

CHAZ. Then give them a summer house in Islamabad!

MIRIAM. But they're already heading to the Isle of Wight!

CHAZ. I'm not so sure about the Isle of Wight . . . Don't you think it's a bit too obvious?

MIRIAM. What do you mean?

CHAZ. The Isle of Wight, the White House . . . you can do better, Miriam! Don't compromise for clichés!

MIRIAM. Honestly, Mr. Goldman, maybe I should just give up writing this play.

CHAZ. Are you nuts?! This play will make us both famous!

MIRIAM. I don't want to be famous, I want to write something good!

CHAZ. Why write something good when you can write something political?

MIRIAM. Because Mr. Goldman, I'm not a political person! I never watch the news, I read only the Arts section of the newspapers and I don't have an opinion about recent events in the world. I'm a simple woman, Mr. Goldman, I love drinking wine, playing dominos and taking my dog out for a nice walk twice a day. I can't offer anything to the world, I barely know how to manage my poor bank account . . . I can't write about politics!

CHAZ. You can and you will! You are gonna have a political play or you won't have a play at all! You're gonna sit down and you're gonna write the damn pages. You're gonna bring every character, every event, every trauma and every misery that you've seen there, in your Third World country, and you're gonna turn it into a smashing hit! You're gonna take the stories of your friends and family and turn them into gold! And hurry up, Miss Miriam Bloom—the world is waiting AND SO AM I!

A loud phone ring.

Lights off.

Scene 3

The phone keeps ringing. Lights up on Miriam, sitting next to her desk, sleeping. Papers are scattered all around her. A half-empty bottle of vodka stands on the table. Finally she picks up the phone.

MIRIAM. Hello?

Lights up on the family—mom, dad, grandpa, Uncle Avram.

FAMILY (*singing together, loudly*). Jerusalem of gold and of light and of silver/ I will always be your slave/ Oh, Jerusalem, Jerusalem, of gold and of light and of silver . . . Shabat Shalom!!! (*They cheer loudly*).

MIRIAM. Yeah . . . Shabat Shalom.

DAD. Miriam? It's dad! Where are you? What are you doing? Who are you with?

MOM. Miriam? It's mom! Stay away from Tompkins Park! I just watched "Law and Order"—a woman was raped and murdered there in broad daylight!

GRANDPA. Miriam, it's grandpa! Did you light candles? Did you buy a gefilte fish? I hope you still observe the Shabat!

UNCLE AVRAM. Miriam! It's Uncle Avram! So?! Did you already sell something? Did you meet any celebrities?

DAD. Are you warm enough?

MOM. Do you need money?

DAD. You sound weird!

MOM. I think she's lonely!

MIRIAM. Mom, I'm not lonely.

MOM (*to the others*) I knew it! I knew it! The girl is lonely!

MIRIAM. I'm NOT lonely!

GRANDPA. Of course she's lonely! She never calls Moishe and Zelda in Brooklyn!

MOM. Why don't you call Moishe and Zelda in Brooklyn?

MIRIAM. Because they are eighty-seven and orthodox!

MOM. Well, no one is perfect!

GRANDPA. I think you should come back here, get married and make babies. What are you doing there anyway?

MOM, DAD and UNCLE. She has this writing thing going on!

GRANDPA. Writing-shmiting. A true writer can write everywhere!

MOM. Oh, you know who I ran into yesterday? Yoni's mother.

Lights up on Yoni and on Yoni's mother.

MOM. She's gained quite a lot of weight.

YONI'S MOTHER. I'm not as pretty as I used to be.

MOM. She wanted to hear how things are going with you—

YONI'S MOTHER (*to Mom*). Did she already sell something? Did she meet any celebrities?

MOM. And she reminded me that this year they'll be having the reception for the anniversary of his death in their house.

YONI'S MOTHER. That way it'll be more comfortable.

MOM. I wanted to talk with her a bit more, ask how she was doing—

YONI'S MOTHER. Sorry, but I have tons of errands to do!

MOM. But she apologized and said she had tons of errands to do.

YONI. Whenever she runs into someone she has tons of errands to do!

Lights off on Yoni and Yoni's mother.

UNCLE AVRAM (*to the rest of the family*). Hey, why won't Miriam call what's-his-name? . . .

EVERYONE. Who?

UNCLE AVRAM. You know . . . the Jew . . .

MOM. What Jew?

UNCLE AVRAM. What's-his-name . . . the feygele . . .

DAD. The one with the angels?

MOM. Who won the Pulitzer?

UNCLE AVRAM. No, he won the Tony!

MOM. He didn't win the Tony, his name is Tony!

DAD. Tony something!

MIRIAM. Tony Kushner?!

UNCLE, MOM, DAD and GRANDPA. That's the one!

UNCLE AVRAM. Why don't you give him a call and tell him that you're an Israeli writer. I'm sure he'll be delighted to meet you!

MIRIAM. Why would he be delighted to meet me?

MOM. Gee, Miriam, sometimes you sound as naive as a real American! Don't you know that they all have a warm spot for us?

MIRIAM. They?!

DAD. The American Jews!

MOM. They feel guilty!

UNCLE. While they make money, we here do all the dirty work for them!

MOM. Don't you think they owe us something in return?

UNCLE. Call Tony, and mention that you were in the army. He'll appreciate a writer who knows how to hold a rifle!

MOM. Tell him that you're the tenth generation from your mother's side to be born in Jerusalem!

DAD. Tell him that your grandfather joined the resistance and sat seven years in jail for being a freedom fighter!

UNCLE. Tell him that your uncle fought in every single war this country's had!

DAD. And that even though your father is fifty-five years old, he still does his military reserve every year!

MOM. And then ask for his help. He won't dare say no!

DAD. And if he will, put him on the phone with me! I'll show him what being an undevoted Jew feels like . . .

GRANDPA. Tony-shmony, Pulitzer-shmulitzer. If my mother, Mina Novodvorsky, may she rest in peace, could see you now, Miriam, she would be very disappointed! She didn't come all the way from Russia to Palestine and dry the swamps with her own bare hands just so two generations later her great granddaughter would run away! I want you to pack your stuff and come back here immediately! This country needs you! AND SO DO WE!!!

Lights off.

Scene 4

Miriam gazes ahead for a while, then takes a sip from her vodka bottle.

MIRIAM. Dear Mina. You don't know anything about me but I've heard a lot about you . . .

Spot on Mina Novodvorsky. She is 35, Russian, wearing the typical clothes of the Russian bourgeois of that time with her hair in a long braid.

MIRIAM. The youngest and most rebellious daughter of the Novodvorsky's, you were the one who changed an entire course of an entire family, MY family, because you made one careless decision. In 1905, while your older sisters were involved in the arts—one a singer, one a ballet dancer and one an actress in The Minsker Yiddisher Theater—you secretly joined the Minsk Daughters of Zion and participated in their revolutionary activities against the Tsar. You were young. You were enthusiastic. You had balls. And so, when a few years later your family realizes the revolution will not help the Jews and that it's time to wave good-bye to Mother Russia and head to the new land of America, you had a realization of your own. In 1921, your parents and sisters sailed to America and watched your figure get smaller and smaller until the boat disappeared. You quickly rushed to pack your few dresses. You had a boat to catch yourself. A boat to Palestine!

Takes another sip from the vodka bottle. Then, in a thick Russian accent.

MINA. My dear sisters. When I open the window of my tiny one-bedroom apartment in Tel Aviv, I see endless yellow sands and a big blue sea. Sometimes camels cross by, carrying gravel. I can reach out my hand and caress them. This place is so warm and innocent that even though I want to see it grow, I sometimes pray it'll stay just the same forever. An untouched, newborn neighborhood where people spend their nights on their balconies, singing along aloud, eating watermelons, talking about politics . . . (*Short pause.*) I know by now that you love America and you love New York. And I know you want me there with you. But I'm happy here more than I've ever been in my whole life and I know that the Zionist dream is about to happen. A Zionist country will be founded and when it happens, I know you'll come to your senses and change your mind. Because this is our true home. This is where we belong!

MIRIAM. Mina, Mina, Mina . . . what the hell were you thinking? . . . True, you were idealistic. But your sisters were . . . (*Short pause.*) Smart.

The sound of a door buzz.

Lights off.

Scene 5

Another buzz at the door. Lights up on Joanna and Edgar. Joanna is wearing a belly-dancer outfit which barely covers her nipples.

JOANNA. Good lord! Charles! Answer the bloody door! (*To Edgar*) Good help is so hard to find these days!

EDGAR. Now listen to me, Joanna. Before we go out to entertain, I have one thing to ask you—under no circumstances are you to mention the bloody serpent!

JOANNA. The serpent?! What on earth are you talking about, Edgar?

Edgar slaps her.

EDGAR. Control yourself, Joanna! This is going to be a long night, and the only way we're going to get through it is if we cooperate!

Mina enters.

MINA. Good evening. You don't know much about me but I've heard a lot about you.

JOANNA. Edgar! Who on earth is this woman?! Another one of your lovers?!

EDGAR. My god, Joanna! I was just about to ask you the same question!

MINA. My name is Mina Novodvorsky, and I come from Palestine.

JOANNA. Palestine? How on earth did you get here?

MINA. I rode my camel. I parked her outside.

JOANNA. Good lord! She'll eat my orchids!

EDGAR. Did you know that the Mayor of Baybrookshire owns the biggest camel collection in all of Great Britain? Bigger than the Pope's!

JOANNA (*to Mina*). I hope you don't mind me asking but—do you have orchids in Palestine?

MINA. No. In Palestine we only have camels. Oranges. Swamps. And malaria.

JOANNA. Good lord! We musn't go there, must we?

MINA. Indeed you must. See, I have to tell you the truth. I came here on a mission.

EDGAR. What on earth are you talking about?! What mission?

MINA. I want the serpent!

JOANNA. The serpent? Oh, did you hear that Edgar? Even she's heard about the serpent!

EDGAR. I said don't mention the bloody serpent! (*Slaps Joanna.*)

MINA. I didn't know the serpent was bleeding!

He slaps Mina. Mina punches him in the stomach. He falls down, holding his gut.

MINA. Now let's get down to business! Edgar, Joanna—pack your
suitcases, serpents and orchids and say goodbye to London.
We're riding to the Middle East!

Pause.

MIRIAM'S VOICE. . . . . *They look at each other, then gaze at the drawer.*
Lights go down slowly. End of first act.

Lights off on Joanna, Edgar and Mina and up on Miriam and Chaz.
He gazes at her for a while.

CHAZ. I LOOOOOVED it!

MIRIAM. You did?!

CHAZ. Loved it, loved it, LOVED it!

MIRIAM. Well, Mr. Goldman, I guess I'm relieved . . .

CHAZ. You added a very interesting layer.

MIRIAM. I did?

CHAZ. Tell me, please. What does Mina symbolize?

MIRIAM. That's exactly the problem. I don't know.

CHAZ. The guilt!

MIRIAM. Of course, the guilt . . . (*Startled*) What guilt?

CHAZ. The Israeli guilt!

MIRIAM. I don't understand—

CHAZ. What a wonderful metaphor! Mina as Edgar's secret lover,
representing the realization of the mistake!

MIRIAM. Mr. Goldman, what mistake?!

CHAZ. The mistake called the "Zionist dream!"

MIRIAM. But the Zionist dream was not a mistake!

CHAZ. While in London, Edgar is having a SECRET AFFAIR with
Mina! SECRET-AFFAIR! SECRET-AFFAIR! . . . Rings a bell?!

MIRIAM. Not to me . . .

CHAZ. The SECRET SERVICE combined with the OFFICE FOR
FOREIGN AFFAIRS?! . . .

MIRIAM. Oh.

CHAZ. And so instead of making love to Joanna, Edgar fucks Mina!

MIRIAM. But if Edgar symbolizes Israel and Joanna symbolizes
Palestine and Mina symbolizes Edgar's conscience, then what
you're really saying is—

CHAZ. That ISRAEL FUCKED ITSELF!!!

Pause.

MIRIAM. Mr. Goldman, are you on medication?

CHAZ. And if that's not a Pulitzer Award-winning message, for a
Pulitzer Award-winning political play, I don't know what is! Now,
the big question, of course, is—what happens in the second act?

MIRIAM. You know what, Mr. Goldman, I'm not sure there's going to
be a second act!

CHAZ. The second act needs to be MORE political!

MIRIAM. More political?! But you just said—

CHAZ. Open your eyes, Miriam Bloom! There's a tough competition
out there! The Middle East is like the '80s—all of a sudden it's
IN again! Everybody writes about it and everybody has something to say! Here, look—(*Opens a newspaper*). The top ten plays
listed by the *New York Times*—plays that will be produced on
Broadway, in 2004–05 . . . Number ten—

Lights are up on journalists.

JOURNALIST 1. "Stones, Rocks and Nothing Else" by Amos Goz.

CHAZ. Number nine—

JOURNALIST 2. "How I Learned to Shoot" by Eyal Negev.

CHAZ. Number seven—

JOURNALIST 1. "Should We? I Wonder" by Sharona Naharan.

CHAZ. Number four—

JOURNALIST 2. "I Wonder if We Should Have" by Ahmed Halil.

CHAZ. Number two—

JOURNALIST 1. "Israelis, Nazis and Everything In-Between" by Shalom Shalom.

CHAZ. And number one, Miriam, the biggest hit of all—

JOURNALIST 2. "Thanks, It Was Nice. Now Goodbye" by Adi Nathan.

Lights off on the journalists.

CHAZ. Now let's do a little bit of math, Miriam Bloom. How old are you?

MIRIAM. Thirty-six.

CHAZ. How old am I?

MIRIAM. Fifty-six.

CHAZ. Together we're—

MIRIAM. Ninety-two.

CHAZ. And how old do you think Adi Nathan is?! (*Short pause.*) TWENTY-TWO! TWENTY-TWO! TWENTY-FUCKING-TWO! (*Tears the newspapers apart and throws them in the air. Then calms himself down.*) Miriam Bloom, you and I are on the right track! But if you want our names printed in this newspaper, you need to be MORE political! You need to shout out loud, you need to shock, you need to rock, and most of all . . . (*Short pause.*) You need to meet Adi Nathan!

Lights off.

Scene 6

Young Miriam and Yoni, eighteen, soldiers.

MIRIAM. I love the night patrols.

YONI. I love the night patrols too. (*British accent*) Did you know that the Parkers decided not to go on their yearly vacation this year?!

MIRIAM. I love how the air smells at four o'clock in the morning.

YONI (*British accent*). They said the Isle of Wight is no longer what it used to be, how ungrateful is that!

MIRIAM. And I love how horny I get around these hours.

YONI (*British accent*). Why darling, I love how horny you get around these hours too.

Short pause. Miriam stops.

MIRIAM. Horny but tired.

YONI (*normal accent*). I'm not tired.

MIRIAM. I am. So tired, I can't even think.

YONI (*British accent*). Why you're a soldier, dear, you're not supposed to think.

MIRIAM. But I do. I think all the time.

YONI (*normal accent*). Then don't. (*British accent*) Did you know that the Mayor of Baybrook—

MIRIAM. Will you stop with the Mayor-of-Baybrookshire nonsense!

YONI (*British accent*). Really, dear, he owns the largest collection of—

MIRIAM. Yoni! I keep thinking bad thoughts.

YONI (*normal accent*). Then don't!

MIRIAM. I can't help it.

YONI (*British accent*). Perhaps what you need is a good cup of tea to calm your nerves.

MIRIAM. It'll calm my nerves if you stop talking with that stupid British accent and start helping me to come up with a plan to get the hell out of here!

YONI (*British accent*). Why, Joanna, don't be stroppy. London might not be the perfect place at the moment but it is our home, and it is our duty to keep it that way. I think we ought to make the best of it. Shan't we?!

MIRIAM. I feel them, watching us. And I know they see us watching them. All the time.

YONI (*normal accent*). So? We watch them, they watch us. Isn't that what being neighbors is all about? (*British accent*) Just like with the Parkers . . .

MIRIAM. It's easy for you. Soon you're done with your service, but I have to stay in this base by myself for one and a half more years! I'll go insane!

YONI (*normal accent*). No, you won't!

MIRIAM. Yoni, I don't want to wear this uniform! I don't want to hold this rifle, I don't want to know how to shoot it and I don't want to tell people what to do, where to go and when to come back!

YONI (*British accent*). Now listen to me, Joanna—

MIRIAM. And stop calling me Joanna, I'm 4599245!

YONI (*normal accent*). You're going to behave yourself, do what you have to and try to do it well! Besides, you'll get used to it.

MIRIAM. No, I won't!

YONI. We all do! I mean, look at me—

MIRIAM. Yeah, look at you!

YONI (*normal accent*). I've spent almost three years in this ridiculous place and I am absolutely perfectly undeniably indubitably level-headed!

MIRIAM. Well I don't want to start counting stupid collections of the Pope of Baybrookshire just to keep my head on straight!

Pause. They try to calm down.

YONI (*British accent*). Personally, I find that the best way to keep your head on straight is to get rogered. Rather fiercely.

MIRIAM (*overlapping*). When I have kids, I'm gonna take this rifle and I'm gonna shoot them in their knees and make them crippled so the army won't want anything to do with them. Then I'm gonna send them off to a place where they can be whoever they want to be and do whatever they want to do!

YONI (*British accent*). Why my dearest crawfish-and-watercress sandwich, I already know who I want to do! (*Pulls her close to him but she pulls away.*)

MIRIAM. Stop it Yoni. I'm just not in the mood.

YONI (*British accent*). TROUSERS OFF!!!

Scene 7

Lights up on Adi Nathan and Miriam. They are in bed together.

ADI NATHAN. So?

Miriam looks at him, tired.

ADI NATHAN. How was I? How was I?

MIRIAM. Have you seen my vodka bottle by any chance?

Lights up on Yoni. He hands her the bottle. She takes it. Lights are off Yoni.

ADI NATHAN. They say writers only know how to make love to their words. But I proved them wrong, didn't I?

MIRIAM. I guess you did.

ADI NATHAN. Can I have a sip of your vodka?

She hands him the bottle.

MIRIAM. Make it a small one.

ADI NATHAN. You know, I'm really happy that Chaz Goldman encouraged you to meet me. I know how tough it is to be a struggling writer and I'm always willing to share my talent with those who are less fortunate.

MIRIAM. Thank you, you're kind.

ADI NATHAN. So why don't you tell me a little bit about yourself?

MIRIAM. I actually think I need to go home.

Lights up on Chaz.

CHAZ. Home?!

ADI NATHAN. Now?!

Lights up on Yoni.

YONI. Why?

Lights off Yoni.

MIRIAM (*to Adi*). Look. You are a nice handsome straight man. Quite rare to find in this city. But I really want to leave.

CHAZ. Don't leave!

ADI NATHAN. Don't leave!

Lights up on Yoni.

YONI. You always leave.

Lights off Yoni.

CHAZ. He has many important connections in the industry!

ADI NATHAN. I have many important connections in the industry!

CHAZ. Stay just few more minutes! For the Pulitzer's sake!

Lights up on Yoni.

YONI. You heard him.

Lights are down on Yoni.

Miriam hesitates. Then sits back on the bed. Lights are off Chaz.

ADI NATHAN. Now tell me a little bit about your background. I'm really eager to hear who you are and where you're coming from.

MIRIAM. Well, OK . . . I was born in—

ADI NATHAN. I suppose you've read MY bio by now, right? Oh, but I'm sorry, I didn't mean to interrupt. Go ahead.

MIRIAM. Well, I grew up in—

ADI NATHAN. Did you read every single detail? Oh, but I'm sorry, I didn't mean to interrupt. Go ahead.

MIRIAM. Well, the first time I realized—

ADI NATHAN. Reading someone's bio is not the same as actually hearing him tell you about himself. Don't you agree?

MIRIAM. Absolutely.

ADI NATHAN. Good. Then take out your pen and notebook.

MIRIAM. What for?

ADI NATHAN. So you can write down everything I say.

MIRIAM. I'm sorry, I don't usually bring a pen and notebook with me to bed.

Adi takes out a pen and a notebook.

ADI NATHAN. Well I do.

He hands it to Miriam.

ADI NATHAN. So . . . where were we? Oh, yes. You were asking me about my life . . . (*Sighs deeply*) My life . . . life . . . life . . . life . . .

MIRIAM. Yes. What about them?

ADI NATHAN. I was born in Tel Aviv, in 1981, to an Israeli mother and a Palestinian . . . mother. Two women who fell deeply in love and had to live through THE conflict on every level of their existence. Imagine how painful it was! I used to hide my problematic yet fascinating background but, deep down, I always felt divided in half. I used to think I'd never be able to find peace within myself. Then, of course, everything changed.

MIRIAM. Why?

ADI NATHAN. The war!

Lights up on Yoni. He and Miriam look at each other.

MIRIAM. What war?!

Lights off Yoni.

ADI NATHAN. I got injured. Shot. It was such a traumatic event . . . but I've survived it! See, even after I was shot, I kept fighting . . . I had to fight. I had to serve the country!

MIRIAM. Wait, what war are you talking about?

ADI NATHAN. I had to watch my friends die. Do you have any clue what it feels like to watch someone you love die? It is one of those things in life that never leaves you. People can know each other for years, and still miss the most important details in each other's life—

MIRIAM. It doesn't make sense, what—

ADI NATHAN. And my most important detail is losing someone that I once loved. And every cup of coffee, every single cone of ice-cream, every good laugh, feels like a betrayal.

MIRIAM. Mr. Nathan, what war?!

ADI NATHAN. What do you mean what war?! One of them, you had so many!

MIRIAM. WE had so many?!

ADI NATHAN. I meant WE had so many . . .

MIRIAM. You got injured in a war but you can't remember which one?

ADI NATHAN. I lost my memory when I got injured!

MIRIAM. Was it the Lebanon War?

ADI NATHAN. Exactly! The Lebanon War! What a tough, horrible, sad defeat!

MIRIAM. But we weren't defeated . . .

ADI NATHAN. What a wonderful, glorious, happy victory!

MIRIAM. It wasn't a wonderful, glorious, happy victory either!

ADI NATHAN. What a tough, horrible, sad defeat!

MIRIAM. And it was in 1982!

ADI NATHAN. So?!

MIRIAM. You were one!

ADI NATHAN. The country was in a crisis! They even drafted little kids!

MIRIAM. Mr. Nathan—who are you?!

ADI NATHAN. I don't understand!

MIRIAM. Who was the first prime minister of Israel?

ADI NATHAN. I don't think I—

MIRIAM. How do you say "you're a fucking idiot" in military slang?

ADI NATHAN. I wasn't into the—

MIRIAM. Name the five best hummus places in Jaffa!

ADI NATHAN. I don't know! I'm allergic to hummus!

MIRIAM (*stands up*). Mr. Nathan! No one in the Middle East is allergic to hummus! (*Short pause.*) You are not an Israeli, are you? And you're not a Palestinian either! You're an impostor! (*Grabs the phone.*) Tell me who you are and your real name before I call the police!

ADI NATHAN. Wait! (*She freezes.*) Please! I'll tell you everything, just don't call anyone. (*Pause. Miriam sits down. He sighs deeply.*) My name is John Johnson and I was born in Wisconsin. I worked as a farmer there. I loved being a farmer but I could never earn enough money. Then, one day, I saw an ad in the newspaper: a $10,000 playwriting grant was being offered. In order to be eligible, you had to be young, contemporary and Serbian but the way I figured it out, two out of three is good enough. So I did some research, I scribbled few pages and I won. The "2002 Serbian Playwrights Award" was mine and so was the $10,000 . . . When the press wanted to interview me, I came up with the character of Slovanov Slovovianiov, a poor Serbian student, and every time they asked me something, I mumbled, "Peace . . . Peace . . . Peace . . ." Next thing I know, I get offered an off-off-off-off Broadway production at the Ooops! Festival for Immigrants. That's where I heard about the $20,000 grant for blind Pakistani playwrights . . .

MIRIAM. Oh no . . . don't tell me that you're—

ADI NATHAN. Tamiliani Tamilianov. Yep. I'm also Leng Lighian, Ibrahim Ibrahimian and many many others. Playwriting is indeed a profitable profession.

MIRIAM. And what about . . . "Adi Nathan?"

ADI NATHAN. My agent advised me to come up with an Israeli character and write a play about self-hatred and guilt. He said that's what the market needs right now.

MIRIAM. So you wrote "Thanks, It Was Nice. Now Goodbye?!"

ADI NATHAN. The most anti-Israeli Israeli play that has ever been written! Two Israeli soldiers stand on a bare stage surrounded by Arab snipers and for two and a half hours apologize to the whole wide world for existing, then use their M-16 rifles to shoot themselves! What a success!

MIRIAM. But how dare you write a play like that? You've never even been there!

ADI NATHAN. I understood from Mr. Goldman that your "Night of the Serpent" includes the very same message!

MIRIAM. Then you understood Mr. Goldman completely wrong!

Lights up on Chaz.

CHAZ. I thought you didn't care about politics! I thought you didn't care about other people's opinions!

MIRIAM. Indeed I don't, Mr. Goldman, as long as their opinions don't contradict mine!

Lights off Chaz.

MIRIAM. Mr. Johnson—you are a liar of the worst kind!

ADI NATHAN. Why? I'm a multi-dimensional artist! I write what deserves to be written. I'm a chameleon! An elusive one, as uncertain as the world itself. Human miseries come in all shapes and forms. I understand them all. Don't you?

MIRIAM. You're a political whore!

ADI NATHAN. But one who happens to own a house in the Hamptons!

Lights up on Chaz.

CHAZ. Don't you see, Miriam? Everyone is wrong and at the same time everyone is right! It'll take forever to figure things out!

ADI NATHAN. But you and I won't last forever!

CHAZ. Exactly! Nothing lasts forever!

ADI NATHAN. Art doesn't last forever. Political views don't last forever.

CHAZ. Borders don't last forever.

ADI NATHAN. Cities don't last forever.

CHAZ. Countries don't last forever.

ADI NATHAN. Even the universe won't last forever.

CHAZ. The only thing in this world—

ADI NATHAN. That does last forever—

CHAZ. Is real estate—

ADI NATHAN. In the Hamptons.

Lights up on Yoni, looking at Miriam.

YONI. And that's the simple truth. (*Short pause.*) Ruth.

Lights off.

A phone rings.

Scene 8

Lights on Miriam, sitting next to her desk, sleeping. The phone keeps ringing. She finally picks it up.

MIRIAM. Yes?

Lights up on Mother.

MOTHER. Miriam?

MIRIAM. Mom?! It's 4 a.m. in Tel Aviv. What are you doing up so late?

MOTHER. I waited for everyone to go to sleep. I wanted to finish telling you the story.

MIRIAM. What story?

Lights up on Yoni's mother.

YONI'S MOTHER. Sorry, but I have tons of errands to do . . .

MOM. I wanted to talk with her a bit more, ask her how she was doing, but she apologized . . .

Lights up on Yoni.

YONI. Whenever she runs into someone she has tons of errands to do.

MOTHER. But this time I followed her, all the way to their house—

YONI (*to Miriam*). Remember the house?

MOTHER. And I knocked on the door. Five times before she opened.

YONI. She never has guests ever since . . .

YONI'S MOTHER. What a surprise. Please, come in.

MIRIAM. What did you do?

MOTHER. We just sat there, on the balcony.

YONI'S MOTHER. In silence.

MOTHER. She offered me lemonade.

YONI'S MOTHER. And some cookies.

MIRIAM. Homemade.

YONI (*to Miriam*). Remember the cookies?

MOTHER. And finally—

YONI'S MOTHER. When the sun started setting—

MOTHER. She said—

    Short pause.

YONI'S MOTHER. Let's go to his room.

YONI (*softly, to Miriam*). Remember my room?

MOTHER. And there was his rifle, leaning against the wall . . .

YONI'S MOTHER. His uniforms on the bed.

MOTHER. His blue pajamas on the floor—

YONI'S MOTHER. Just like he left it the weekend before.

MOTHER. And look at this photo—

YONI'S MOTHER. It's him. He's five. And there's one from the trip he took to the north.

MOTHER. And this one I remember taking myself. I have a copy too. Right on my wall.

YONI'S MOTHER. They would have made such a nice couple . . . wouldn't they?

MOTHER. Then she pulled out some letters.

YONI (*to Miriam*). Remember the letters?

YONI'S MOTHER. They were his, but perhaps—

MOTHER. And she gave them to me.

Lights off on Mother and Yoni's mother.

YONI. My dear Edgar . . .

MIRIAM. In just eight days your never-ending military service will end . . .

YONI. . . . And you'll be free to join me, for some mushrooms—

MIRIAM. Cigarettes—

YONI. Coffee—

MIRIAM. And sex. (*Short pause.*) Yours, Joanna. Toodle-doo. Can't wait.

Lights off.

Scene 9

Lights up on Joanna and Edgar.

JOANNA. Oh, good lord, where on earth did you put the serpent?

EDGAR. Why Joanna, I was just about to ask you the same question! The serpent was your responsibility!

JOANNA. I hope you didn't forget it in London! The fact that we're in the Middle East does not mean I will give up the serpent!

Mina enters.

MINA. Good evening. I came to see how you're settling down, here in little Palestine.

JOANNA. Well I must admit it is not half as horrible as one might imagine! I absolutely adore the weather!

EDGAR. And what a view! So different than London!

JOANNA. Camels instead of chimneys!

EDGAR. Yellow sands instead of gray clouds!

JOANNA. Strong Arab coffee instead of pale British tea!

EDGAR. And the watermelons!

JOANNA. Good lord, the watermelons! Makes one wish he could eat them seven times a day!

EDGAR. Did you know that the Mayor of Baybrookshire owns the largest watermelon collection in the world?!

A knock at the door.

MINA. Guests already?

JOANNA. Oh, it must be Charles. I allowed him to take the afternoon off. Who needs a servant in such a small place anyway?!

Yoni enters, wearing his soldier uniform. He is bleeding.

EDGAR. Good lord! And who are you?

YONI. Good evening. My name is Yoni, also known as Edgar of Hampstead Heath.

EDGAR. Wait a second! That's not right!

YONI. I just got injured in the war. A sniper shot me.

JOANNA. Why, what on earth are you talking about?!

YONI. I'm not going to last for much longer. I'm running out of blood.

EDGAR. And I'm running out of patience! Who exactly are you, what the hell do you want from us and why do you keep using my name?!

YONI. My dear Edgar. Deep down inside this masculine soldier's body hides the kind soul of a Londoner. Unfortunately for both of us, there's no time for teas and chats and cats and whiskers. There's a war going on. I've come to draft you for the military.

JOANNA. A war?!

EDGAR. The military?!

YONI. Hurry up! We need every young man and woman! Everyone, including serpents!

EDGAR (*to Mina*). You mentioned camels, gravel and watermelons but you forgot to mention war!

JOANNA. And ridiculous young soldiers who think they're my husband!

MINA. I did, didn't I?

YONI. There's a war going on here 24/7. We die young but brave.

MINA. Besides, do you know how many watermelons you could eat by the time you're eighteen and ready to get shot by someone?

EDGAR. Did you know that the Mayor of Baybrookshire owns the biggest dead bodies collection in the world? Bigger than the Pope's!

JOANNA. I don't want to die! At least not without the serpent!

EDGAR. Leave the damn serpent out of it!

Edgar slaps her. She slaps him back. Mina slaps Edgar. He slaps her back. She slaps Joanna. Joanna slaps Yoni. Yoni slaps Edgar who slaps Yoni back as lights shift and go up on Miriam and Chaz while she's describing the scene:

MIRIAM. Edgar slaps Joanna, she slaps him back. Mina slaps Edgar, he slaps her back. Mina slaps Joanna who slaps Yoni who slaps Edgar who slaps Yoni back who's grabbing his rifle trying to shoot Edgar who grabs the rifle back, accidentally shooting a member of the audience who gets upset, grabs the rifle himself, shoots the actor playing Edgar but misses him by an inch, hitting

Mina. Blood flies all over the stage, everyone screams as they start shooting each other: actors shoot real people, real people shoot actors. By now the whole theater space is dripping blood, people are panicking, running from side to side, trying to figure out what's going on: who's shooting whom, where the injured are, how many are dead, how many can be evacuated from the scene, and WHO THE FUCK GAVE THE FUCKING ORDER TO OPEN FIRE! They all just want to get the hell out of there! Out of this hell! They can already see the headlines in the news-papers: "Another Incident Ending with Heavy Casualties on Both Sides!" But it's too late and they know it, they know there's no chance they'll get out of there alive, so they close their eyes and give the world one last look, full of acceptance: they behaved themselves, they did what they had to and they tried to do it well . . . It's the type of acceptance only eighteen-year-old kids can have . . . END OF PLAY.

Long pause. Chaz gazes at her.

CHAZ. I haaaaaaaaaated it! (*Short pause.*) Hated, hated, hated, hated, hated it!

MIRIAM. Well, I—

CHAZ. Melodramatic, noncommercial, boring, but most of all— UNCLEAR! Really, Miriam Bloom, I couldn't follow! Weird metaphors! Strange symbols! Everyone shooting each other with-out really knowing why . . . You wrote a pathetic joke that isn't even funny! Miriam Bloom, are you on medication?

MIRIAM. Mr. Goldman, I can explain!

CHAZ. Explain?! Is that what you gonna tell the people when they're running out of the theater? That you can explain?!

MIRIAM. Well, you told me to find the political play within myself. I did!

CHAZ. What political play?! Who wants to hear about politics?

MIRIAM. What do you mean?! You're the one who told me to be MORE political!

CHAZ. That was two and a half weeks ago, Miriam! (*To himself*) Maybe it was a mistake to work with a foreigner after all . . .

MIRIAM. I don't understand—

CHAZ. My dear child. The world of theater, like life itself, is a capricious one. What's right today is wrong tomorrow. And as an artist, you have to be able to be one step ahead of everyone, not one step behind . . .

MIRIAM. Mr. Goldman, you don't understand! I had a revelation! I *am* a political person and I actually do have something to say!

CHAZ. Nonsense. Who cares what you have to say? People don't go to the theater to listen to important shit being said out loud. They go to the theater because they want to be entertained! They want to laugh for a couple of hours and go home happy and optimistic. Now, why don't you write something funny?

MIRIAM. Funny?!

CHAZ. How about a farce? Something sexy, about relationships and heartbreaks and human beings . . .

MIRIAM. I can't! Not now, not when I'm finally writing MY political play!

CHAZ. Miriam Bloom! I'm going to say it one more time—

MIRIAM (*stands up*). No, Chaz Goldman—I'M going to say it one more time. I, Miriam Bloom, a playwright, currently working on my new play called "The Night of The Serpent." A political play, with a political message! Two and a half hours with no intermission about war and sex and heartbreaks and chaos! (*Pause.*) Besides. Maybe it's time to move on. For both of us, I mean.

CHAZ. I don't understand.

Short pause.

MIRIAM. Maybe I need to take a little break. Rest a little. Do some thinking.

Lights up on family.

MOTHER. Maybe it's time to come back home.

FATHER. Maybe meet someone new.

UNCLE. Fall in love again.

GRANDPA. Or even make a few babies!

Lights up on Yoni.

YONI. And maybe, if you hurry up, you can still make it on time to the reception for the anniversary of my death.

Lights up on Yoni's Mother.

YONI'S MOTHER. This year we'll do it in our house. That way it'll be more comfortable.

MOTHER. Please hurry up, Miriam. Make it on time this year.

YONI (*British accent*). Put a cucumber sandwich and a nice cup of tea on my grave. A rare treat up here in heaven.

Miriam looks at Yoni, standing close to him.

MIRIAM. Good lord, Yoni. (*Short pause.*) The anniversary of your death . . .

Lights slowly down.

Scene 10

Young Miriam and Yoni.

YONI. I hate "the one final" patrol.

MIRIAM. I hate "the one final" patrol too.

YONI. I hate goodbyes.

MIRIAM. I hate goodbyes too.

YONI. I hate it especially if it's from someone that I love.

Pause.

MIRIAM. I love you too.

Pause.

YONI. So . . . where will you go? What will you do?

MIRIAM. I'm leaving on Friday, bought a ticket to India, where I can quietly have some coffee, mushrooms and sex.

YONI. Oh. Well, good luck.

MIRIAM. The coffee and the mushrooms are kind of urgent but I can wait for you with the sex.

YONI. You'll have to wait eight months. That's 156 more patrols!

MIRIAM. That's not that many. I'll wait.

YONI (*British accent*). Just for the record, I find it absolutely despicably outrageous that they just released you from the service! After a mere twelve weeks!

MIRIAM. They didn't. I released myself. I had to put a lot of effort into it . . . third degree with the doctor. I thought he'd never run out of questions. Then a comittee, three psychologists and a psychiatrist with a humiliating look of disbelief.

YONI (*British accent*). Darling, quitting the battle right in the middle while we brave servants manage to endure is somehow . . . unbearably disappointing. (*Pause. Then back to normal accent*). Besides, you're not the only one who deals with bad thoughts. I have them too, you know, morning, noon and night.

MIRIAM. Then stop having them.

YONI. And do what instead?

MIRIAM. Leave!

YONI. Like you?

MIRIAM. Why not?

YONI. And who's gonna stay and watch our little Hampstead Heath?

MIRIAM. The Pope of Baybrookshire.

YONI. There is no Pope of Baybrookshire. There is only us. Edgar and Joanna.

MIRIAM. Not even.

YONI. There's still time to change your mind.

MIRIAM. No, there's not.

YONI. Go back to the committee, apologize, explain that it's a mistake—

MIRIAM. But it's not.

YONI. They'll be delighted to have you back, they'll just erase your file—

MIRIAM. No, they won't.

YONI. All you need to do is—

MIRIAM. BUT I WON'T!

Short pause.

YONI. You know how in the movies, someone is just about to start fresh when the worst thing happens to him? Or, like in all those stories, where the parents and the friends are being interviewed on television, to talk about someone who died, and they say, "He was just about to go on patrol for the last time, when"—

MIRIAM. Yoni—

YONI. —You'll be in some village in India, you won't even know that my parents and my friends are gathering together for my funeral, and—

MIRIAM. Yoni—

YONI. —And I'll be here, dead, and you'll be there, alive, and not with me and I won't be with you and we won't be together and after I die, we won't even know how much we missed, and—

MIRIAM. —Yoni!

YONI. What!

She pulls him over to her.

MIRIAM (*British accent*). Please! The guests will arrive any moment now! And once they're here, we are going to have the most superb tea party ever, and then even get rogered, rather fiercely! Right? Right?!

Yoni finally smiles faintly.

MIRIAM. TROUSERS OFF!

Lights up on Mina.

MINA. May 14, 1948. My dear sisters. A few months ago the UN voted in favor of the existence of the state of Israel. In only a few hours the British Mandate will be over and the state of Israel will be announced by David Ben Gurion, the first prime minister of a nation which is yet to be born. In every house, families are gathered around the radio, waiting with anticipation to hear him. I wish you could be here with us and feel the great excitement in the air. I wish you could witness, along with me, this monumental moment in history. (*Short pause.*) The state of Israel will finally be a dream coming true. We'll be finally able to look towards the future and know that the world is about to become a better place. Our sons and daughters, and their sons and daughters, and their sons and daughters will grow up in a better, easier reality. A reality in which they won't have to fight anymore. Fifty years from now, there are not going to be any wars. There are not going to be any borders. There are not going to be any countries. Peace will rule not only the Middle East but the whole wide world . . . Amen.

Mina turns the radio on.

Fade-in the recording of the UN vote, 1947, followed by the 1948 recording of David Ben Gurion, reading the Declaration of Independence, as the entire cast joins her on stage, listening to it with anticipation.

Lights slowly off.

The End

Sofia Ahmad as Delilah and Bridgette Loriaux as Tamam at the Magic Theatre. Photograph by Bill Faulkner.

THE BLACK EYED

BY

BETTY SHAMIEH

I began writing *The Black Eyed* after September 11. This is my most directly political work to date. I wanted to address my experience as a Palestinian-American playwright living and working in New York City at the time. I refer to this play as a tragicomedy.

CHARACTERS

CASTING REQUIREMENTS   4 women

AIESHA
DELILAH
TAMAM
ARCHITECT

ACT I

The stage is very sparse. Aiesha is onstage, facing the audience.

AIESHA. Unanswered questions,
Unquestioned answers.
I do someone good dead.
I do someone dead good.
What is the point of the revolution that begins with the little hand?
Any little hand?
(*Lifts her right hand and looks at it*) This little hand?

Aiesha can repeat the dialogue above until Tamam and Architect appear and enter the stage. Delilah follows them onstage a few steps afterwards. For this section, these three characters will read the lines of the chorus.

AIESHA. Tell me who you are and I'll know why you're here.
Tell me who you are—

CHORUS. And you'll know who we're looking for.

TAMAM. My name is Tamam.
It means enough.
I need to see the thing that started out smaller than me
and got bigger.
I need to see my brother.

DELILAH. Women were his only weakness.
I was his only woman.
They called me Delilah.
I want my Samson.

ARCHITECT. Hands, movement, change!

TAMAM (*to Architect*). Answer her questions, girl. She may help us.
(*To Aiesha*) I don't know her name.

ARCHITECT. I will be known only as
the architect of the unseen, underlying structures
and buildings that have never been built.

TAMAM. I don't know who she's looking for.

ARCHITECT. I'm here for answers from the only one who can give
them to me.

CHORUS. Let us in.

AIESHA. Go right ahead.
They're waiting for you.
(*Motions towards the audience*) The door is unlocked.

CHORUS. We're afraid.

AIESHA. Tell me why and I'll tell you if you have good reason to be.

Delilah, Tamam and Architect all attempt to speak at once.

DELILAH (*overlapping*). Women were his only weakness.

TAMAM (*overlapping*). Started out smaller than me and got bigger.

ARCHITECT (*overlapping*). Unseen underlying structures!

*They glare at each other but Delilah continues. At this point, Architect
and Tamam make up the chorus.*

AIESHA. Women and weakness?
You'll speak first.

DELILAH. Women were his only weakness
And I was his only woman.

CHORUS. Yeah, right.

DELILAH. OK, the only one that mattered.
And I asked—

CHORUS. Did you have him?
Did you want him?
Did you love him?

DELILAH. I asked him—

"What makes your strength weak?
Show me the crack in your armor, so I may lick and seal it
together.
Let me who loves you whole know all.
Only to keep you safe from
those who hate you and wish you dead."

AIESHA. So you refused to put out till he told you, right?
Crudeness is necessary for clarity.

DELILAH. Basically.

CHORUS. It comes down to the basics.
You knew the only power
you had over men was sexual.
Those were your means.

DELILAH. I intended to use them.

I long for madness,
for the strong that comes from the sweet
letting go,
like a snip of the lock
from the hair
where the power to slaughter my people
lay nestled in his whorls,
His long curls tangled up
with mine every morning.

AIESHA. You acted justly, Delilah.
You saved your people.

DELILAH. My people!
My people called me a whore.
I overheard a young man from my own clan say—

CHORUS. "The whore did her job and she did it well."

DELILAH. He didn't call me
a daughter of an honorable man,
or a good woman who loved her people—

CHORUS.—but a whore.

DELILAH. But not at first

No, not . . . of course.

The elders came to me after my brother died.

The elders knew I was alone,
they knew I intended to stay that way.

CHORUS. So they made you seduce Samson.
They forced you into it.

DELILAH. Worse.

They made me think it was my idea.

They asked me to take my father's place at their meetings,
even though I was a girl,
because my only brother was dead.

We talked of many things.
They listened as if they thought my opinions mattered,
as if I mattered.

They were polite.

CHORUS. Too polite.

DELILAH. I told them my ideas about how to prevent the cattle from
dying
and why our well always ran dry.

Suddenly, my father's best friend brought up Samson.
We rarely talked about Samson in our villages.

CHORUS. The problems that are the most pressing
are the ones you tend to ignore.

DELILAH. He stated the obvious.
He said if Samson wasn't stopped—

CHORUS. It wouldn't matter whether we had enough to eat next
season.

DELILAH. Samson did need to be stopped.
You realize that, don't you?
He needed to be stopped.

CHORUS. We realize it.

DELILAH. Then my father's friend said our men can't win against him.
"We don't want to lose more men like your unparalleled brother,
your brother with a face like the moon."

TAMAM. I want to see my brother.

AIESHA. Let the girl tell her story.

DELILAH. He said the only weakness that man has is for—

CHORUS. —women.

DELILAH. And in perfect time they all turned their heads and looked
at me.
It was then that I offered to try.

CHORUS. You offered?!

DELILAH. You have to understand.
I trusted who my father trusted.
Father trusted them.
I should have known by the way they were talking
that they wanted something from me.
And they sure knew how to get it.
They told me—

CHORUS. "We loved your honorable father.
He was a pillar that was knocked down too soon."

DELILAH. His friend took me aside after the meeting,
as if he had a secret to share about my father.
But all he told me was what my father himself told me often
enough—

CHORUS. "If I had known I could make daughters like you, Delilah,
I would have wished for a dozen."

DELILAH. Their words were honey.
Sweet—

CHORUS. —without substance in heat.

DELILAH. The grief over Dad's death was still fresh after seven years.
   Everyone thought I did it,
   because my brother had been killed by Samson in the last battle.
   My brother was the first of a hundred men to charge at Samson.
   Being in the front was dangerous,
   almost suicide.

CHORUS. Suicide!

DELILAH. Someone had to be in front
   if there was to be a fight at all.
   Samson snatched up my brother first—

ARCHITECT. Hands, movement, change!

DELILAH. —but killed him last,
   made a game of dangling him,
   choking him in the crook of his arm,
   while he
   with his other iron fist
   continued to knock the heads off the necks
   of all my cousins, neighbors and friends.

CHORUS. Not only everyone I loved, but everyone I knew lost
   someone.

DELILAH. A wife of a man killed charged at Samson,
   roaring, livid, full of a uniquely female fury
   that when you witness
   makes you sure
   this woman can punch through a wall,
   kill a lion if it chanced on her path,
   till a man flattens her with a half-of-his-strength hit.

CHORUS. He hit her?

DELILAH. That would be tacky.
   Samson was a lot of things but he wasn't tacky.
   He grabbed her and kissed her passionately.
   and she scratched and bit and pushed at him.
   He told her—

CHORUS. "I like 'em kinky."

DELILAH. It was then that I saw my brother was not moving.

CHORUS. Now your story makes sense.

DELILAH. I haven't begun to tell the story.
    so none of it can make sense.

AIESHA. It makes perfect sense.

CHORUS. You were sad about your brother,
    that's why you seduced Samson,
    that's why you're here,
    you want to see your brother now.

DELILAH. I am not here to see my brother.

TAMAM. My brother!
    Have you seen him?
    He looks like me,
    Black hair, black [eyes]—

AIESHA. Hold on, you! Wait your turn or I won't listen.
    (*To Delilah*) So who are you here to see?

DELILAH. I told you before. Samson.

AIESHA. To spit in his face, right?

DELILAH. He might kind of dig that, but no.

CHORUS. Gross.

DELILAH. That's my Samson. He's quite special.

AIESHA. How did you wrench from him the secret of where his
    power lied?

DELILAH. You mean, what's so bewitching about little ole me?
    I'm a pretty woman.
    It's not a boast, it's a fact.

CHORUS. But pretty enough to die to have?

DELILAH. But you want to know precisely
what he loved about me?

So you'll understand why he told me his dark secret?

Do you want to know why he put the power of his fate
in the nest of my interlaced hands?

AIESHA. Obviously we want to know. We already asked you, bitch.

DELILAH. What does it matter?
What good does it do for you to know?
We're all dead.

There's no hope of using the knowledge to seduce.

CHORUS. But it can't hurt.

DELILAH. Women, what do you do when you want a man?

This is what I did and this is what I suggest.
Go to where he frequents.
Dress well, dress in a way that makes it obvious you are a woman.

CHORUS. Men can never tell the difference
between a beautiful woman and a person dressed like one.

DELILAH. He'll take you,
because you're there and available.

Then, he'll probably leave you alone,
like Samson did to me,
immediately and for days, weeks, months, years.

CHORUS. Or did it just feel that way?

DELILAH. Either way, the waiting killed me. What's the difference
between a thing that feels like it kills you and the one that actually does?

CHORUS. Plenty. But go on.

DELILAH. I almost went back to my people,
gave up.
But then one morning,

I opened my door and there he was, about to knock.
He didn't say hello. He just announced—

CHORUS. "You can live with me for a while."

DELILAH. And I said, "Yes, I can."

I didn't know that there would be his other lovers living there too,
all Philistine women,
like myself.

I had never met any of them before. They were poor girls.
At home, we did not run in the same circles. Do you understand?

CHORUS. We understand.

DELILAH. I was surprised, my pride was wounded.
But I wrestled with jealousy and I grabbed it by its throat
before it grabbed me by mine.

CHORUS. How did you win against jealousy?

DELILAH. Women, you want to cease to be jealous.
Every time you see your man looking at another
think this to yourself—

"I am in the process of erasing you
I will watch you cower and then crumble
into dust before me."

CHORUS. "You will pay for every pleasure you exact from my pain."

DELILAH. Believe that and it's surprisingly easy not to be jealous.

My indifference made me different
so he began to prefer me.

CHORUS. Preference is the first domino of feeling.
Hit it hard and it knocks over "like."
"Like" tilts,
wavers between "preference" and "love."

DELILAH. Preference or love.

CHORUS. Gravity and a little luck make it fall in love's direction.

"Love" brings down "need" with it.
They're closer together than the others.
One follows the next so quickly
it's as if they're struck at the same time.

DELILAH. I need to go inside.

TAMAM. Go, I'll follow.

DELILAH. I'm scared.
(*Motions towards the audience*)
He's in there. I know it. It's like I can feel him watching me.

(*Addresses the audience as if she sees Samson*)
Samson!
I begged my people not to hurt you.
They promised, I almost believed.

When they blinded you, I could not see,
how to show you though I loved my people more,
I still loved you.

Surrounded by darkness, I knew you
who loved me, without lights on,
would—

CHORUS. —recognize my touch.

DELILAH. I touched, muttering a skeleton of apologies.
You sliced through the bone saying—

CHORUS. "Leave! Your presence torments me."

DELILAH. I stayed, you cursed me.
I fled your cries and the cruelty you learned from me.
Outside, looking in,
I saw you framed in the doorway
of that great hall.

CHORUS. The one that stood so tall.
The one that seemed as if only God's hand could make fall.

DELILAH. There you were,
with your head cocked as you watched me with your ears.

Your arms stretched out.
The pillars exploded.
The world went flat.
You spared me.

Your people dug and found you
under the layers of mine.
I prayed that you would rest softly in their soil.
I wished your God could have kept you safe
from she who loved you,
(*pause*) but still wished you dead.

AIESHA. Nice story.
But I don't suggest you stick to it
if you really want to get in there.

DELILAH. Why not?

AIESHA. Trust me, you won't be welcome in there if you tell that
story.

DELILAH. How do you know?

AIESHA. Maybe because I've been in there.

DELILAH. What?

TAMAM. Did you see my brother?

AIESHA. I wouldn't know him if I did.

Delilah joins the chorus again.

CHORUS. How did you get in? Why did you leave? Tell us.

AIESHA. It's a long story.

DELILAH. I don't believe you.

AIESHA. Don't believe me. Go in. Tell your story. See what happens.

DELILAH. If it's true you went in
why didn't you stay?

AIESHA. Like I said, it's a long story.

ARCHITECT. Why is everybody always talking about length? There
   are other factors to consider.

   Pause.

AIESHA. What?

TAMAM. Excuse her. She's not very articulate.

DELILAH. You'll get used to her.

TAMAM. She means to ask why do people mention the length of a *story*
   as a reason not to tell it?

   When there are far more important factors to consider—
   like how bad we need to know it.

AIESHA. How long have you been together?

CHORUS. A long time.
   Not long enough to hate one another,
   but long enough to know we eventually will.

TAMAM. I've seen everyone I loved except my brother.
   Please try to remember if you've seen my brother.
   He was about this tall
   (*frantically indicates a height that would suggest a tall man*) and had—

AIESHA. What was his name?

TAMAM. Muhammed.

AIESHA. Muhammed? Do you know how many Muhammeds are in
   there?

CHORUS. No more than there are Johns.

AIESHA. True.

TAMAM. My brother is one of a kind.

DELILAH. Hold on, Tamam.
   Don't anyone let her start talking about her brother.

TAMAM. I shouldn't have let you follow me here.

DELILAH. I didn't follow you here.
  Do you want to talk about your brother
  or do you want her to help you get in there to see him?

TAMAM. You're right.

CHORUS. Everyone has heard a rumour.
  When you believe a rumour, it makes it true.
  We heard that all the martyrs were
  sitting in the one room in the afterlife.

ARCHITECT (*points to the audience*). The one right there!

CHORUS. The room no one knows anything about,
  the room no one but martyrs have dared to go into.
  And no one who goes in comes out.

AIESHA. Except me.

CHORUS. Huh?

AIESHA. I was a martyr.
  (*Pause*) Do you doubt it? Do you dare doubt it?

CHORUS. We believe it.

AIESHA. Swear that you believe it with your whole heart.

CHORUS. We believe it.
  That's all we need to say.
  Everything about the afterlife
  each of us believes to be true
  ends up being true
  to the extent we believe in it.

ARCHITECT. Even if what we believe about the afterlife contradicts
  itself.

AIESHA. That's right. All I have to do is believe I was a martyr.
  That I did what my people needed me to do.
  That by my death, I gave my people a chance at life.

CHORUS (*speaking as if it is a prayer*). Help us take our first step
  towards that room.

Water goes from solid to liquid,
people don't just cease.

Our loved ones are allowed an afterlife,
just like every other misguided soul who murdered and raped.

Some of our martyrs were mistaken, cruel, even insane.
But the fact remains,
they are not worse than the worst of them that are here.

We believe in
our loved ones
who are sitting in that room in front of us.
(*Pointing to the audience*) That room!
And we only need to go in
to see our brothers, our lovers, our fathers, our friends.

AIESHA. Ourselves.

CHORUS. We are in heaven. And when we woke up here,
   there was mint on the pillow
   beside the one we slept on
   and a note that had fallen off the bed.

   The note said—

AIESHA. "Welcome to heaven,
   where everything you believe to be true is true."

ARCHITECT. The only problem is we can't control what we believe.

AIESHA. That's what makes our heaven such hell.

CHORUS. That's in the fine print, of course.
   So we don't know what we really believe lies waiting for us
   in that room.
   None of us are brave enough to find out.

TAMAM. But you know, so go in and find my brother—

AIESHA. Hold your horses, Tamar.

TAMAM. It's Tamam.

AIESHA. Whatever.

DELILAH. I'm sure you're planning to go back in sometime. You'll
notice Samson. He's the big guy. He'll probably hit on you.
Ask him to come out and get me.

AIESHA. First of all, no matter how much he loved you and misses
you still,
no martyr will ever leave that room to come get you.
You've got to go in there alone.

CHORUS. We're in heaven
and it has all the same contradictions we faced in life.

AIESHA. But in heaven we've learned how to live with them.

ARCHITECT. That's what makes it heaven.

CHORUS. We've learned how to live with them.

DELILAH. I don't care. I want to see Samson. I'm sure they'll let me
in the room where the martyrs are staying, if they know how
much I loved him.

AIESHA. If you think I'm wrong,
go first, Delilah.
Go inside.
See what happens.

ARCHITECT (to Aiesha). What's your name?

AIESHA. Aiesha.

ARCHITECT. Were you famous?

AIESHA. Yes, but you wouldn't know me.

ARCHITECT. Maybe I do. When were you alive?

AIESHA. Listen, half-wit. I said you didn't.
You speak out of turn again and I'll make you go stand with one
of the other groups of women that are around here.
But they probably won't have you either, so you'll be all alone.
You want to be alone?

Don't look at your friends. Keep looking at me.

They're not going to help you.
They know I'm right.
Look at me and answer my questions.
Do you want to be alone?
(*Architect shakes her head.*)
That's what I thought, you stupid worthless waste of a human soul.
Now, I'm going to ask you again—do I look familiar?

ARCHITECT. Whatever you want me to say, I'll say.

AIESHA. That's what I thought.

CHORUS. What you think, we think.

TAMAM. You're certainly not a religious figure.
If you were, I would recognize you instantly.
I've taken advantage of my time in heaven,
especially the ability to read without getting tired.

I have scoured the holy books of every religion that ever existed.
Looking for a trace of what all the world religions say happens
to martyrs, so I can figure out where my brother might be.

Do you think you can go in and ask about him now?
If you wouldn't mind . . .

DELILAH. Forget her brother. Ask about Samson first. I've looked at
all those books too. I did just as much work as she did.

TAMAM. You dirty liar. You didn't. You followed me here.

DELILAH. I didn't follow you!

TAMAM. You were wandering.
You saw that this girl (*points to the architect who stares out into the
audience and does not seem to be listening*) was following me.
I told her she could come with me as long as she didn't get in
my way and stayed quiet. And she does, usually,
except when she screams of hands, movement and change.

ARCHITECT. Hands, movement, change!

TAMAM. Like that.

> She won't explain who she's looking for.
> I'm not sure if she knows herself.
>
> I went to talk to all the gods and prophets
> of all the religions that ever were.
> They tried their best to tell us where to locate the martyrs in the afterlife.
> But they could not.
> Some forgot, some didn't know where to begin.
> Finally, we got in touch with this god the humans prayed to
> before they made it to the sapien part of the homo sapien.

AIESHA. It was at the homo erectus point in the chain of human development.

DELILAH. Homo erectus?

TAMAM. You'd know that if you did the research.

DELILAH. Okay, I didn't do all the research you did.
> I just stood around and said,
> (*flirting*) "I need a little information.
> Does anyone want to help me out?"
> Then this monkey-like man appeared,
> ready to, you know, help out.

TAMAM. I found the Monkey God in some corner,
> drinking banana wine and chilling out with Persephone,
> they're lovers now.

The chorus is Tamam, Delilah and Architect.

CHORUS. Persephone finally got rid of that piece of shit Hades.

AIESHA. Is it true that she walked out one day and said, "Stilettos are on sale. I'm going shopping" and never came back?

CHORUS. No. She bought a pair of steel-toed boots
> and kicked his head in while he slept.
> The sun of the summer of forever shines above
> Demeter and her daughter

who have tied up brain-damaged Hades
and now take turns shoving pomegranates up his ass.

AIESHA. That's what I call divine justice.
Demeter no longer wakes up screaming—

CHORUS. "Where is my daughter?
Where is she?
I'll chill your hearts in your chests with my cries till you tell me!
What corner of hell has he taken her to and what is he doing to
her there?
Where is my child?"

TAMAM. So, I spoke to Persephone's new love—the Monkey God.
His name is Oo-oo-oo.

DELILAH. That's what he called himself!

TAMAM. Oo-oo-oo told me I was the only person he was going to tell
about where he thought the martyrs might be.

DELILAH. It wasn't easy to get it out of him. It took a lot of persuasion.

TAMAM (*ashamed*). You persuaded him too?

AIESHA. You're obviously pretty good at persuasion, Delilah.

DELILAH. It has been said that I am.
I got him drunk on banana wine at the first moment his ghoulish
girlfriend wasn't at his side. Then he began to talk. He said—

Delilah can join chorus again.

CHORUS. "Look, I'm going to get into trouble for telling you this.
I don't like to mess with the martyrs.
No one does. But there was this room at the corner of heaven,
where the Columbus monkeys who sacrifice themselves"—

AIESHA. —"who run towards the predators"—

CHORUS. —"so their loved ones have time to get away"—

AIESHA. —"who run towards their predators
so the weaker ones aren't certain prey."

CHORUS. "They used to hang out in this room, long before humans
were invented.
We gods have talked and we figured out this is the place where
the human martyrs must be too."

DELILAH. That's the story he tells if you persuade him enough.

CHORUS. Yes.
But banana wine is cheap and persuading a monkey is easier
than you might think.
The Monkey God likes all kinds of women.

So women of all different cultures and all centuries wait here.
(*Point to different areas of the stage.*)

TAMAM. There are the Japanese women, whose men kamikaze-d
their way here and haven't been seen since.

DELILAH. Over there are Iranian mothers who helped convince their
children it was their duty to run through land riddled with landmines.

ARCHITECT. Here are the Tamil women, sisters of the Black Tigers
who sit for centuries, waiting.

TAMAM. There! Those are the Buddhists,
mostly mothers of monks who made love to fire
and died in its embrace.

DELILAH. The Irish girls are over there,
whose fathers starved themselves in the hope of tasting freedom.
They tend to sing to pass the time.

ARCHITECT. There are the Jewish ladies,
the relatives of the unsung
heroes of the Holocaust
Unnamed, because anyone who might have seen or heard or
been told about their brave acts died almost immediately after
them.
Unknown, except to those women who will not rest
till they find them again.

CHORUS. There is no hatred here.
Each of us wishes each of them well.
Though, here we wait in heaven, at the gate of the martyrs' door.
None of them seem to have discussed it or decided upon it,
but somehow they have managed to separate themselves
into the groups, the races,
we identified with while we are alive.

AIESHA. Waitaminute. I know you're Arabs but are you Palestinians?

CHORUS. Yes. We're among our own kind.
Even in heaven, you can breathe more easily with your own people.
Here we are
and here we have segregated ourselves almost by accident it
seems.

AIESHA. All except for her.

DELILAH. Philistine is how you pronounce Palestine in Arabic in my
day and in yours, Aiesha. You know that.

AIESHA. All I know is that you like kosher dick, bitch.

ARCHITECT (*covers her ears*). Ugly! Ugly! No hands, no movement, no
change!

Tamam puts her hand on Architect and she stops shouting.

TAMAM (*to Architect*). Stop yelling, woman.
(*To Aiesha*) Aiesha, I want your help in finding my brother.
But that kind of talk is not necessary.

AIESHA. It's not necessary to speak my mind
but I'm going to do so anyway.

DELILAH. Don't worry, Tamam. I can handle her. I like men and all
the different flavors they come in. And trust me, when they do
come, it is in different flavors.

AIESHA. The flavor of forbidden fruit rots quickly.
But you didn't have the chance to know that, did you?
You know why he liked you so much?

ARCHITECT. No!

DELILAH. You don't know anything about what he felt for me.

AIESHA. Because, while having you,
    he was able to relive murdering all your men.

ARCHITECT. I said no!

AIESHA (*to Architect*). You shut up!
    (*To Delilah*) So why don't you go join the Jewish women, Delilah?

TAMAM. Aiesha, that's enough.

Architect goes over and stands by Delilah.

DELILAH. Just because I love someone else doesn't mean I become
    something else.

AIESHA. Whatever. Now, if I were the two of you, I'd say maximize
    your chances of getting into the room of the martyrs safely.

DELILAH. What does that mean?

AIESHA. Well, most martyrs are religious.

DELILAH. So?

AIESHA. Almost every religion requires one to be pious and that
    means chaste.
    And associate only with people who are pious and chaste.

DELILAH. What? Are you saying we've got to pretend to be virgins or
    something?

TAMAM. Just don't advertise, okay?

DELILAH. I spent way too much time pretending to be a virgin on
    earth. Must I do it here too?

ARCHITECT. You mean you can pretend to be a virgin?

Delilah and Tamam nod. Architect slaps her forehead as if to say "stupid me."

TAMAM. We were friends before we got here, Delilah. Let's be
    friends again.

I want to walk in that room with you.
But, for our sakes, in case it causes harm
don't mention Samson and—

DELILAH. Don't worry.
I am a virgin.
I'll tell that to anyone who asks me.

TAMAM. Good.

AIESHA. Well, I wouldn't want to walk in with a liar if I were you.
The martyrs won't like it.

DELILAH. Why are you making such a big deal of this?

AIESHA. I'm just trying to help you all out.

TAMAM. What does it matter if she lies?
No one doublechecks stories.
We're in heaven, remember?
In heaven, people figure that if you lie,
you must have a good reason to do so, so they let you be.

DELILAH. But I'm not lying.
It's the truth. If they ask me, if it matters, I'll tell them I am a
virgin.

AIESHA. That innocent ole "of-course-I've-never-done-this-before"
stuff might have worked with Samson. It ain't gonna work with
you in there.

TAMAM. What if it's different in the martyrs' room than it is in the
rest of heaven?
We've never been there, Delilah.
If they don't buy our story, they aren't going to let us in and I've
got to get in.
My brother needs me.

DELILAH. I am a virgin.
because I destroyed the only man I ever loved.

CHORUS (*without Aiesha*). I think that counts.

AIESHA. It doesn't matter what we think. It matters what they think.

DELILAH. How do you know what they will think of me or anything else?

AIESHA. Because I've in been there, remember?
I'm the first female suicide bomber.

CHORUS. What?

ARCHITECT. How could you . . .

AIESHA. Easy.
I built something more intricate than the human heart,
hugged it to my chest,
and walked into the biggest crowd I could find . . .

DELILAH. No one cares how you killed yourself.
What I want to know is why,
how could you end yourself that way?
It's so angry.

CHORUS (*without Aiesha*). It's so male.

AIESHA. Let's put it this way.
Oppression is like a coin-maker.

TAMAM. That's what my brother said!
He said, "Oppression is like a coin-maker."
That's what my brother said.
That's exactly what he said.

AIESHA. Can you keep it to yourself, Reham?
I'm trying to tell my story.
I suggest you listen to it. It may be of some interest to you and yours.

TAMAM. Sorry. It's Tamam, by the way.

AIESHA. You should be.
The truth is I was a martyr.
Unlike some people, I didn't stand on the sidelines,
seducing my way into saving my people's skin

DELILAH. It worked.

AIESHA. Not for long.

DELILAH. No one tells the rest of my story.
That Samson only killed the Philistines in the banquet hall,
had he lived and had I not wrung his secret from him,
he would have slaughtered us all.

Check your sources, remember who wrote them.
If you do, angry woman, you might find out
you're closer to me than you think.

I might be your ancestor.

AIESHA. We've heard enough out of you.
Go hang out with the Jewish women.

DELILAH. Religion doesn't mean anything here, remember?
I was born before your religion even existed.

TAMAM. Well, we are still separated, Delilah.
(*Indicating difference places in the audience*)
Look at us, we women are still in the groups we lived and died
for while on earth.

CHORUS. We're all trying to get in that room where the martyrs live,
we should go up to each of the groups of women and ask if they
want to work together.

TAMAM. We are like these other women in at least one way, for sure.
We are the only ones who are still searching for our martyrs.
Everyone else, even people like my mother,
has given up looking for them.
Looked around for a millennium or two, and then let it go.
But I can't.

DELILAH and ARCHITECT. None of us can.

TAMAM. I've thought about
going up to and speaking with those Iranian mothers,
who begged, ordered and somehow convinced their children to
run through minefields in order to clear them.

Iranian mothers who are looking for those children now.
They want to see their loved ones as badly as we do.
(*To Delilah*) Go ask if they want to walk in with us.

DELILAH. No.
What kind of woman could send her child to certain death?

TAMAM. They had to. There was no other way to clear those fields full of mines.

ARCHITECT. I'd run through myself instead.

Aiesha joins the chorus and Tamam drops out.

CHORUS. Be a martyr.

TAMAM. And let your children die of starvation or worse?

CHORUS. What's worse that letting a child blow herself up in a mine-field?

TAMAM. Sending a child to fight in a war that everyone admits is only about oil.

AIESHA. If everyone sacrificed one child, the minefields would be clear. I would send my favorite child.

TAMAM. There are no favorites when it comes to children.

CHORUS. If you believe that, I've got a peace process I can sell you.

AIESHA. I would send my favorite child.
So none of the children who are left can accuse me of favoritism

DELILAH. I still say I could never send a child to die.

AIESHA. Who are you to talk, whore?

DELILAH. Words like that don't mean anything here,
because up here we know
there isn't a woman alive who doesn't sell herself—

Pause.

CHORUS. —short.

TAMAM. So, Aiesha, you shouldn't call her that or talk to her that way.

Aiesha drops out of the chorus. Tamam joins in.

AIESHA. I'll talk any way I please.
  I took matters into my own hands and got my reward.
  The minute I got to the afterlife,
  I had a hundred men of every hue.
  That's what I believed I'd get.

CHORUS. So that meant that's what you got.

AIESHA. Maybe I also believed that maybe killing people was wrong,
  even if those people were massacring mine at a maddening pace.
  Maybe the thought crossed my mind.

CHORUS. And in heaven what you believe is true becomes true.

AIESHA. Maybe I spent a fleeting time in the hell I feared.

CHORUS. There is no eternal hell. No one believed in it enough to
  make it true.
  If there was one person who truly believed in eternal hell
  instead of just feared it,
  it would exist. But there isn't and it doesn't.

AIESHA. Wanna make a bet?
  None of you know what you're talking about!

Pause.

CHORUS. We know enough.
  We know all religions are wacky and, if you don't buy that—

ARCHITECT. —you haven't read
  your own book with honest eyes.
  Know that you're picking and choosing what's convenient
  about your own religion—

AIESHA. —before you start talking about someone else's.
  I believed my book
  when it said
  heaven is indescribable in human terms—

CHORUS. —i.e. you just won't get it.

AIESHA. So, to describe indescribable delight.
it said that men who live virtuously—

CHORUS. —don't literally get to have a bunch of sexy women—

AIESHA. —but they have pleasures
that will feel like—

CHORUS. —what can only in inferior human terms
be understood as
hanging out with a bunch of houris,
virgins whose virginity is continually renewed,
also known as—

ARCHITECT. —the Black Eyed.

AIESHA. I interpreted that to mean that if I blew myself up and took
others with me,
because no one would give a shit about my people's plight unless
I did,
I would have a hundred men of every hue.
who were lined up like fruits at the market.

CHORUS. Ready for the picking and the plucking.

AIESHA. Men,
forever chaste with their chastity renewing throughout eternity,
untouched, eager.
I had them all.

CHORUS. In that room?

AIESHA. No. Nothing like that goes on in the martyrs' room.

TAMAM. In what religious text did you find that if you blew yourself
up you'd have a hundred men of every hue?

AIESHA. Okay, my interpretation is a rather loose one.
But, hey, it's heaven.
That's what I believed, that's what I got.

CHORUS. Men. Men. Men. A hundred men.

ARCHITECT. Why are you here then?
How could you leave a hundred men of every hue?

AIESHA. You're not only stupid, you're a virgin, which is kind of the same thing. Tell me, are you or are you not a virgin?

ARCHITECT. According to whose standards?

AIESHA. Not according to the standards of Delilah, that's for sure.
You aren't a virgin too, are you?

TAMAM. No. I had children.

AIESHA. Then, you know what I'm talking about.

TAMAM. I do.

AIESHA. No idea? (*Architect shakes her head*)
Okay, stupid.
Did you happen to miss that I said that these men had no sexual experience?
How many times can a woman scream—

CHORUS (*without Architect*). "That's not it.
That's not near it.
That's so far away
you might as well be rubbing the soles of my shoes,
without them even being on my feet.
I might get a little more satisfaction that way."

AIESHA. And the worse thing about it is,
if you get a little desperate,
and give it a go.
Spend a spell
training a pretty dumb angel—

CHORUS. "I like it this way, do it that way."

AIESHA. But every hour on the hour,
their virginity is renewed.
You know what that means?
It means their eyes glaze over with a dull vapid look.

All the time you spent training them is in vain,
and they are back to aiming at your belly-button.

Architect laughs to herself.

AIESHA. It isn't that funny. Why are you laughing?
(*To Tamam*) Make her stop.

DELILAH. Actually, it is funny.
You're a pretty girl, Aiesha.
It's not a compliment. It's a fact.
And you blew yourself up
and ended up with a hundred male virgins in heaven—

CHORUS. —when any girl could have twice that number on earth if
she wanted to.

All three women laugh at Aiesha.

AIESHA. Shut up. Shut up.

DELILAH. And now you're hanging out with us,
because for some reason, the martyrs don't want you back in
there with them.

AIESHA. I could go back in there any time.
Unlike out here, there is no separation according to race or
religion.
But it's a boy's club in there.
I got the sense that they didn't want me around.

TAMAM. They're not supposed to do that.
They're not supposed to make you feel unwelcome.

AIESHA. Welcome to heaven,
where a lot of things that aren't supposed to happen do.
I thought we could all burst in together
and make them make room for us.
But you're weaklings,
Useless.
In other words, women. Mere women.
Get out of my way.
I'm going to go inside.

DELILAH. Please ask our loved ones if they want us to visit.

AIESHA. Why do you doubt that they do?

CHORUS. Our loved ones haven't sought us out
    in all this time.

AIESHA. The door is unlocked.
    Why are you afraid?
    Just walk in.

CHORUS. Just because a door is unlocked
    doesn't mean you should go in.
    We don't know what lies there.
    No god but Oo-oo-oo has been inside.
    He says that the martyrs aren't used to visitors
    He's afraid of them. Why shouldn't we be?

AIESHA. Because there are people you love in there.
    Don't you have faith that they'll protect you?

CHORUS. We don't really know what to expect.
    Why would every martyr from every religion and race
    from every point in time
    congregate there?
    And never choose to come out.

AIESHA. It's just another place, like any other in heaven.

CHORUS. Help us and we'll be in your everlasting debt.

AIESHA. Everylasting debt is overrated and hardly ever paid in full.

TAMAM. I can't take it anymore. Go in there right now and ask about
    my brother!

AIESHA. Quiet. Do you want everyone else to hear that I've been in
    there?
    If the other groups of women know I can go in and out of the
    martyrs' room, they'll all be clamoring for me to go in and find
    their loved ones too.

TAMAM. You go in there right now.

ARCHITECT. Stop fighting. Stop everything. Just stop everything!

AIESHA. We're not fighting, retard. I'm ignoring her.

TAMAM. Go find my brother. Tell him I want to see him.

ARCHITECT and DELILAH. Hold on a minute.
We agreed.
We're in this together.
If we're asking her to go in, she should ask about all our loved
ones.

TAMAM. No, you're going to ask about my brother first, before you
look for anyone else

AIESHA. Heyam, I don't care about you or your stupid—

*Tamam grabs Aiesha's hair. At this point, Delilah and Architect will par-
ticipate in the chorus.*

TAMAM. —My name is Tamam.

(*Letting go of Aiesha*)
It means enough.

I was called that because my family wanted no more daughters.
I am the last of seven sisters, good luck for the family.
After me, there were two brothers
and now there is only one.

CHORUS. Why do our people rejoice when a boy child is born?

TAMAM. Because we understand the power of might.
We know what it means to be weak—

CHORUS. —to cement a settlement of resentment,
brick by brick,
in our own ravaged hearts and shell-shocked minds.

Times like these call for soldiers.
The ones we had have fallen.

TAMAM. A birth of a girl is different from a boy.
A girl is a gift that's too precious,

a reminder that soft things don't last long
in our world.
Arab parents fool themselves,
thinking a boy child has at least almost
a fighting chance
or a chance to fight
the Europeans and their holy war,
crusading against we people who lived here before,
and will live here afterwards.

I want to talk about something smaller than me
that became bigger.

I want to talk about my brother.

If you've heard stories about him, don't believe them.
I was far more religious than he.
I never had the heart to wake him to pray
He was hoping to study medicine while working
for nothing,
so we could eat.

CHORUS. I let him sleep through the call.

TAMAM. My brother was caught with a weapon in his hand
   and a curse on his lips.
   I went to the jail to arrange a ransom for his release

CHORUS. Installment by installment—

TAMAM. —I paid as much as we could of the price that they asked
   for the life of my brother.

   Most of my people looked at the Crusader guards
   with every ounce of hatred a human heart can hold—

CHORUS. —their faces twisted not like they tasted something bitter,
   like something bitter was forced down their throats.

TAMAM. I was smarter than that.

   I knew I must navigate through the maze of might,
   and did my best to be kindly, polite.

Challenges western ideas of
middle eastern women)

Hoping perhaps that I would
remind them of a woman
that they knew.

CHORUS. Or would have liked to know.

TAMAM. So when they beat my brother,
that thing that started out smaller than me and got bigger,
they would, perhaps for my sake,
lighten their touch.

I am a pretty woman.
It's not a boast.

CHORUS. It's a fact.

TAMAM. Looks are a commodity, an asset, a possession I happen to
possess.
It's why my grandmother said no,
when my sister's brother-in-law asked for my hand.
The family that was good enough
for my plain sister wasn't good enough for me.
I'm a pretty woman.
It's not a boast.

CHORUS. It's a fact.

TAMAM. And I smiled my best smile
when the soldiers opened the gate for me.
Weighed down with baskets of food,
I brought extra,
hoping to create the illusion
that that dirty jail was one place
where there was enough and extra for all
the guards to eat twice.
Otherwise, my brother would get none.
unless there was enough and extra.

CHORUS. They thanked me for the food.

TAMAM. And they raped me in front of him,
forcing my brother's eyes open so he had to watch.
They wanted to know something.

CHORUS. He preferred not to tell them.

TAMAM. They skewered the support for their argument into my flesh.

> I'm told they believed rape would enrage our men.
> Enraging a man is the first step on the stairway
> that gets him to a place
> where he becomes impotent,
> helpless.

> They not only refer to us as the cockroaches,
> they examine us, experiment upon us,
> as if we were that predictable, that much the same—

CHORUS.—that easy to eradicate.
> They know Arab men value the virtue of their womenfolk.

TAMAM. They know something within me was supposed to be inviolate.

> Say what you want about Arab men and women
> and how we love one another,
> there is one thing that's for certain.
> There are real repercussions for hurting a woman in my society.

CHORUS. There are repercussions.

TAMAM. When the first hand was laid upon me, we both screamed.
> The evolutionary function of a scream is a cry for help.
> They tied down the only one who could
> so I silenced myself.
> That was the only way to tell my brother
> I didn't want him to tell.

> I flinched when I had to,
> but I kept my breathing regular.
> My brother tried to look every other way,
> but realized I needed him,
> to look me in the eyes
> (*pause*) and understand.

> They thought making us face one another
> in our misery would break us.

But we were used to misery.
It's like anything else.

CHORUS. You can build up a tolerance for it.

TAMAM. Someone else told them what they wanted to know,
so they released my brother two weeks later.

That's when he joined a rebel group organized in a prison.

CHORUS. The group sent each man alone at the same time—

TAMAM. —to a different part of the crowded Crusader marketplace,

ARCHITECT. No hands, movement or change!

TAMAM. Each with a knife and a double-ball battle mace.

CHORUS. Is that an arm?
Who does it belong to?

TAMAM. Full of men, women, children

CHORUS. No, it's a spine. Look at the ridges.
Who does it belong to?

TAMAM. Pilgrims—not warriors.
People—not parts of flesh strewn everywhere,
until my brother and the others got there.

CHORUS. Who does it belong to?

TAMAM. The killer and the killed.
My brother's parts mixed in
with the people he believed could not stand him.

CHORUS. Because he believed they could not stand him.
Who does it belong to?

TAMAM. Killing as many of them as he could
until he himself was . . . torn apart.
I was not allowed to bury what I gathered—

CHORUS. —what I believed to be—

TAMAM. —parts of him.
That I recognized and kissed

The Crusader mourners pulled
the one hand that—

CHORUS. —I was sure was his—

TAMAM. —out of mine.
    They smeared it and his head with pig fat,
    as they did to desecrate the bodies of our soldiers.
    They hung my brother's head and hand with them
    on pikes above the city walls

TAMAM. The head I barely knew,
    but I wanted to bury the hand

CHORUS. To show who it belonged to.

TAMAM. The day he did it,
    he told me over breakfast—

CHORUS. "Oppression is like a coin-maker.—

TAMAM. —You put in human beings,
    press the right buttons and
    watch them
    get squeezed, shrunk, flattened
    till they take the slim shape of a two-faced coin.
    One side is a martyr, the other a traitor.
    All the possibilities of a life get reduced to those paltry two.
    The coin is tossed in the air
    it spins once for circumstance,
    twice for luck
    and a third time for predilection
    before it lands flat.
    The face that points down
    towards hell
    determines not only who you are.
    But how you will become that way."

What he was really saying was goodbye.

Had I known, I would have said something more than—

CHORUS. "Brother, it's interesting
    you think oppression

makes us turn into a form of money, a currency.
How odd."

TAMAM. Listen, I don't agree with killing innocent people
under any circumstances,

CHORUS. Ever.

ARCHITECT. There might have been Arab children in that crowd too.
(*Looks at Aiesha who looks away.*)

TAMAM. I want to feel sorrow when *anyone* is suffering,
No matter who they are or what their people have done to mine,
no one's life should be snuffed out.
I am the kind of human being
who refuses to get high on the drug of hate.
In my opinion—

CHORUS. —that's the only kind of human being there is.

TAMAM. In other words, no one is going to reduce me to a coin.
There are absolutes,
it's wrong to kill, period.

ARCHITECT. Children who will never be born.

AIESHA (*to Tamam*). No, it's not!

TAMAM. I should have known what my brother was bound to do,

CHORUS. I could have stopped him.

TAMAM. I said every time he went out to fight,
"Don't go.
We'll achieve peace by peaceful means.

CHORUS. "Don't be a pawn."

TAMAM. "Let others risk their lives.
With all their weapons,
these foreigners can never truly win—

CHORUS. —they can't kill us all."

TAMAM. I'd always say—

CHORUS. "Don't go."

TAMAM. But I didn't say—
    "You are the most precious thing in the world to me.
    The fact that you exist makes the earth spin on its axis,
    it's rolling for joy because you are here.
    The sun shows up to see you,
    and the moon chases the sun off to be in your sky
    and none of them love you like I do, brother.

CHORUS. Not even close.

TAMAM. There is no goal, no political means,
    worth wrenching your life from mine.
    If heaven on earth is what you want,
    heaven on earth is here.
    Heaven on earth is my brother being by my side
    and screaming for joy when I have my firstborn
    and—

CHORUS.—living long and laughing loud—

TAMAM.—with me
    over hot tea and warm bread,
    each morning,
    which is all we can afford
    but, if you are by my side,
    it is more than enough.
    If you think this is a gift for me,
    the box will be empty, brother.

CHORUS. How can it not be?

TAMAM. Everything will be empty, if you're not here.
    Don't hurt yourself and others in my name or for my sake.
    I will not forgive you if you leave me.
    I will not be comforted.
    I will not be."

    Instead I said—

CHORUS. "Don't go."

TAMAM. And I didn't say it loud.

> They burned down our entire village
> because you killed those people.
> In all this, I didn't realize what true fear, true dread, was
> till I watched our younger brother
> watching them destroy our homes—

CHORUS. —witnessing the smoke curl and churl—

TAMAM. —with more anger in his eyes than I had ever seen in yours.

> I was engaged to be married
> to the love of my life and the richest man any of us knew.
> My father went to his house
> and told his father what had happened to me.
> My father didn't want scandal if we went ahead and married
> and it was found I was not . . . as I was before.

CHORUS. My love left me.

TAMAM. Because of his father's insistence.
> His mother, who never liked me anyway,
> took him and married him to a girl from her town.
> He moved to Damascus with her
> and I . . .

CHORUS. . . . haven't seen him since.

TAMAM. I try to convince myself
> that I wouldn't want to be married to a man
> who could ever betray me.
> I try to convince myself I'm better off without him.

CHORUS. Try is the operative word.

TAMAM. His cowardice was a violence
> that hurts and haunts me more than what the guards did to me.
> Because I have no one to blame but my own people,
> which is as hard to do as blaming yourself.

> I married my sister's brother-in-law,
> who was made aware that I was not . . . as I was before.

My husband and I understand one other,
which is not exactly a good thing.
My husband never lets me live it down that my family once
rejected him,
He calls me a whore—

CHORUS. —when he is angry—

TAMAM. —and stuck up—

CHORUS. —when he is not.

TAMAM. He gets angry often,
    especially when I tell him he is worthless—

CHORUS. —not a real man—

TAMAM. —when he can't find enough food.
    It's the only way I know how to make him steal it.
    Like I said before . . .

CHORUS. We understand one another.

TAMAM. I think of my first love who deserted me.
    Every day, I visualize a new way I'd tell him
    what a traitor he was to leave me,
    in case I happen to ever see him again.
    It makes me sad that,
    though he wronged me in more ways than one,
    he'll only have ears to listen to the first words I say.

    You only get—

CHORUS. —one chance—

TAMAM. —to tell people they are wrong,
    You get that chance because it takes people a minute or two
    to realize you're telling them stuff they don't want to hear.

CHORUS. Then, they shut you out—

TAMAM. —though they might be still standing before you—

CHORUS. —smiling—

TAMAM. —they make sure the door between the ear and the heart is locked
and they forever take away your key.

Because they know if they—

CHORUS. —keep listening—

TAMAM. —they might not change,
but it will be a little harder
to stay the same.

If I saw him today, I would tell him,
"You should have married . . .

CHORUS. . . . me.

TAMAM. I was still a virgin, even after what the guards did to me.
I was still a virgin,
because I don't consider the men who raped me human and,
if you had any inkling of what a true man was
or how to be one,
neither would you."

My name is Tamam.
It means enough.

Aiesha begins to clap.

AIESHA. Bravo! Bravo. That was a wonderful performance. You had us all in tears.

CHORUS. Boo-hoo. Boo-hoo. Boo-hoo.
What a horrible life you had on earth.

AIESHA. Get over it. The Crusades were nothing compared to the Palestinian and Israeli wars I lived through.

TAMAM. But, the solution to that one was so easy.

CHORUS. Yes, the Palestinian-Israeli problem was solved centuries ago.
One state called
the United States of Israel and Palestine.
Pal-rael for short.

DELILAH. The posters for travel agents everywhere boast first-class
   packages
   to Pal-rael that say—

CHORUS. "Come to Pal-rael.
   It's safe
   because the Palestinians and Israelis are now real pals."

   Come see the Pal-rael museum of the centuries of war.

   It was built so both peoples of Pal-rael could be reminded of
   their dark past.
   It was built so all people could remember that there was a time
   —in that land of too much religion and too little faith—
   where humans would have lives snuffed out for no good reason
   at all.
   You go to remember that all the killing and struggling on both
   sides was in vain.

AIESHA. Your struggle—in vain . . .

CHORUS. The death of your loved ones—

AIESHA. Ourselves.

CHORUS. In vain.

AIESHA. There are other hot spots in the world.

CHORUS. Flash points of pain.

AIESHA. The Swedes have now gone buck wild,
   are angry that the Maltese continue to make fun of the fact that
   they have no eyelashes.

CHORUS. The Swedes insist they have eyelashes, but they are blond
   and therefore invisible to the naked eye.

AIESHA. The Maltese will have none of it.
   At the last UN conference, a Maltese diplomat
   took the Swedish ambassador aside,
   told him there is only one way to prove to the world
   that the Swedes had eyelashes.

The Maltese diplomat promptly plucked off an eyelash of the
Swedish ambassador,
and held it up for the world to witness.

CHORUS. Those in the back couldn't see.

AIESHA. So, he plucked one eyelash off the Swedish ambassador for
each diplomat and gave it to him,
proving that the Swedes indeed have eyelashes,
but only to those present.

CHORUS. It was a set-up, of course.
The newly eyelash-less ambassador was taken hostage by the
Maltese, who use him as proof that
the Swedes have no eyelashes.
War ensued.

AIESHA. And they've been fighting every since.
The UN has called again and again for the Maltese to stop
killing Swedes and then plucking the eyelashes off their corpses,
but the world only heeds the UN when they want to.

CHORUS. You see, it comes down to money, resources.

TAMAM. This all began when diamonds were discovered in Sweden.
The Maltese wanted a piece of the action,
which required occupying and settling upon Swedish land.
They believed if they proved to the world that the Swedes have
no eyelashes—

CHORUS.—they don't blink like you and I, they aren't fully human,
their blood is cheap—

TAMAM. —they could take the diamonds without the world taking
notice.

CHORUS. Well, they notice but they don't care.
When they notice, all the Maltese have to say is,
"For God's sake . . .

TAMAM. . . . they don't even blink like we do!"

CHORUS. It may sound kind of amusing.
   And you can laugh and laugh,

ARCHITECT. Unless . . .

CHORUS. You're a Maltese mother who watched her son die
   or a Swedish sister whose brother walked out one day and never
   came back.

TAMAM. Unless you lost someone who was everything to you, like I did.
   Now you know my story. Now you know why I need to get in
   there.

AIESHA. Yeah, I know.
   But I don't care.
   Your story is not unique.
   No one cares about rehashing stories about old conflicts that
   have been resolved centuries ago.

TAMAM. Then, why don't I have my brother with me?

AIESHA. What?

TAMAM. I've been in heaven for over hundreds of years.
   I have seen every person, even the guards who raped me,
   who apologized profusely.

   And, what they believed,
   what they feared even as they raped me,
   would eventually happen
   did happen.

   I was the first person to greet them in the afterlife
   and I was allowed to cut off their genitals.

   But I chose not to and said I'd be back to do it later,
   because I didn't want to hurt them once and be done with it.
   I wanted them to fear me forever.
   I have no intention of doing it.

ARCHITECT. Every night—

TAMAM. —I stand over them—

ARCHITECT. —every night.

TAMAM. She knows. I cast my long shadow as they cower,
   and sharpen my knives.

CHORUS without TAMAM. For your own sake,
   wouldn't you rather let it go, Tamam?
   It would be a sign that you have grown, healed, moved on.

TAMAM. Hell no. I look forward to it all day.

   Those soldiers killed more than my brother did, I'm sure.
   And, aside from my nightly visits, they are here roaming free.

   So I have seen everyone,
   except the dearest person in the world to me.

   So, if the war I suffered under is truly over,
   why is my brother in that room?
   Why is he not with me?

ARCHITECT. Tell her.

AIESHA. I don't know.
   Let it go.

TAMAM. I can't.

ARCHITECT. Tell her and tell me why did I have to die like that?

AIESHA. I don't know how or why you died.
   I'm getting tired of you, you little idiot.

ARCHITECT. I may be inarticulate.
   Have always been.
   It's not that I'm not thinking clear thoughts,
   I'm thinking too many of them.
   (*To Aiesha*) Murderer!
   But not of me!

TAMAM (*to Architect*). That's enough, honey.

ARCHITECT (*to Aiesha*). I know your face.

AIESHA. Do you have something to say?

ARCHITECT. Yes!

At this point, Architect drops out of the chorus. It may make sense for Delilah, Tamam and Aiesha each to play one of the voices of the characters (Half-Breed, Boss, Fiancée, other passengers) in the chorus.

ARCHITECT. But can I say it? No.
 Why must I speak in words when I think in images?
 I'm an architect of unseen structures
 and buildings that will never be built.
 I am the mother of children who will never be born.

CHORUS. The lover of men who will remain unloved.

ARCHITECT. Or rather men who are loved beyond compare,
 but will never know it.

CHORUS. Or how their lives would be changed if they did.

ARCHITECT. It was all Half-Breed's fault.
 I had to meet that son of a bitch who killed me.
 This, like so many things, all started with a—

CHORUS. —job interview.

ARCHITECT. He had an Arab last name.

CHORUS. Half-Breed.

ARCHITECT. I was always falling for the half-breeds.
 I can even see him in front of me now.

 (*Addresses Half-Breed as if he's in front of her*)
 I walked into your office, Half-Breed,
 applying for an assistantship.

 I read all about you in *Architectural Digest*.
 Your daddy's Palestinian.
 And your mama's white.

 You're a son of bitch with that sideways smile,
 that you flash when I walk in.
 You were discussing Gehry's new museum with your minions.

Nice as hell you were,
asking me what I thought of the new museum,
as if my opinion mattered
as if I mattered . . .
You were polite—

CHORUS. —too polite—

ARCHITECT. —to someone applying to be an assistant.
And everyone in the room knew it.
Sidelong glances, and smirks from your minions
"He's at it again," their eyes say.

CHORUS. "I'm at it again"—

ARCHITECT. —your eyes say.

I'm glad you asked me.

Architecture is the only thing I can be articulate about.

"I think Gehry's work is over . . . "
Your eyes never leave mine as
your head cocks to one side.
(*Other actors cock their heads to the left.*)

" . . . indulgent . . ."
I meant to say "rated."
I think to myself.
Your eyes don't leave mine
as your head cocks to the other side.
(*Other actors cock their heads to their right*)

CHORUS. "Why do you say that?"

ARCHITECT. The answer is: you make me nervous.
You make me say over-indulgent when I meant overrated.

If you didn't, I'd still be articulate
about the one thing I can be articulate about.
If that flash in your eyes wasn't signaling—

CHORUS. "We don't have to be here.

You and I.
We could, in fact, be somewhere else"—

ARCHITECT.—while your lips are asking me . . .
   "How would you—

CHORUS. —do it?"

ARCHITECT. If I was articulate, I'd say, "Hire me and find out."

   But I'm not so I pull out the drawing I happen to have,
   the draft I made on the train coming over,
   You see I do little projects.

CHORUS. I take the requirements and dimensions—

ARCHITECT.—that clients give to overrated white men like Gehry to
   make a museum—

   —and make my own drawings
   of how I would do it—

CHORUS. —if someone gave me a chance.

ARCHITECT. And on the ride over to meet you, Half-Breed.
   I happened to be working on
   my version of the museum
   you and your minions—in your jealousy—were denigrating.

CHORUS. An exercise—

ARCHITECT. —you might say, if you didn't know
   how desperate I get on trains.
   I have what I call . . .

CHORUS. —day-mares.

ARCHITECT. Every time I step on a train, I think
   what if—

CHORUS. —what if—

ARCHITECT. —what if
   I'll always be stuck in this place
   where no one is allowed to talk to one another
   while trying to get to a place where people do?

So I take out a piece of paper and sketch
and scrap and sketch again.

I never show the work I do on trains to anyone,
why I gave it to you, God only knows.

You appraise it, the way you appraise everything in your path,
including me in my well-tailored suit.

If you were to touch me, Half-Breed,
I would pull out handfuls of your hair.

CHORUS. Not against—

ARCHITECT. —but towards me.
    I can already feel how your hands
    will work.

CHORUS. Sculpt.

ARCHITECT. Grasp.
    Fingers full of my flesh
    like clay in your arms.
    I'll want to tell you
    "It's like you're shaping me! You're shaping me!"

But I'm not articulate, so I'll probably just—

CHORUS. —pant.

ARCHITECT. I'm thinking all this while you are
    still staring at my draft, my exercise.

CHORUS. Buying time.

ARCHITECT. Even though there might be none for sale.
    I would marry you—

CHORUS. —in a heartbeat.

ARCHITECT. And, though, half-breed that you are,
    our children will have an Arab last name
    and I will raise them in the culture you do not know
    and you will not understand why I'm still a virgin at thirty.

CHORUS. My father's tongue is not my mother tongue.

ARCHITECT. I don't speak hardly a lick of Arabic either,
   but I understand the morsels that count.
   My parents never insisted on me speaking back to them.
   Took it for granted I would know what they knew.

CHORUS. But I didn't.

ARCHITECT. You will not understand
   that the only thing you've got going for you is
   you have a chance of understanding
   the two languages
   I was born to learn and love.

CHORUS. Arabic and architecture.

ARCHITECT. My first-closest-thing-to-a-real-love-affair involved a
   man who only knew one.

CHORUS. Arabic.

ARCHITECT. A mother brought her son to the Arab church to see me
   He was Lebanese, but born here like me.
   But, unlike you, Half-Breed, he knew how things worked.
   Mothers love me for their sons.

CHORUS. They mistake inarticulacy for submissiveness.
   I soon teach them the difference.

ARCHITECT. And he came up to me while I was serving coffee
   and cups of sweetened grain and candy.

CHORUS. Our fingers touched—

ARCHITECT. —as I handed him a cup.

CHORUS. We spoke.

ARCHITECT. He said—

CHORUS. "I wanted to let you know of a scholarship for Arab female
   architects. It's an enormous sum of money."

ARCHITECT. "Really? How come I haven't heard of it?"

CHORUS. "Well, it's been fairly recently established.

Today, actually, because it's the first day I've met you and fallen
in love.
I've decided to establish this scholarship
for beautiful young Arab architects.
All you have to do is marry me.
I commission you to build us a house,
any way you want it."

ARCHITECT. "That's no scholarship," I thought.
But I was intrigued nevertheless.

He was studying to be a surgeon of the heart,
and it's so fucking bourgeois of me.
It's such a moment of intersection where I don't know
if these are my thoughts
or ones that my mother planted in my head,
but—

CHORUS. —I've always wanted to marry a doctor.
and how cute is it that he fixes hearts.

ARCHITECT. And before I know it.
I'm engaged.
And I'm already spending holidays where he wants me to.

It's Easter Sunday.

Christ has risen, and we Christian Arabs eat brunch.
I'm there with his family and him
at the top of the tallest building in the city.
Everyone is trying to "correct" my Arabic.

CHORUS. Rid me of my Palestinian accent in the few Arabic words I
do know.

ARCHITECT. His father spears a tomato and holds it in front of my
face.
He asks me—

CHORUS. "What is this? Say it in Arabic."

ARCHITECT. And I look at him

and he knows that I know what
he's saying.
You see Palestinians and Lebanese pronounce words differently.
Sometimes it feels like a whole different language.

CHORUS (*sing-song*). Palestinians say tomato, Lebanese say tomato.
Tomato, tomato.
Potato, potato.

ARCHITECT. So, during the civil war in Lebanon,
when Lebanese soldiers cornered someone who was alone
and wanted to find out—

CHORUS (*menacing*). "Are you a Palestinian? Are you?"

ARCHITECT. They'd show him a tomato.
and ask the poor soul—

CHORUS. "What is this?"

ARCHITECT. And if he said tomato instead of tomato.
They'd know he was a Palestinian and . . .
(*cocks a gun and points at audience*) Bang!

CHORUS. Let's call the whole thing off.

ARCHITECT. So I'm staring at the face of this man
who no laws are going to make any form of a father to me,
I know the point of all this was his father had to let me know—

CHORUS. "You will say things the way I want you to. Or else."

ARCHITECT. I looked at the boy I intended to marry,
who, with his eyes downcast, made it clear.
he knew what his father was doing.
He wasn't defending me
He could stop the human heart—

CHORUS. —and start it again—

ARCHITECT. —but he couldn't stand up to his father, even when he
was wrong
For me.

CHORUS. For you?

ARCHITECT. For me.
    That wasn't the main reason why I ended the relationship,
    it was only the point in time that I realized I probably would.

CHORUS. The scholarship had fine print you didn't read.
    There is a risk that your first commission can be your last.

ARCHITECT. So I didn't marry that man and waited for real scholar-
    ships, real commissions.

CHORUS. And when they didn't come?

ARCHITECT. I still wasn't sorry. Most of the time.

    My second-closest-thing-to-a-real-love-affair involved a man who
    spoke the other of the two languages I was born to learn and
    love.

CHORUS. Architecture.

ARCHITECT. My current boss.
    You know him, don't you, Half-Breed?
    He's your rival
    in more ways that one.

    His name is just under mine on my résumé next to the exercise
    you haven't looked up from since I handed it to you.

    I hoping that you'll hire me, Half-Breed,
    so I can never see him again.

    Not because I don't like him, but because I do.
    He was the first man that hired me out of school.

    He said he believed in me, that my work was—

CHORUS. —exceptional.

ARCHITECT. Men lie about such things—

CHORUS. —when it suits them.

ARCHITECT. But I didn't know that then.

I would never tell a person their work is good when it's not.
That's the only time it's useful that I'm so inarticulate.
I had a drink with him in his office after a big project.

CHORUS. Happy—

ARCHITECT. —we discussed my work on it.
My contributions.
His wife called. He told her he was working on a project
and would be home late.

CHORUS. But the project was over.

ARCHITECT. I know. We continued talking about my work.
Then his colleague came in without knocking and gave me—

CHORUS. —the eye.

ARCHITECT. I didn't know what to do with it.
The eye was seeing and signaling—

CHORUS. "You're at it again"—

ARCHITECT. —to my boss who smiled back as if to say—

CHORUS. "I'm at it again."

ARCHITECT. I realized there was a joke being made
and I was somehow—

CHORUS. —the butt—

ARCHITECT. —of it.
I took off hastily.
I left the two men—

CHORUS. —smiling at each other.

ARCHITECT. I was running away from the woman I was about to
become.
It looks like I haven't run far enough,
because I am here
asking you, Half-Breed
for a job,

a chance,
that you can give me and probably will.

The problem is . . .
I'm getting tired of running.
I live with my parents—

CHORUS. —always have—

ARCHITECT. —always will till a man takes me from my father's house.
You don't understand that concept either, Half-Breed,
staring at my work which you know is original.

CHORUS. Perhaps even better than yours?
You're buying time.

ARCHITECT. Though I don't intend to sell.
Half-Breed!
Can I explain why if you want me
it's important your people come to my home on the day we
marry,
so that you know I do not come from nothing?
The bejeweled old peacock women of my clan
who you pray I won't look like in forty years—

CHORUS. —though I'd be proud to have half the strength and seren-
ity of the least of them—

ARCHITECT. —will come to my house to make their presence known.
to trill and clap, but really to show you
that if you hurt me . . .
these bejeweled old women
can fly up like birds and peck out your eyes.
What they're saying by showing up to my house early,
witnessing your people escort me from it is,
"We are watching . . .

CHORUS. If you fuck with her, you fuck with us."

ARCHITECT. But you won't know our customs.
Half-Breed!
Your mother wasn't Arab.

CHORUS. Mothers teach their children early
the customs and morals and supersitions that stick.

ARCHITECT. My mother always told me—

CHORUS. "Marry an Arab man. They have a little sense of decency."

ARCHITECT. She means they don't often abandon their families.
My mother thinks if a man doesn't leave you,
that means he loves you—

CHORUS. —in the way men know how to love.

ARCHITECT. I would marry you in a heartbeat, Half-Breed,
and hope you learned how to be a man from your father.

CHORUS. I have designs on your heart.

ARCHITECT. But I don't know how to execute them.

Why can't love be as easy as architecture?
Half-Breed, you like me and I like you.

I wish I could just show you
a draft of the nest I would build for us,
with a room for each child I want to have.
A house with no master bedroom.
A house with no masters.
The only thing I'll have to say is . . .

CHORUS. "Do you like this house? Just say yes or no."

ARCHITECT. And you will understand my question to mean—

CHORUS. "Do you want to live here with me forever? Yes or no."

ARCHITECT. "Put the plans in motion or no.
Lay down the first twig of our nest in the nook of a tree
that won't be felled . . .

CHORUS.—or no."

ARCHITECT. All this I think of as I look at you looking at my draft.
You clear your half-bred throat.

CHORUS. "Ahem."

ARCHITECT. The job interview isn't over.

> You haven't looked up from my draft,
> but the bell for the minions to leave has been sounded.

> I stare at you, Half-Breed.

> And from the time it takes you to lift your eyes
> from the page to mine,
> this is what I think on . . .

> Will our children have your doe eyes or my black ones?

> I think of how I will stop making drafts on subways,
> because I want our youngest son to recite for me his ABCs and
> 123s.

> Our daughter is so arrogant already.
> Just like me.

CHORUS. Arrogance is confidence that is snuffed out,
resuscitated,
and is never quite the same again.

> Weaker and meaner.

ARCHITECT. Unrecognizable.

CHORUS. Arrogance is what happens to a confident girl
when the whole world, or even just her mother,
tells her that she's nothing and she finds out
she's really something.

CHORUS. Really something.

ARCHITECT. I'll tell myself
it's no big tragedy that I rarely sketch anymore.
It's my choice, really.
You tell me to get a nanny.

CHORUS. "If you want to . . ."

ARCHITECT. As if what I want ever has anything to do with what I get.

I want to slice myself in half,
one side for my work,
one side for my children.

But that's too difficult to articulate so I tell you—

CHORUS. "I don't want to."

ARCHITECT. Men like Gehry and you, half-breed husband, design
museums
I wipe asses,
because they are the most beautiful perfect little asses imaginable,
and no one would WIPE THEM THE WAY I DO!

I content myself with helping you,
showing you where you falter, and you falter often enough.

CHORUS. "It's not sound. It's not sound,
and it's being built on a fault line.

Was your head up your ass when you did this?!

Or was it up someone else's?"

ARCHITECT. But I can't say that.
I'll have to be vague and suggest—

CHORUS. —a reinforcement or two.

ARCHITECT. I have to be careful not to bruise your ego.

CHORUS. Because we all know what happens when that happens.

ARCHITECT. You have your women,
but you never leave me,
That's cold comfort and I'm in the winter of my life.

CHORUS. But it's comfort just the same.

ARCHITECT. I'm like cement.
You pour me, I fit the mold of a wife, and stay until I crack.
I'll smile softly when I overhear them saying about me—

CHORUS. "She's an architect in her own right too."

ARCHITECT. In my own right, they will say,
    which always makes me think,
    my relationship with you makes—

CHORUS. —what is my right—

ARCHITECT. —somehow in question.

CHORUS. Why must one speak in words when she thinks in images?

ARCHITECT. Now the last minion steps out.
    You've sent them away without a word, Half-Breed.
    You lift your head from my page,
    weighing your words so carefully
    you can't come up with ones.

CHORUS. Welcome to how I feel all the time.

ARCHITECT. Your eyes finally meet mine.
    You tilt your head so slightly again,
    (*Chorus cocks their head to the left side for a moment*)
    look at me sideways
    and smile.

CHORUS. I can make you fall in love with me—

ARCHITECT. —and never feel secure in that love.
    I know that, if I encourage you, twenty years—

CHORUS. —from now—

ARCHITECT. —I will be sitting on the toilet
    in a hotel ballroom
    on the night you get some award
    for a project I did at least half the work on.
    Two girls will enter,
    about the age I am now,
    and one will be bragging in a sing-song voice to the other . . .

CHORUS. "I did it with him again on Sunday. In his office."

ARCHITECT. She won't have to say his name for me to know,
    which him she's singing about.

My half-breed husband
My mind will flip back to Sunday afternoon
when you said—

CHORUS. "I'm going to the office to finish up the project I'm working on."

ARCHITECT. Sunday is my day.
You take the children and I do my work
But I don't insist, you usually give me my Sundays.
I don't complain because the one time I tried.
You told me—

CHORUS. "Give me a fucking break.
Whose work pays the bills? Who pays the bills?"

ARCHITECT. I don't cost much to feed nowadays.
You're a big fat motherfucker now.
I weigh much less than the day you married me
because I have to stay
thin,
gaunt,
hollow.

CHORUS. Take up less space.
Take up less space

ARCHITECT. I stay thin so no one can say that I'm not trying!

CHORUS. To be in control.
Stay in control.
Who pays the bills?

ARCHITECT. If I was articulate, I would say
"I do."
I organize every aspect your life
so you can do your life's work.
But I know that's not what you mean.

Most people ask for one day of rest, I beg for one day of work
and you—

CHORUS. —can't give it to me!

ARCHITECT. But I don't complain on that Sunday
    and you go to work on—

CHORUS. —your project—

ARCHITECT. and that was the day I slapped my daughter hard
    across the face.
    (*All four actors making a slapping sound at the same time*)
    She gave me a look that said—

CHORUS. "I did not deserve that."

ARCHITECT. I will not forget that you did that to me and I didn't
    deserve it.

CHORUS. Not even the day you die."

ARCHITECT. That was last Sunday.
    I step out of the toilet.
    and make my way to the table of—

CHORUS. —honor.

ARCHITECT. You smile when our eyes meet from across the room.
    I think of what you told me on the way over here.

CHORUS. "My wife's still a pretty woman.
    It's not a boast, it's a fact."

ARCHITECT. I smiled stiffly.
    I hate it when people talk about me in front of me in the third
    person.
    Like the client we had over last week who,
    when I—

CHORUS. —stood to serve—

ARCHITECT. —dessert, said to you—

CHORUS. "You've got a regular geisha girl, don't you?"

ARCHITECT. I think he meant—

CHORUS. —harem girl.

ARCHITECT. But he said—

CHORUS. —geisha girl.

ARCHITECT. But if the difference doesn't matter to him,
   why should it matter to me?
   I even smiled, took it as a kind of complement.
   It's been many years since I thought of myself as—

CHORUS. —a girl.

ARCHITECT. I sit next to you.
   You can tell I'm upset.

CHORUS. Everyone can tell. You cock . . .

ARCHITECT. . . . your head to the side,
   questioning at first—

CHORUS. "What's wrong, honey?"

ARCHITECT. Then you see the look in my eyes, you don't ask again
   You . . .

CHORUS. Let it go.

ARCHITECT. And when I ride in silence on the way home
   and slam the door behind me
   I say out loud, something articulate,
   something that's been crystallizing in my mind
   since practically the day I met you.

   "I just want you to know—

CHORUS. —you son of a white bitch—

ARCHITECT. —without me, you might be something
   but you wouldn't be much."

   I'll tell myself to just lighten up and get over it.

CHORUS. There are people dying in Palestine.
   There are people dying in Palestine.

ARCHITECT. And I very easily could have been one of them.
   In marriage, there are worse crimes than infidelity.

CHORUS. He still falls asleep stroking your cheek.

ARCHITECT. I now even think it's endearing that he is jealous of my
work,
that he needs all my time and attention when he's home.

CHORUS. Like a child.

ARCHITECT. Soon enough, I'll be staring at you in your coffin.
Our three-quarter breed children will be crying . . .

CHORUS. "Baba!"

ARCHITECT. Because I made our three-quarter breed children use
the Arabic words for family members. Always.
They'll be screaming . . .

CHORUS. "Excuse me, would you like to go somewhere and *(pause)*
have coffee?"

ARCHITECT. Your question interrupts my thoughts, Half-Breed.
It startles me.
I didn't notice you were done looking at my exercise and hold-
ing it out for me to take back.

I think to myself—
Why are you talking to me?
Can't you see I'm in the middle of envisioning our future together?

I realize that I've done it again.

In my mind, I planned a whole life—

CHORUS. Birth, death and remembrance—

ARCHITECT.—with a guy
before he even asks me out.
Why does my mind flip a lifetime ahead?

We might go out and not hit it off.

I mean, for God's sake, you could be gay
I could be reading all the signs wrong.
It has happened to me before.

You've just asked me for coffee.
Why am I imagining your funeral
with our children standing before you screaming

CHORUS. "Baba!"

ARCHITECT. Why am I sure
as I stare into your eyes, trying to decide if I want to have coffee
with you,
that, if I say yes, one day
I'll be staring at your corpse in your coffin,
thinking a thousand thoughts,
not the least of which will be—

"There lies your body. Your flesh,
that you valued more than my heart, my love, our family, and
my life.
Let. It. Rot!"

Pause.

CHORUS. "I said, would you like to have coffee with me?"

Pause.

ARCHITECT. "No! No! No!"

CHORUS. "Tea?"

ARCHITECT. And I decline that too, saying I have to go right back
home.
We worked together for a summer and he's always—

CHORUS. —polite—

ARCHITECT. —but he never offers to quench thirsts with me again.
(*Pause*) Then, I was murdered.
And, as a result, I died.
Do you understand now?
Do you see now that she's lying?

DELILAH and TAMAM. No.

AIESHA. Ha! I knew you were a half-wit.

ARCHITECT (*to Delilah and Tamam*). She's going to try to distract you
    She's going to keep you here.

AIESHA. All right you two.
    Either you're staying with her
    or you're coming with me.

ARCHITECT. Stop pretending you're going to
    eventually lead them through that door.

AIESHA. Stop pretending you know something about me.

DELILAH (*to Tamam*). What should we do?

ARCHITECT (*to Aiesha*). I'm getting to how I know who you are.

TAMAM (*to Delilah*). Listen.

TAMAM and DELILAH. What does this encounter with a half-breed
    have to do with this woman?
    Why shouldn't we trust her?
    Can you tell us in a way we will understand?

ARCHITECT. Yes.
    My contract with the Half-Breed's company was not renewed.
    I was told I was not a team player.

CHORUS. Five years passed.

ARCHITECT. I stayed friends with his assistant so I could keep tabs on
    Half-Breed.
    On my thirty-fifth birthday, I called him.

    You see I had promised myself
    If I'm not married by thirty-five,
    I would stop being precious and just have sex
    with a man I wanted to love me,
    whether or not he did.

CHORUS. Why thirty-five?

ARCHITECT. Because it's no longer cute
    that you're a virgin at thirty-five.
    I went to lunch with his assistant that week.
    He was away at a business trip.

I stole the number of his hotel from his assistant's desk.
When she was in the bathroom.

CHORUS. I called him.

ARCHITECT. I told him my name. He said—

CHORUS. "You're the girl who worked as an assistant that summer,
   who walked into the interview
   with a plan for a museum,
   right?"

ARCHITECT. "I want to come see you. I want to come stay with you."

CHORUS. "Get on the next flight."

ARCHITECT. And I do so.
   I've got two fantasies, day-mares, about flying.

CHORUS. First fantasy I have as I'm going through the security check
   on my way to see Half-breed.

ARCHITECT. It's totally stupid, okay?
   But you've got to understand,
   I grew up watching American movies
   and so I've got this fantasy.
   That I'll be on a flight, okay, and it'll be hijacked by my people,
   Arabs.

CHORUS. Sounds stupid.

ARCHITECT. I already admitted it was.
   But in my fantasy
   I'll hear the shouts first in my mother's tongue
   that my mother never bothered to teach me to speak.

And I understand what they're saying:
I realize the power of language—
that being able to listen and understand is a different kind of
articulacy
and one I possess.

Like how I can't speak Arabic, but I can comprehend—

CHORUS. —and know what's going on before everyone else does.

ARCHITECT. In my fantasy,
all the men are fit and handsome.
They don't intend to kill anybody.
They've lived lives that would break the hardest of men.
They only want to be heard.
Dramatic music will play.

I will stand up,
perfectly manicured and dressed to the meet the press,
my hair will have obeyed me that day
and be everything that I had no choice but to want to be.

CHORUS. Light and straight.

ARCHITECT. I will say in perfect Arabic to the men.

CHORUS. But you can't speak Arabic?

ARCHITECT. This is my fantasy, goddamn it.
And in it, I speak perfect Arabic.
I will stand up
and talk those men out of their plans.

I will tell them
"So what if terror is the only thing that brought down apartheid
in South Africa?"

CHORUS. "So what if the Black Panther Movement got civil rights
workers moving
just a little bit quicker?

So what if the American government plants puppet leaders
who are corrupt and corrupting in our countries,
and kill hundreds of thousands of us
when those leaders don't do
what they say
when they say it?"

ARCHITECT. I would say to them—
"You're hijacking this plane full of people who are ignorant,
who are looking at you and saying—

CHORUS. 'Why are they trying to hurt me? What kind of people could do such violent, cruel things?' "

ARCHITECT. They don't know that it's the kind of people
their government has been doing
just as violent, cruel things to
in their name for generations.

Maybe they don't care.

But they're not worth killing yourself over.
They call us terrorists, they are wrong.
We're too good a people to do such harm.

I would tell them
I am a Palestinian.

I lived like an Arab in America.

I even only dated my own kind,
because I wanted someone who understood
the first words my family taught me to mean love.

CHORUS. *Ha-beeb-tea.*

ARCHITECT. Even after I realized,
just because a man knows the right words
doesn't mean that he will say them
and even if he says them,
it doesn't mean that he means them.
I will tell them.

CHORUS. I was never ashamed of who I was.

ARCHITECT. I knew I had to synthesize all the signals about who I was
in a way
that made me not want to be anything else.

I knew if I was not proud to be a Palestinian,
I could not live a life with dignity.
I knew if I did not I love my people, no one would.
I would tell them all this—

CHORUS. —and more.

ARCHITECT. And, when I tell them about my life, it will seem like it
 has a relevence,
 a grace, an arc.

CHORUS. A worth—

ARCHITECT. —that I didn't realize it had before.
 They will realize it too.

 I would no longer resent being a bridge between two cultures,
 or ask myself . . .

CHORUS. "What does a bridge ever do except get stepped on?"

ARCHITECT. Because I was so articulate in my perfect Arabic,
 the plane would touch down safely.

 All the Americans in the plane would listen to the grievances of
 the men who were willing to kill and die to be heard.

 They would be moved by stories of those they feared.

 In fact, they'll refuse to get off of the plane,
 until Palestinians are allowed the right to self-determination,
 Iraqis are not killed so their oil can be stolen.

 The people on the plane don't buy the crap
 they try to sell us
 about trying to secure human rights . . .

 having the gall to use human rights—
 as an excuse to bomb those human beings

 while being allies—

CHORUS. —bedfellows—

ARCHITECT. —with the oppressive Saudi royal-pain-in-the-ass regime
 because—

CHORUS. —they give us their juice.

ARCHITECT. When all those conditions are met, everyone on the
 plane leaves safely.

There will be a movie made about me.
I would end up on Oprah, telling my story.

CHORUS. I will be articulate.

ARCHITECT. One of the audience members will tell me—

CHORUS. "Julia Roberts does a great job playing you in the movie.
I'm glad she acknowledged you at the Academy Awards.
But I've got to say that,
We, the PTA board members of Lansing, Michigan,
think you're even prettier than Julia is."

ARCHITECT. Of course, I'll blush and smile benevolently and Oprah
will say—

CHORUS. "More importantly, she's also a brilliant architect."

ARCHITECT. But she won't have to say "in her own right."

Before the first commerical break,
it'll be clear that Oprah and I are now best friends.

I'll let her announce that I've been commissioned to design
the new United Nations building
since the old one obviously wasn't engineered to work right.

CHORUS. It had the master bedroom syndrome.

ARCHITECT. And, in my fantasy, the love of my life
who may or may not be the Half-Breed,
because maybe when my people are no longer under siege,
no longer a dying breed,
I won't feel I owe it to my people to mate with my own kind.

I'll be free in the most important way it is to be free.
I'll be free to love who I love.

And whoever that man who I love is,
he will be sitting in the audience.

Our eyes will connect for the slightest second
We'll remember—

CHORUS. —we don't have to stay here much longer.
 You and I, we will soon go somewhere else.

ARCHITECT. I'll feel a shot of warmth in me,
 like a dying fire that with one breath he can keep aglow.

 Like Oprah

 I'll live with the man I love
 but I won't need to marry.

CHORUS. Because I know he'll love me forever.
 Because he would never want to leave me.
 Because some things don't change!

ARCHITECT. I will be a hero like Dr. King or Gandhi
 But no one shoots me.

 Pause.

 Did everyone hear that? No one shoots me.
 That's not part of the fantasy I have as I go through the security
 check on my way to lose my virginity to the Half-Breed.

 I don't want to die that way.

CHORUS. Does anybody want to die that way?

ARCHITECT. I think what a stupid fantasy that is.
 I've clearly been watching too many American movies.

 I will refuse to watch the one on the flight.
 I think that to myself as I give the girl at the counter my ticket.

 I'm afraid to fly,
 though I do it every chance I get.
 So much of my life is lived in the space between—

CHORUS. —fear and desire.

ARCHITECT. It's kind of funny.
 Flying makes me understand—

CHORUS. —the allure of suicide.

ARCHITECT. I think to myself,
   "If this plane I'm on goes down, at least I won't
   have to finish that project I'm working on,
   or—

CHORUS. —wake up—

ARCHITECT. —sweaty
   with the knowledge
   it is possible that
   my ambition overreaches my abilities,
   or have to—

CHORUS. —face the fact—

ARCHITECT. —that the structures I build with my hands
   will never be like the ones I see in my head.
   Or that I'll die alone.

CHORUS. Or married to a man who makes me wish I was.

ARCHITECT. If the plane goes down, it'll be a—

CHORUS. —relief.

ARCHITECT. Mine will be a life full of potential—

CHORUS. —cut short—

ARCHITECT. —rather than a life fully realized and—

CHORUS. —found wanting.
   I won't have to work or face failure.

ARCHITECT. But if it were to go down, there is one thing I would
   regret."
   And that leads me to the next fantasy I have while settling in my
   seat
   on a plane
   which will take me to the place
   where I will lose my virginity to the Half-Breed.
   I look for the straps of my seat-belt.
   Knowing I'm a beast—

CHORUS. —animal—

ARCHITECT. —beast, but to have been a beast with only one back all
my life.
To die a virgin!

CHORUS. What a tragedy that would be.

ARCHITECT. Tell me about it.
So my fantasy as I strap my seat-belt on—

CHORUS. —click—

ARCHITECT.—is that if I somehow figure out that
this plane is going to crash.
And I realize I'm going to die a virgin.
I'd stomp up to the—

CHORUS. —cock—

ARCHITECT. —pit—
And who says language isn't everything?
And once I get to the

CHORUS. —cock—

ARCHITECT. —pit, I'd get on that loudspeaker and say,
"Unfasten your seatbelts—

CHORUS. Motherfuckers!

ARCHITECT. If this plane is going down,
someone is going down on me!"

CHORUS. But I never have the guts to act out my fantasies.
So even if the plane went down—

ARCHITECT. —by accident—

CHORUS. —technical failure instead of the emotional kind—

ARCHITECT. —I probably would not go up to the—

CHORUS. —cock—

ARCHITECT. —pit and say that.
  I would have sat in my seat like I —

CHORUS. —sat in the seat in disbelief—

ARCHITECT. —when I actually did hear those men shouting in my
    mother's tongue
    and it wasn't a fantasy.

  It was real.
  It was my life.
  It was awful.

  I knew what they were saying and I knew what they were doing—

CHORUS. —before anyone else did.
  Though my mother's tongue is not my tongue.

ARCHITECT. One of them passed by my row and I thought to myself
    as if I was an American with ancestors on the Mayflower
    and had no understanding of America's history
    in the Middle East.

  I thought to myself—

CHORUS. "What kind of person could do such a thing?"

ARCHITECT. The one who ran past me was chubby—

CHORUS. —like my brother.

ARCHITECT. Stupid me, always thinking—

CHORUS.—inappropriate thoughts.

ARCHITECT. Thoughts that make me thank heaven I am so inarticulate.

CHORUS. As the man tied up a stewardess . . .

ARCHITECT. I was thinking, "I like chubby men."

  I don't trust men if they're too thin.
  I don't trust men
  if they aren't susceptible
  to the least pernicious of appetites.

CHORUS. I think you just don't trust men.

ARCHITECT. He passed my row and our eyes met.
     Perhaps because I was the only one looking up,
     not crying.
     He froze.
     The way Arabs outside the Arab world do
     when they recognize that someone here—
     (*steps towards Aiesha, forcing her to take a step backwards*)

CHORUS. —is one of my kind.

ARCHITECT. He waited for me to speak
     and when I couldn't,
     he went on his way without a backward glance.

     From the look in his eyes,
     I lost all hope that any of us would live.

     I took out my sketchbook
     and sketched for the first time—

CHORUS. —without fear.

ARCHITECT. I took out my sketchbook,
     did my work
     and saw that it was good.

     I'm here to find that man who passed me and knew I was an
     Arab.

     He's in that room in front of us.
     I know it.

     Just like I know that I could have stopped him
     before he did what he did
     if I had the right words.

CHORUS. There are no right words.

ARCHITECT. Goddamn it. There are!

CHORUS. Don't blame yourself.

ARCHITECT. What's the point of being articulate when no one
    can hear anything they aren't ready to hear?
    It's not about blame.

    It's not about blame.
    It's about knowing
    that there are always words—

CHORUS. Words that work like spells—

ARCHITECT.—something you can say
    that will stop someone from doing something—

CHORUS. —awful.

ARCHITECT. We tell ourselves that there aren't such words,
    but that's because we don't
    know them
    and probably can't
    know them,
    but it doesn't mean they don't exist.

    I doesn't mean I couldn't have used them then.
    I still want to know what those words are,
    so I can be articulate.
    The man who killed me is the only one who can tell me—

CHORUS. —what those words are.

ARCHITECT. I'm here to ask him.
    They better let me in
    If they give me trouble while I'm trying to get into the martyrs'
    room to see him, I will tell them.

    I died a virgin, but that was just bad luck.

    While I was alive, I did the hardest thing imaginable,
    more wonderful than a million buildings that will one day crumble.

    I am a woman who was born with a good heart
    and I designed and executed my life in a way that made sure
    that's how I would stay.

The image I had in my mind
during the last moment I was alive
was of your face.

I died thinking I hope people won't see me where I saw you.
I know your story, Aiesha, and it isn't the one you've been telling.

TAMAM and DELILAH. What is it?

AIESHA. She's lying. She knows nothing about me.

ARCHITECT. The night before I boarded that plane and died on it,
 I had insomnia.
 It was my—

CHORUS. —last night as a virgin.

ARCHITECT. Or so I believed.
 I couldn't sleep.
 I was on my computer

CHORUS. —using search engines

ARCHITECT. to seek out the sites of hate that cry "Death to Arabs."

 Sites that call for the destruction of
 all the people who look and pray and love like I do.

 I seek out the places
 where people think it's amusing to
 tell stories of Palestinians like you
 and post your pictures and laugh and laugh and laugh.

CHORUS. How can you stand to look at those websites?

ARCHITECT. Because I need to remind myself that I am hated for
 committing no crime
 but being who I am.

 I look at those sites to remind myself that every breath I take is a
 victory,
 that the reason I work so hard at architecture—

CHORUS. —and drive myself to the point of collapse—

ARCHITECT. —is so I will one day create a work that defies gravity
   itself.
   And all who look upon it will say
   we can't possibly
   be known as the ones who discount—

CHORUS. —drive out, plunder, occupy, make invisible—

ARCHITECT. —people who can make things like that.
   I think, maybe, if I work hard enough.
   and create something worthwhile, something of value.

CHORUS. Something!

ARCHITECT. People
   might look at it
   and see—

CHORUS. Something—

ARCHITECT. —that makes them understand
   we are just as human, we exist, we matter.
   The number of our dead and dying will suddenly actually
   mean—

CHORUS. —something—

ARCHITECT. —because people like us will suddenly actually count.

ARCHITECT. Then, I remember I can't control what people will think.

   But I can point to the buildings I'll make and ask,
   "Do you want to be remembered
   as the murderers of people
   who make things like that?
   Ask yourself."

CHORUS. Answer me!

ARCHITECT. I go to those websites and check for updates to see what
   I am up against and sometimes I see stories like yours that read
   "Palestinian female suicide bomber's only victim is one of her
   own kind."

They show your picture and they show hers,
because they think its funny.
She was a little Palestinian girl

AIESHA. I didn't mean to kill her.
   I wanted to kill an enemy.
   Don't look to the specifics of my life
   to understand why I did it.

   Others around me had lived more terrible lives
   and still wanted to live.
   All I knew is I couldn't breathe.

CHORUS. No one hears our cries.

AIESHA. I can't breathe.

CHORUS. No control over our own destiny.

AIESHA. I can't breathe
   and if I can't breathe
   then no one should be allowed to breathe easy.
   But, when the time came, I was scared. I was so scared.
   I intended to get a crowd of children.
   I had seen too many of our own die to care for theirs,
   but —

Architect joins the chorus.

CHORUS. Timing is everything.

AIESHA. The crowd I was leaning towards suddenly moved away
   at the same second
   I detonated myself.
   They knew to get away, all except for this little girl with big black
   eyes
   and a heavy key around her neck.

CHORUS. She couldn't have been more than nine.

ARCHITECT. The website said seven.

CHORUS. Her mother took her with her across two hours of Israeli
   checkpoints,

so she could work as a maid.

ARCHITECT. Her mother was proud.

CHORUS. The women in the refugee camp thought she was arrogant.
    She never let them forget she was once richest girl in her town.

ARCHITECT. The town of Ras Abu Ammar. The town that no longer
    exists. Have you heard of it?

AIESHA. Of course.

ARCHITECT. It was the place this woman once lived in
    before her family fled to Gaza.
    She's only allowed to get near her town with a worker's permit.

CHORUS. She's only allowed to go back to be the maid.

ARCHITECT. She was proud.
    She hated to make her daughter
    watch her clean toilets.

    She named her only daughter Amal.

CHORUS. It means hope.

ARCHITECT. And she felt hope as she hung the heavy key of the door
    to the house
    she once lived in
    around her only daughter's neck.

    It didn't matter that the house no longer stood there.
    It was her house.
    Her daughter would know that—

CHORUS.—she had a house.

ARCHITECT. The mother hated to make her daughter
    watch her clean toilets.

    She hated it even more that day,
    because her daughter offered to help
    and, even though she said no, Amal took a dripping brush in
    her hand.

Amal's mother slapped her.
(*All four actresses clap their hands once while making a slapping motion.*)

Amal's mother thinks to herself as she watches at her daughter trying to swallow her tears—

CHORUS. "When my daughter grows up and can understand, I will apologize for that."

ARCHITECT. Amal's mother imagines how she will one day tell her daughter—
"Everything one cannot say with a mop in your hand
and work to be done—

CHORUS. —before the curfew is called."

ARCHITECT. But, years later, the mother
will still *be* sorry,
not just say or feel or act it—

CHORUS. —but become sorrow itself.

ARCHITECT. She imagines when Amal is sixteen or so,
they will be laughing.
Her mother will look at her and ask—

CHORUS. "Do you remember that time I slapped you for no good reason?"

ARCHITECT. Amal will shake her head as if to say—

CHORUS. "No, I don't remember. No, that didn't happen. No."

ARCHITECT. And Amal's mother will tell her—

CHORUS. "You did not deserve that.
Is it possible for you to see that as something I did once,
not someone who I was?"

AIESHA. Amal will nod
and the mother of hope
will know that she taught her daughter the most important lesson,

the lesson you have to learn
to survive this life with your humanity intact.

CHORUS. She taught her daughter—

AIESHA. —how to forgive.

ARCHITECT. That is how I will apologize to Amal when she grows older,
when she can understand.
It's not something Amal's mother normally allowed.
But on that day, she sent her outside with the teenager of the
house,
who doted on her . . .

CHORUS. Look at those big black eyes.

ARCHITECT. The teenager and her friends bought Amal a falafal
sandwich,
because what else do you feed little Arab children?

Amal saw the janitor at the shop was Palestinian.
She smiled at him,
so he would recognize that she was one too.
The man didn't smile back.
Amal thinks to herself as she took the first bite of her falafal
sandwhich—

CHORUS. "When I grow up, I will remember what it's like to be a
child.
When I grow up, I will greet children as if they are people.
When I grow up and have children, if people don't greet them, I
won't speak to them either."

ARCHITECT. Amal thinks the sandwich the teenager gave her was lousy,
not enough parsley.
But she didn't want to hurt her feelings.
so she thanked her
and forced herself to eat it.

They bought her an ice-cream cone—

AIESHA. And they ran and left her for dead when they saw me coming.
I don't think they meant to, but that's what they did.

It was too late to stop everything,
the one step I took back was my last.
The little girl didn't understand she was going to die.
She smiled at me.

ARCHITECT. The last image I had in my mind
before I died was of her picture next to yours.
And underneath it were the words—

CHORUS. "Finally, they are killing one another."

ARCHITECT. I thought to myself—will they put my picture next to
the man who ran past my row?
Under our pictures, will they write the words . . .

CHORUS. "Finally, they are killing one another."

TAMAM. So, the reason the martyrs don't want you in there
has nothing to do with you being a woman.

DELILAH. It's because you're no good at being no good.

ARCHITECT. No. That is no room for martyrs.
Or maybe it is?
We won't know till we go in that door.
But we can't believe what we've been told.
This can't be heaven.
Heaven is not a place where people segregate themselves
according to religion or race.

TAMAM. We're in hell.
Hell is a place where we have to look for the ones we lost.

DELILAH. No. Earth.
Earth is a place where—there is a door—
where no one who goes in comes out.

The lights should shift to become unnaturally bright.

AIESHA. No, you're in heaven.
Stupid fools.
Heaven. Doesn't it look like heaven to you?

CHORUS. Heaven is not a place you have to be convinced that you're in.
Heaven is not a place where people don't know the answers.

Half the lights on the stage should dim.

AIESHA. You know a lot about what heaven is not,
But you don't know what heaven is.

Neither do I.
The only thing real is that door.

I don't know what's beyond it.
I've never been.
If you don't spend your life asking hard questions,
you spend your eternity with no answers.

My job—which I took upon myself—is to distract you from moving forward.

CHORUS. You keep people here.

AIESHA. Each of the groups of women here has—

CHORUS. —someone like you.

AIESHA. Someone from their own race.

CHORUS. Someone they feel they can trust.

AIESHA. Someone who keeps them in line.
It usually works.
My job is to keep Palestinian women here.
You want real answers,
First ask harder questions.
I try to make each of you—

CHORUS. —spend an eternity—

AIESHA. —asking the easy one.

ARCHITECT. Aren't they just a little different? Greedy? Backward?

TAMAM. Am I supposed to feel sorry for what my great-grandparents
did before I was born?

DELILAH. Isn't the only way we can assure we're never oppressed
again is to oppress other people?

ARCHITECT. Wouldn't they do the same to us the minute they had
the chance?

CHORUS (*without Aiesha*). Why is violence only wrong when we use it?

CHORUS (*all four women*). Isn't violence the only thing these people
understand?

AIESHA. I keep you asking the wrong questions

CHORUS. So, we'll stay with you.

AIESHA. Instead of going on the only quest
to find the answer to the only question.

CHORUS (*all four women*). How do you survive in a violent world and
not be violent?

AIESHA. Key word . . .

CHORUS (*all four women*). Survive.

ARCHITECT. This place feels too much like limbo.
I've been limbo in all my life.
I'll go first, you two can follow.

DELILAH. Well, if Samson really wanted to see me,
he would seek me out.
Maybe he's angry.
I would be.
You can forgive someone for
breaking every promise
except those whispered in the dark.

TAMAM. Yes. I'm not sure I should go with you either.
How would it look?
My brother knows it's *his* duty
to come find me.
To take care of me.

ARCHITECT. What?!

TAMAM. You know, like a man should.

ARCHITECT (*to Aiesha*). Then, you come with me.

AIESHA. I'm not allowed in there.

ARCHITECT. Who says?

AIESHA. I say.
    What I did was right.
    I'm not going to a place where I might have to question that.

ARCHITECT. Do you know why I keep searching?
    What I need to tell the man who murdered me is that,
    "They rate our lives at nothing,
    when we kill ourselves in the hope of hurting them,
    we show that we agree,
    that we feel our lives are dispensable.'

AIESHA. *Our* lives?!
    Ha!
    He's going to laugh at you.
    What have you suffered?
    Did someone make fun of your parents' accents?
    Didn't get an award or two because of racism?
    Poor you!

    Live my life on earth
    in my dirty, crowded refugee camp
    in the place where your parents—

CHORUS (*all four women*). Ran and ran and ran like cowards from—

AIESHA. —spend one day
    Live like that for one day
    knowing that the people—

TAMAM and DELILAH. —you love most—

AIESHA. —have no choice
    but to live like that
    every second of their living lives.
    Then, see if you think limbo

is the only honest place to be.
I am no privileged little—

CHORUS (*all four women, Architect looks down while she says it*).
Hypocrite.

AIESHA. You can go around searching for heaven,
I wasn't born to have that luxury.
Maybe that door is back to earth.
Who knows?
Maybe you and me would return there together.
Maybe then we could see
which of us does any goddamned good?
Down there I didn't even have the chance to ask
who makes more of a difference,
in the long run

CHORUS (*without Architect*). Artists or militants?

AIESHA. People like me or people like you?
Because I never had the chances
you had to do anything different
than what I did.
Unlike you.

CHORUS (*without Architect*). If only everyone had the chance to be a
hypocrite!

AIESHA. So don't you judge me.
I don't get to make pretty drawings and such . . .
and pray people
will maybe look
and maybe see
and maybe think of me as human.
No.

CHORUS (*without Architect*). I am human.
I will be treated as such.

AIESHA. Or else,

ARCHITECT. My life and what I do with it is worth something.

AIESHA. Because you had a life worth living.

ARCHITECT. I can't stay here in limbo.
I've been in limbo all my life.

CHORUS (*Aiesha, Delilah, Tamam, chanting*). Here I only have unanswered questions.
Because, there, 1 only had unquestioned answers.

ARCHITECT (*speaking with resolve as she exits*). Hands, movement,
change.
Hands, movement, change.

The three other women watch her exit.

CHORUS (*all three women*). What is the point of the revolution that
begins with the little hand?
Any little hand?
(*Each lifts her right hand and looks at it*) This little hand?

Delilah and Tamam then look at each other.

AIESHA (*returns to chanting in a drone-like manner*). Unanswered questions.

CHORUS (*all three women*). Unquestioned answers.
I do.

TAMAM. No one.

AIESHA (*at the same time*). Someone.

*Aiesha gives Tamam a dirty look. Tamam makes a motion like "What do
you want from me?" then rejoins the chorus.*

CHORUS (*all three women*). Good dead.

CHORUS (*all three women*). I do

DELILAH. No one.

AIESHA (*at the same time*). Someone.

CHORUS (*all three women*). Dead good.
What is the point of the revolution that begins with the little hand?
Any little hand? This little hand?

TAMAM. Waitaminute. Waitaminute
  I know the answer to that.

DELILAH. Answer to what?

TAMAM. *The* question.
  What's the point of the revolution that begins with the little
  hand?

AIESHA. You can't know the answer.

DELILAH. Yes, of course.
  The point is
  (*pause*)
  it pushes,

TAMAM. —forces—

DELILAH and TAMAM. —the big hand forward!

AIESHA. With enough movement, the times will change.

TAMAM and DELILAH. Right!

CHORUS (*all three women*). Little hands, enough movement, times
  change.
  Hands, movement, change.
  Wait!

The End

Liana Pai as Yuki and Billy Crudup as Robert. Photograph by Carol Rosegg.

AMERICA DREAMING

A PLAY WITH MUSIC

BY

CHIORI MIYAGAWA

MUSIC BY TAN DUN

I have two second languages—Japanese and English. My first language may have been burnt in bonfires all across California in 1942 when my people were terrified of being identified as an enemy; they set on fire books written in Japanese, letters from Japan and family photographs. During this time, if an Issei (immigrant) mother said to her Nisei (American-born) daughter, "Nothing bad can ever happen to you. You're an American citizen," she would have been wrong. But do I truly have the right to claim these women as my people? After all, my parents and grandparents were nowhere near the bonfires. They were in the snow country of Nagano. Racism and the US government's inability to distinguish Japanese in Japan from Japanese and Japanese-Americans in the US caused 112,000 people to be uprooted and incarcerated in concentration camps during World War II. Yet today I want to be both. Even though my English is imperfect and my Japanese is that of a child, I want to claim things old and beautiful as my heritage and have the freedom to loudly criticize the US government as my right as a citizen. Unlike those who came long before me, the fear of a collective malice has not crushed me, though with the Patriot Act I sense the danger just around the corner.

Set against a backdrop of revisionist history, *America Dreaming* is a time-traveling love story. Yuki is an amalgamation of the confusions I have lived with all my adult life—being Japanese, being Japanese-American, being American, and yet not being able to declare that I'm a card-carrying member of any particular tribe. The entire story of the play happens in a few seconds when, at her wedding, Yuki hesitates to say "I do" to her fiancé Robert. At that moment, she is propelled into the past, a distorted version of American history, in which the Great Depression never happened, no government sponsored anti-Japanese hate campaign was launched, no war was fought in Vietnam. As an outsider, Yuki is the only person who can see the strange processions that represent truth in this false world. Time warps continuously and Robert appears, disappears and reappears in Yuki's whirlwind journey.

Interwoven in the fake events is Robert and Yuki's longing for each other, a love that seems impossible in any rendition of history. At the end of the journey, they move forward to 2094, where Yuki is incarcerated in a future camp for Japanese-Americans as Robert is preparing to go to war in the Pacific. Their love has become unsustainable because no lessons were ever learned from history. The very next moment, Yuki and Robert are back in the present, just before Yuki is to say "I do." Instead, she joins a madly dancing procession that is multi-racial multi-class, and finally, she understands, uniquely American.

By writing *America Dreaming*, I don't think I achieved the optimism and abandon that Yuki did. Years later, I'm still angry about the Executive Order 9066 that President Roosevelt signed, which made refugees out of my people. I set out to write a political play about America's shameful acts with *America Dreaming*, and ended up writing a personal story. There is a scene in which Yuki keeps sleeping and her brother David enters three times to wake her up: on December 7, 1941, except what struck Pearl Harbor was an atomic bomb; on July 20, 1969 when Armstrong landed on the moon, except it's Jupiter; and in present time when he calls Yuki a whore for betraying her culture. Obviously none of those things happened in my real life, but I now realize that I wrote an autobiography. I wrote about destruction, progress and love. I wrote that these aspects of humanity were all the same and that they were about me. By doing so, I think I wanted to forgive myself for not belonging, forgive the history of the land that I chose as my home. No, I'm not forgetting the crimes that my grandparents' generation committed in Asia before and during World War II. I have not written about it, so perhaps I'm not ready to forgive. And then there is Iraq. There is so much, so much, that is wrong about us.

Yet, I can still encounter countless languages, bend time, reverse memory, meet ghosts and make political statements, all from where I live. New York City. The city where I am allowed to be nothing and everything. I'm not free from my confusion and outrage, but I think Yuki is. She has been free since 1995 when Liana Pai (who played Yuki) danced off and left Billy Crudup (who played Robert) alone on the stage of the Vineyard Theatre.

AMERICA DREAMING was commissioned by Music-Theatre Group and premiered at Vineyard Theatre in co-production with Music-Theatre Group in December 1994, with the following cast: P. J. Brown, Shi-Zheng Chen, Billy Crudup, Joel de la Fuente, Beth Dixson, Ann Harada, Aleta Hayes, Michael Lewis, Liana Pai and Virginia Wing with musicians David Cossin and Elise Morris and with the following design/artistic team: Scenic Design by Riccardo Hernandez; Costume Design by Michael Krass; Lighting Design by Michael Chybowski; Stage Management by Crystal Huntington; Music Direction by Bruce Gremo; Choreography by Doug Varone and Direction by Michael Mayer.

CHARACTERS

CASTING REQUIREMENTS	4 women and 2 men
YUKI	Young Asian American woman
ROBERT	Young Caucasian man
PROFESSOR/NEIGHBOR/ OLD WOMAN/ENSEMBLE	Older Caucasian woman
DAVID/MAN LISTENING TO THE RADIO/WOMAN IN THE DESERT/MAN AT THE BANQUET/ENSEMBLE	Young Asian American man
WOMAN IN THE DESERT/ WOMAN AT THE BANQUET/ WOMAN LISTENING TO THE RADIO/ENSEMBLE	Asian American woman
WOMAN IN THE DESERT/ WOMAN AT THE CAFÉ/WOMAN AT THE BANQUET/ENSEMBLE	Older Asian American woman
WAITER/ENSEMBLE	Young Caucasian man
PRIEST/MAN AT THE CAFÉ/ENSEMBLE	Older Caucasian man
CHORUS OF THREE SINGERS	
TWO LIVE MUSICIANS	

Note: The dialogue and lyrics in quotation marks are based on interviews, found texts and historical documents.

The piece is meant to move swiftly. Lighting should be used to signal changes in both time and place.

The chorus should be interracial in a way that reflects the different ethnicities present in the US. They sing three love-song versions of "America the Beautiful," each with a different melody, and Yuki sings one love-song version of "The Star Spangled Banner" also set to a different melody.

The chorus participates in all the processions and functions as ensemble players.

In the original co-production at the Vineyard Theatre with Music-Theatre Group in January 1995, director Michael Mayer chose to use minimal sets and a sand floor to create the sense of a universal location and underscore the disjunctions of time and space that occur throughout the play.

Each scene is discrete in time and place. Scenes contain false memories, historical inaccuracies and fragments of truth.

Scene 1

Pipe organ church music.

Brilliant lights up.

There is a wedding in the center: An Asian American woman in a simple modern white wedding dress and a Caucasian man in a dark suit. Upstage, there is a priest.

Music stops abruptly.

PRIEST. Dearly beloved, we are gathered here today to join this man . . .

Sudden music, mostly percussion.

A procession—of characters who will appear later in the play—goes by, dancing wildly. Only Yuki sees the procession.

Music stops abruptly.

PRIEST. . . . and this woman in holy matrimony. Repeat after me.

Yuki coughs. Lights change.

The first love song. The words are that of "America the Beautiful."

Scene 2

Spotlights upon Yuki and Robert sitting at school desks. A university classroom. Yuki and Robert talk to each other.

YUKI. When I was in junior high, I often stayed up late to study. Mostly to impress my parents. Those nights my mother made me midnight snacks. One of my favorites was a slice of white bread dipped in milk and egg and pan-fried. I ate it with soy sauce. It wasn't until many years later that I realized what she made for me was French toast and I was supposed to eat it with syrup. I don't think my mother knew either. Today, I still have the urge to pour soy sauce on my French toast but I know now that it's wrong and I will be punished for wanting such a thing.

ROBERT. I'm interested in trying Japanese food. It looks pretty. I would like to take you out on your birthday. When is your birthday?

YUKI. I'm uncomfortable on my birthdays. It's the one special day out of the 365 ordinary days you should be guaranteed love. But birthdays always make me unhappy. I test the universe by not announcing to anyone that my birthday is coming up. It's a trivial social ritual anyway, I think, on the morning of my birthday. I don't buy into it. Yet I can't believe I get only one birthday card, no phone calls and no surprise party. This is injustice. I'm entitled. I don't even like the one card I got. I dress up but the black dress doesn't fit right today, and I even notice a faint stain on my chest. I feel like crying, but I don't know why. Is it because my dress is ruined? Or because I realize that the universe is so enormous and there is no guarantee. . .

ROBERT. Happy birthday, Yuki. I want to take you out of the universe. Take you out of the loneliness. Take you out to dinner. I got you a present. A teacup. Blue. I know the colors you like. They are my colors.

YUKI. No. They are my colors. Different.

ROBERT. Blue.

Lights up on the rest of the classroom. Students are taking notes.

PROFESSOR. Seventeenth-century Puritans held that marriage was a civil contract which could be broken.

YUKI. What are you afraid of most?

ROBERT. Running out of time.

YUKI. I'm afraid of dying, too. Every night as I fall asleep, my heart feels like a cold stone sinking down my body and I'm scared I won't ever wake up.

ROBERT. I will be there every morning to wake you up. I will make sure you wake up every morning.

PROFESSOR. Divorce was permissible on several grounds including adultery, long absence, and cruelty.

YUKI. It's lonely here, isn't it?

ROBERT. Let's go have Japanese food. I'll like it. I know I will.

YUKI. I'll teach you how to use *ohashi* if you promise not to pour soy sauce over white rice. Taste the rice. White rice.

PROFESSOR. However, only a few hundred colonists in the New World actually obtained divorces. Instead, thousands simply deserted their spouses.

ROBERT Let's live together. We love the same music. We'll spend cold nights in front of a fireplace, listening to our music. I love cold nights. I will keep you warm and safe.

YUKI. It's not important that I don't know what music I like. It's not important that I'm afraid of cold nights. I won't be lonely anymore. You will make it all right.

They kiss passionately. Time warps.

PROFESSOR. In principle, both men and women could obtain divorces, but in practice, "Any state has the power to exclude an undesirable immigration."

Only Yuki notices the shifts of subject matter and time period in Professor's lecture.

STUDENT 1. "That is founded in natural law."

PROFESSOR. So there existed, not surprisingly, a sexual double standard. "It is based, of course, upon the right of a state to preserve itself. The American people consist largely of the Caucasian race."

STUDENT 1. "They assimilate."

YUKI (*alarmed*). Robert?

PROFESSOR. "As a result?"

STUDENT 2. "There is a strong and a composite race known as the American people." But what about homosexuality in the colonial world?

PROFESSOR. In every colony, homosexual activity was a capital offense. At least five men were executed during this time. And "the Chinese are an undesirable immigration because?"

STUDENT 1. "They are incapable of that assimilation."

YUKI (*in a panic*). Robert. Robert!

ROBERT. You and me against the world. Hey, maybe you'd like to bleach your hair a bit. You'll look beautiful with light hair.

STUDENT 2. "There has been in this state no law forbidding the intermarriage of whites and Chinese."

STUDENT 1. "Until this last year, 1900, when the legislature enacted a law adding the word 'Mongolian' to that of 'Negro and Mulatto,' forbidding intermarriage."

PROFESSOR. "I am informed by the Police Department and by the Chinese Mission that there were a few of such marriages."

STUDENT 2. "Their children have invariably been degenerates."

PROFESSOR. Yes.

Lights change.

The classroom disappears.

Scene 3

Music of the wind.

Desert. Women come in and set up the tea ceremony. One of the women is the same actor who will later appear as Yuki's brother. This group of women should be cast non-traditionally. The woman who sings is African American. They are wearing kimono, and they perform in silence for a few minutes. Yuki watches.

WOMAN 2. Bad things are happening in the world you know. I hear in Germany, Jews are put in concentration camps. (*It's obvious she doesn't know what that means.*) I hear Jews are dirty and corrupt. That's why they are dangerous.

WOMAN 1. Concentration camps. In *The Webster's Dictionary* it means: "A camp where persons as prisoners of war, political prisoners, or refugees are detained or confined."

WOMAN 3. "Race prejudice, war hysteria and a failure of political leadership."

Women notice Yuki.

WOMAN 1. We have company. Would you like some tea?

YUKI. Where am I . . . (*finding herself in a fictitious World War II period*).

WOMAN 3. This is Manzanar, California.

WOMAN 1. Please join us for some *ocha*. We are the Japanese Picture Brides' Club. We meet once a week for tea. It's 1942. This is the best time of our lives.

YUKI. Picture brides?

WOMAN 2. Yes. What is the correct term? Oh, yes, "an uncivilized 'Asiatic' custom." (*She is proud that she remembered this.*)

WOMAN 3. Life wasn't any better in Japan. I was already twenty-nine and not yet married. My uncle sent my picture to California to a man who was lonely and looking for a Japanese wife. He liked my picture and sent for me. What could I have done?

WOMAN 2. It's a strange thing. My husband, he serves me red raw meat sometimes. Then he says I'm not one hundred per cent American if I don't eat it.

WOMAN 3. I live in a dirt-floor shack. But we have a bed, a stove and a table. Those are good things to have.

WOMAN 1. You are new. What does your husband do? A small fruit stand? A share-cropper? That's how it is.

WOMAN 2. Ohhh. You are new. Then you must have an English lesson by our kind neighbor.

A nice white woman enters with a shopping cart full of canned food. It's the professor from the previous scene. She takes out a milk crate and sets up some food.

NEIGHBOR. Now. This is tomato soup. Tomato. Say it. All right. This is Del Monte. Peas. Canned Mushrooms. Yummm. Chicken Noodle. Say it. Beef Vegetable. Say it. Aha. Can of tomatoes. Tomatoes. Say it. Oh, here is something special. Spam. S-P-A-M. It's made of . . . let's see . . . pork shoulder, ham, salt, sugar, and sodium nitrite. Yummmm. Spam. Say it. All right.

WOMAN 2. Thank you, thank you.

NEIGHBOR. Now, Let's learn how to read. Here, take this story. A fairy tale. I read. You follow. All right. (*Reads as if it is a bedtime story.*) Long ago, an old man and an old woman were happily in love. But they had no children. "All radios and lights of every kind in all evacuees quarters shall be turned off by the occupants not later than 10.30 p.m." The old man went to the mountains every day to cut wood and the old woman went to the river every day to do laundry. "The possession of or serving of foods which require heating or cooking will not be allowed in the quarters of the evacuees." One day, the old man found a little girl inside a radiant bamboo tree. On the same day, the old woman found a giant peach floating in the river. Inside was a little boy. "Parents are required to properly and thoroughly instruct their children in these regulations and the necessity for obedience thereto." OK, time's up.

WOMAN 3. Thank you. Goodbye.

Neighbor exits.

YUKI. Do you know about World War II? The relocation camps for Japanese Americans? In California and Arizona and . . . ?

WOMAN 1. No such thing. Couldn't happen. Everything is all right.

YUKI. What?

WOMAN 1. Don't be upset. Your husband is not as handsome as he looked in the picture when you decided to cross the ocean and marry the stranger, isn't that right? He is not even rich. He lied in his letters. *Shikataganai Shikataganai.* This is the fate of picture brides. You'll be all right.

YUKI. I'm sleepy.

WOMAN 3 (*sings as if it is a Japanese lullaby*). Bound to an enemy nation
    by strong ties of race
    a tightly knit group
    unassimilated
    racial
    racial
    strong ties of race

    a menace
    a menace
    has to be dealt with
    a frontier
    a frontier
    vulnerable to attack
    loyalties unknown
    time is of the essence
    a Jap is a Jap
    bound to an enemy nation
    a Jap is a Jap
    bound to the enemy

Lights change.

Scene 4

Yuki sleeps. A young Asian-American man enters. He is dressed casually. Each time he enters, he is dressed slightly different: first in the style of the 1940s, then the late 1960s, then the 1980s.

DAVID. Yuki. Wake up. Mother and father are crying in the living room.

YUKI. Why?

DAVID. The Japanese dropped an atomic bomb on Pearl Harbor.

YUKI. An atomic . . . ? (*Pause*) David, when I don't talk for a long time,
I forget what my voice sounds like. And I can remain silent forever.

DAVID. Mushroom cloud! The ocean is red with blood. People are
wandering about with half-melted faces. Babies burnt crisp like
pieces of charcoal. The putrid smell of rotten skin falling off in
chunks. The city is gone. People are crying without eyes. It's
over. Remember Pearl Harbor!

YUKI. What are you saying? Why do you talk so much?

Blackout.

Lights.

Yuki is sleeping. David enters.

DAVID. Yuki. Wake up. Mother and father are crying in the living room.

YUKI. Why?

DAVID. America just landed on Jupiter.

YUKI. Jupiter. Majestic mystery. Why invade it?

DAVID. Now there is an American flag on it. We are the first. Hot
dogs and baseball. Canned soup. Frozen vegetables. Mowing the
lawn. Christmas gifts. We are Number One.

YUKI. What are you saying? Why do you talk so much?

Blackout.

Lights.

Yuki is sleeping. David comes in.

DAVID. Yuki. Wake up. Mother and father are crying in the living room.

YUKI. Why?

DAVID. Because you are a whore. You don't understand what it
means to mix blood. "The good Lord created five races and if

He intended to have only one He would have done so. It was never intended that the races should be mixed."

YUKI. You don't know, David, how Robert collects small nails and screws in a glass jar as if they are precious and uses them when they are needed. Only I know that. He doesn't ever throw them away. You don't know.

DAVID. After looking into his blue eyes for a long time, you will forget that yours are black.

YUKI. I will always remember. Because my black eyes are reflected in his blue.

Music.

A procession of Japanese Picture Brides goes by, carrying an odd assortment of suitcases and bundles as if being herded onto a train.

The chorus sings their second love song.

Lights change.

Scene 5

Memory music. Robert comes in and sits beside Yuki.

ROBERT. When I order eggplant parmesan, I really like it when the mozzarella cheese gets burnt at the edges. I enjoy peeling paint off things. I can do that for hours. I eat potatoes for every meal, but prepared differently. Hash browns in the morning, French fries for lunch and baked potatoes for dinner. I don't like to stop reading a book in the middle of a page. I have to get to the end of a paragraph as close to the end of a page as possible before I quit. What does this all mean?

YUKI. You don't even like potatoes. You just insist on thinking that you do.

ROBERT. Stay with me.

YUKI. Stay with me.

Lights change.

Scene 6

Future. Three Asian Americans are having a banquet. The table is covered with a heap of food and drinks. Throughout the scene they constantly pass food to each other and eat and drink excessively. Yuki is serving the food. She is wearing a blonde wig.

MAN. I hear the Cotton Group averaged 125 on the most recent testing.

WOMAN 1. The only reason they improved their score is because now the Half-Cottons are in their group.

WOMAN 2. They stopped testing the Chestnut Group.

MAN. There is no need, I guess.

WOMAN 1. What about the other group?

WOMAN 2. The Coal Group? Last I heard their scores are even lower than the Chestnuts. Something like 115.

MAN. The question is not how each group can improve but how society can be best constructed accordingly.

WOMAN 1. But it is possible to implant Golden genes to other groups, isn't it? To improve human existence as a whole?

MAN. There are ways to improve their genes without actually using Golden genes. That way we will benefit from the improved efficiency from each group without diluting ourselves.

WOMAN 2. I hear they are in the process of mixing the Cotton, Chestnut and Coal groups. The ultimate goal is to create two classifications: Pure Gold and Assimilated.

MAN. That makes good sense to me. (*Making a toast*) To human progress!

Everyone toasts.

MAN, WOMAN 1 and 2 (*singing an angry rap song*). The congress congress?

congress recognized
that a grave injustice was done

as described
as described
as described by the
commission on war
commission on war?
commission on war
commission on
wartime
relocation
done to all citizens
of Japanese descent
Japanese descent?
Japanese descent
Japanese descent
ancestry

evacuation
relocation
internment
of civilians
during world war two
world war two?
world war two
internment of civilians
during world war two

enormous?
enormous damages
done to all citizens
of Japanese descent
Japanese descent?
Japanese descent
Japanese descent
ancestry

material

material?
material
losses
material
losses
intangible

significant
significant?
significant
human
significant
human
suffering

education
job training
appropriate
compensation has not been made
not been made?
not been made
compensation
compensation
compensation
compensation
compensation
compensation
has not been made

fundamental
liberties
fundamental
liberties
basic civil
liberties
violated
violated?
violated
basic civil

liberties
violated

on behalf
of the nation
on behalf
of the nation?
on behalf
of the nation
apology
apology?
apology

on behalf of the nation
apology
congress
congress?
congress
(Japanese)
congress
(Japanese)
apology

During the song, Yuki bends down to pick up a plate and notices her own blonde hair. She is horrified. While they sing, she tries frantically to rip her hair out.

YUKI (*screaming*). No, no, no, no. Not true! Robert! Robert!

Lights change.

Scene 7

Street music.

1935. Yuki and Robert on the town. Occasionally, other couples go by.

ROBERT. Hey, are you OK? What shall we see? Marlene Dietrich? *The Devil is a Woman? Night at the Opera? Mutiny on the Bounty?* Or would you like to stay home and listen to *Little Orphan Annie?*

YUKI. I want to see a musical.

ROBERT. Then *Top Hat* it is.

YUKI. Can we afford this?

ROBERT. It's only 25 cents. My treat, anyway. I'll even buy you pop-corn. When you turn thirty, I'll buy you a luxury car. I promise. Let's get married. We like the same movies. Life is romantic. Adventures are ahead. You and me.

YUKI. You and me against the world.

ROBERT. The world is good, Yuki. It's cozy and comfortable. People are in love. Can't you feel it?

'30s-style music is heard. Robert dances with Yuki. Others join them. They are very cheerful. It looks like a dance party.

Dark procession music.

A procession of The Grapes of Wrath *migrant workers goes by. There is a striking contrast between them and the well-dressed people on the streets. Nobody except Yuki sees the procession. As the procession exits, the '30s-style music resumes but quickly disintegrates.*

YUKI. I remember one summer night, I was out on the balcony. Old, crowded with geraniums and dried radishes. Paint peeling off the railing. I think I was thirteen. My father came out and stood next to me. I thought maybe this one time he would understand. So I said, "Papa, I'm burdened. I'm burdened."

ROBERT. I remember playing baseball when I was a boy. Koster Park. Long Island. But my parents never came to see the games. They were both exhausted from working at the factory making play-dough all day. Every day. Then my father hung himself.

YUKI. Do you still play baseball?

ROBERT. No. I stopped playing a long time ago. Are you still burdened?

YUKI. My father said, "You need sleep. That's all."

ROBERT. When you turn thirty, I will buy you a luxury car. I will buy you a Pierce-Arrow. I promise.

Lights change.

Scene 8

A beautiful 1960s city. Pristine. Green trees. Prosperity and peace are in the air. Yuki takes a chair at a street café. A Caucasian man comes to take her order.

WAITER. Hello, fellow human being. What may I serve you today? Café Equality? Racial Harmony tea? Turn-the-Other-Cheek muffin?

MAN AT THE CAFÉ. Racial Harmony should be just your cup of tea, honey.

YUKI. Do you have ice-cream?

WAITER. Of course. Love-Your-Neighbor-five-different-color-flavor. Perfectly separated in an enormous dish so you can enjoy each flavor.

YUKI. OK. It's beautiful here.

WAITER. Oh, are you a traveler? From China?

MAN AT THE CAFÉ. I know something about China myself. It's a beautiful country. Cats are a delicacy there, right dear?

YUKI. I don't know. I'm from New York. What city is this? (*Not recognizing where she is.*) The air is so fresh.

WAITER. Detroit.

YUKI. Detroit? Detroit, Michigan?

MAN AT THE CAFÉ. Yes, we owe this beautiful city to President Kennedy. He really came through. No crimes, no bums, no drugs. Good education for the kids. Paradise. Yes, indeed.

YUKI. Kennedy . . . Aren't we at war with Vietnam?

WAITER. Vietnam? Is that in China?

YUKI. No. You know Kennedy spent 140 billion dollars fighting . . .

MAN AT THE CAFÉ. Against crimes and poverty. 140 billion dollars spent on urban renewal for every major city in America.

YUKI (*very carefully*). I thought 58,000 American soldiers died . . .

WOMAN AT THE CAFÉ. No such thing. Couldn't happen. Everything is all right.

YUKI. Is Kennedy still the president?

MAN AT THE CAFÉ. Little girl, are you a citizen? It's 1965, of course he's still the president. Greatest president in American history.

WAITER. I bet he saved lives with his urban renewal projects. I bet he saved 58,000 American lives.

YUKI. . . . I bet.

WAITER. Would you like a banana with your ice-cream?

YUKI. No. I changed my mind. I'd like French toast.

WAITER. What would you like with it?

Pause.

YUKI. I would like . . . some maple syrup.

WAITER. OK.

YUKI. Thank you, fellow human being.

Waiter exits as cheerfully as he entered. Yuki is comfortable in the environment. An old homeless woman enters. It's the professor/neighbor. She is quite out of place. Yuki is startled. Nobody else sees her.

OLD WOMAN. Yuki, that means snow, doesn't it. Ha! Snow. White. Ha! Temporary. Meaningless. Unsubstantial. Well . . . Your mother had no idea how to adjust to life without a lot of money, did she? Married at nineteen. Her mother-in-law made sure she starved good.

YUKI. You . . . I don't know you!

OLD WOMAN. Husband drinking, kids screaming. She didn't have anywhere else to go anyway. Her mother didn't want her back. There were eleven girls in the family. Good riddance, that's it.

YUKI. You don't even exist!

OLD WOMAN. Well . . . Your mother saved money and bought a little table, didn't she. The family sat around it and had dinner. Your father didn't amount to much, she thought later. That's your history. Well . . . *Akiramenasai.* Nothing to be done about that. But you, you go to college.

YUKI. It was never like that! It never happened! Never happened!

Lights change.

Scene 9

1954. A young Asian couple is listening to the radio—news about the Korean War. They are obsessively cracking peanut shells and eating throughout the following scene. They talk to the radio, not to each other, and do not see Yuki. This is Yuki's childhood displaced in a false setting. Robert enters. He is in the present. He does not see anyone but Yuki and is unaware of the warped environment that Yuki is trapped in. Yuki interacts with Robert across time and spaces.

YUKI (*unsure*). Mother?

ROBERT. Happy birthday, Yuki. I want to take you out of the universe. Take you out of the loneliness. Take you out to dinner. I got you a present. A teacup. Blue. I know the colors you like. They are my colors.

YUKI. What?

WOMAN. We should have a television set. Mrs. Yokokawa told me they are getting one. She was soooo proud. Her husband doesn't make that kind of money. She even invited me to come watch. Their television.

MAN. *Yakamashi.* It's not natural. We don't need it.

WOMAN. Need! Is that what you want me to say to Mrs. Yokokawa?

MAN. What do you want me to do? Huh? What?

ROBERT. I got you a teacup because you need it. You like to drink tea in the mornings.

YUKI. And at nights.

WOMAN. You are important. An intellectual. You must realize, people think you make more money than you really do. We have to live up to that image. We must have a television set. I want a television set.

MAN. You are crazy.

ROBERT. I got you a blanket because you need it. You get cold at nights.

YUKI (*annoyed*). And in the mornings. Robert, I wanted flowers. Why can't you ever get me flowers? I hate it that I can always count on you to fix any electric appliances in my apartment but can't count on you to pick orchids over apples. I hate it that you can drive me anywhere in this country without getting lost but can't remember how to say "I love you" in Japanese. I hated it that my father couldn't talk about what a hard day he had at work because my mother became immediately critical of him.

ROBERT. Would you rather live with a broken toaster and get lost somewhere in Alabama? Yuki, it's OK with me if you have a hard day.

YUKI. I hated it that when my mother was lonely, my father was out drinking. I hate it that everything you give me has a purpose.

ROBERT. You hate meaningless knick-knacks, too. I think you should choose. Choose between yesterday and this minute. Between memories and poetry. Between soy sauce and syrup. Between me and the pain.

YUKI. I'm all of those things. Still, you're supposed to guarantee me love because it's my birthday. And you're my only card.

ROBERT. Why aren't teacups and blankets love? What is love then?

YUKI. Flowers. Not a small table you save your money to buy so you have something to eat dinner on. Not paying the rent. Not buying a TV set. I want flowers.

WOMAN. Don't you care when we have children, they may grow up to be the kind of people who will be friends with cab-drivers' kids?

MAN. Don't let them.

ROBERT. Yuki? Happy birthday.

Yuki is now concentrating on the couple and does not pay attention to Robert.

WOMAN. What if they grow up and want to marry Koreans?

MAN. You are really crazy.

ROBERT. Yuki, flowers will just die. You can keep the teacup and the blanket.

YUKI (*frustrated, to the couple*). Why are you so ignorant?

The couple doesn't hear her.

Robert fades away.

WOMAN. Koreans. You know, the little dirty corner store is owned by Koreans. It smells bad in there. I think they cheat, too. The government should do something about them. To protect the national security now we are at war with Korea. "The hours between 8 pm and 6 am hereby designated as the hours of curfew. Effective at 12 noon, P.W.T., June 2, 1942."

MAN. 1954.

WOMAN. 1954. "All persons of Japanese . . ."

MAN. Korean.

WOMAN. "Korean ancestry, both alien and non-alien, residing or being within the said California portion of Military Area No. 2, shall, during the hours of curfew, be within their places of residence. Their racial characteristics are such that we can not understand or trust even the citizen Japanese."

MAN. Korean.

WOMAN. "The citizen Korean. A viper is nonetheless a viper wherever the egg is hatched."

They crack peanut shells in silence and keep eating for awhile. The radio keeps playing. A long pause. Yuki sits beside them. They don't see or hear her.

YUKI (*sobbing*). I'm sorry. I'm sorry there are things that make you unhappy. I wish you had a television set. I wish I could have gotten you one.

The Picture Brides' procession enters again. The chorus sings the third love song.

Lights change.

Scene 10

Yuki is gardening in a pool of light.

YUKI. Instead of roses, I'll plant teacups. Instead of orchids, I'll plant blankets. Because I need them.

Out of the ground emerges Robert.

YUKI. Instead of stars, I'll grow Robert.

Lights up on the barbed wires surrounding the ground. Then lights down on the garden and Robert. Yuki moves into the visiting room. She is surrounded by the chorus.

CHORUS (*sings as her inner voice*). In the fabrics of the stars
          Maya's cosmic time
          unfolds in a circle
          step on the wave
          remember
          mixing blood
          yours and mine
          in the future
          back
          back
          back
          at the beginning

Future. Yuki is in a war relocation camp. Robert enters wearing a military uniform. They are divided by the fence. This is an intimate love scene.

ROBERT. How are you?

YUKI. . . . What?

ROBERT. . . . I miss you.

YUKI. I dream about you.

ROBERT. Isn't this a beautiful day, Yuki? Almost like Spring.

YUKI. I can hear the family in the next cell, yelling at each other, crying and yelling all night long. Every day.

ROBERT. My niece had her fifth birthday last month. She had a new dress on at the party. A pink one with lace. Everyone says hello. Have you had any birthday parties in here?

YUKI. There are no dividers for the communal toilets. We are exposed. Exposed to strangers.

ROBERT. My brother bought a car. Can you imagine? He loves it. He sends his love.

YUKI. Sometimes they cook mutton for dinner. Those days the bloody smell fills the camp. Older people go hungry.

ROBERT. Please, Yuki. Why can't life be easy with you? Tell me about the dance parties and the movies you see. Tell me about the wonderful vegetable garden your parents now have the time for. Tell me about the good things. Let me hear you laugh.

YUKI. I see many movies. Love stories. New movies about what love is in 2094. People fall in love with others who look like them. Have you noticed that married people begin to look alike after some years?

Silence from Robert.

YUKI. Look at me, Robert. What are you afraid of? Are you afraid of running out of time? Time for what? Birthday parties? Graduation parties? Tupperware parties? How much time do we need not to remember? Where am I? Look at me. (*Silence*) I have no memories anymore, Robert. No memories of my childhood. I don't remember the path I walked to school. I don't remember faces or names of children there. I don't remember any school trips or volleyball games. Instead, all the small events that made me what I am bleed inside me. They continue bleeding until one day I give birth to a bloody cyst, putrid with rotten memories.

ROBERT. Next week I ship out to the Pacific. You know the Japanese are about to invade California. Their force is powerful because they own so much land and business here. Who knows what kind of network exits for their purpose already. We are prepared to use nuclear destruction on Japan. This is the beginning of the end.

YUKI. You may run into my brother in the Pacific, Robert. David is with the Japanese Army now. He wanted to be a whole person who belonged to a whole country. (*Bitterly*) Give him my love if you see him. His birthday is coming up.

Pause.

ROBERT. I made a mistake, Yuki. I love you, but you eat fish and rice for breakfast. That's not right. Not eating breakfast food for breakfast is not normal. Not eating cereal and toast for breakfast is too difficult. Life with you is too difficult. I'm sorry.

YUKI. Poor Robert.

ROBERT. Goodbye.

Yuki sings a heartbreaking love song to departing Robert. The words are that of "The Star-Spangled Banner."

Lights change.

Scene 11

Back to the wedding. The setting is identical to the wedding in the first scene, but this time Yuki is wearing a Japanese wedding head-piece instead of the veil.

ROBERT. Yuki, I want to take you out of the universe. Take you out of the loneliness. Take you out to dinner. I got you a present. A teacup. Blue. I know the colors you like. They are my colors.

YUKI. No. They are my colors. Different.

ROBERT. Won't you like red hair?

YUKI. Like your sister's?

ROBERT. What? Oh . . .

YUKI. No. I would like purple hair. Purple like you've never seen on anyone. Purple that doesn't make sense. Unrecognizable. That's what I would like.

Wedding music.

The priest enters.

PRIEST. Dearly beloved, we are gathered here today to join this man . . .

Sudden music.

The same procession as the first scene enters and dances wildly around Yuki and Robert. The priest and Yuki join in.

Music stops abruptly.

ROBERT. Stay with me.

YUKI. Come with me.

Music suddenly starts again.

The procession exits. Yuki exits with them.

Music stops abruptly.

Robert is left alone on the stage.

Silence.

Blackout.

The End.

NOTES ON CONTRIBUTORS

CATHERINE FILLOUX'S plays include *Lemkin's House* (McGinn-Cazale Theatre, 78th Street Theatre Lab, New York City & Kamerni Teatar, Sarajevo, Bosnia); *The Beauty Inside* (New Georges, New York City & InterAct); *Eyes of the Heart* (National Asian American Theatre Co., New York City); *Silence of God* (Contemporary American Theater Festival); *Mary and Myra* (CATF & Todd Mountain Theater Project); *Arthur's War* (Theatreworks/USA, New York City); *Photographs From S-21*, a short play performed worldwide; *Escuela Del Mundo* (The Ohio State University); *The Beauty Inside*, translated into Arabic for a workshop in Rabat, Morocco. Her operas include *The Floating Box* (Composed by Jason Kao Hwang; premiere at Asia Society, New York City; CD by New World Records); a commission from Cambodian Living Arts for opera libretto *Where Elephants Weep* with composer Him Sophy. Her awards include the Peacewriting Award (Omnicenter for Peace), the Kennedy Center Fund for New American Play's Roger L. Stevens Award; the Eric Kocher Playwrights Award (National Playwrights Conference, O'Neill Theater); Callaway Award (New Dramatists), Fulbright Senior Specialist (Cambodia & Morocco); James Thurber Playwright-In-Residence; Asian Cultural Council Artist's Residency; Filloux has won the Nausicaa Franco-American Play Contest and been the recipient of the Rockefeller MAP Fund (for a project with Southern Rep. in New Orleans) and is a four-time Heideman Award finalist (Actors Theatre of Louisville). Her oral history project with the Cambodian Women's Group, St. Rita's Refugee Center, Bronx is titled *A Circle of Grace*. Filloux's plays are published by Smith & Kraus, Playscripts, Inc., Vintage, & Dramatic Publishing. Her articles have been published in *American Theatre, Manoa: In the Shadow of Angkor, The Drama Review* and *Contemporary Theatre Review* (Routledge/UK). She has received an MFA. in Dramatic Writing from the Tisch School of the Arts, NYU, and a French Baccalaureate with Honors from Toulon, France. She is a member of New Dramatists, Writers Guild of America, New Georges, The League of Professional Theatre Women and a co-founder of Theatre without Borders.

CAROL MARTIN, Ph.D. is an Associate Professor of Drama at Tisch School of the Arts, NYU. Martin writes on contemporary American and Japanese performance as well as performance and globalization. Her essays and interviews have appeared in academic journals in the US and abroad and in *The New York Times* and have been translated into French, Polish, Chinese and Japanese. Her awards include a Visiting Professor Fellowship at Tokyo University; Best Issue of the Year by Professional/Scholarly Publishing Division of the Association of American Publishers for a special issue of *TDR* on Japanese Performance and the De La Torre Bueno for her book, *Dance Marathons*. Grants received by her include the Fulbright; National Endowment for the Humanities; Mellon and Tisch Senior Faculty Development grants. Martin's books include *Brecht Sourcebook*; A *Sourcebook of Feminist Theatre*: *On and Beyond the Stage* and *Dance Marathons*: *Performing American Culture of the 1920s and 1930s*. She has lectured and presented papers on theatre and performance in many parts of the world including Singapore, Shanghai, Tokyo, Hong Kong and Paris. Martin has appeared as an academic specialist on the American History channel discussing popular performance in the 1930s and on the BBC, discussing female playwrights and literature. Her current work is on documentary theatre.

CHIORI MIYAGAWA was born in Nagano, Japan. She travels in time and space in her life and in her plays. She interviewed men on death row in Huntsville, TX (*Broken Morning*, supported by TCG's Extended Collaboration Grant and Dallas Theater Center); traveled to Bath, England, where the first recognized woman astronomer lived in the 18th century (*Comet Hunter*, supported by EST/Alfred P. Sloan commission) and explored life in Chekhov's Russia (*Leaving Eden*, supported by The Meadows School of the Arts at Southern Methodist University). Her deepest inspiration comes from the forty-five minute private audience she spent with The Dalai Lama in Dharamsala, India, in 1998. Miyagawa's other plays include *Nothing Forever* (published in *Positiv/Negative Women*), *Yesterday's Window* (premiere: New York Theatre Workshop, published in *Take Ten*); *Woman Killer* (Crossing Jamaica Avenue in co-production with HERE, published in *Plays and Playwrights* 2002), *Jamaica Avenue* (premiere: New York International Fringe Festival, published in *Tokens? The NYC Asian American Experiences on Stage*), *FireDance* (Voice and Vision), *Antigones*

Red (published in *Take Ten II*), *Red Again/Antigone Project* (Women's Project) and *Thousand Years Waiting* (Crossing Jamaica Avenue in co-production with PS122). She has been awarded many grants and fellowships including the New York Foundation for the Arts Playwriting Fellowship; McKnight Playwriting Fellowship; Van Lier Playwriting Fellowship and Asian Cultural Council Fellowship. Miyagawa is a member of New Artists, the Co-Artistic Director of Crossing Jamaica Avenue and a board member of the Alliance of Resident Theaters of New York. She lives in New York City with visual artist Hap Tivey.

BETTY SHAMIEH is a Palestinian-American writer and actor. Her play *Roar* had its off-Broadway premiere at The New Group under the direction of Tony-nominated Marion McClinton, starring Annabella Sciorra and Sarita Choudhury. *Roar* was selected as a *New York Times* Critic's Pick for four consecutive weeks. Her play *The Black Eyed* premiered at the Magic Theatre in May 2005. Betty performed in her play of monologues *Chocolate in Heat—Growing-Up Arab in America*, which had three sold-out and critically acclaimed off-off-Broadway runs and subsequently toured over twenty universities across the United States. She has been awarded an N.E.A. grant; the New Dramatists Van Lier Fellowship, a residency at the Rockefeller Foundation's Bellagio Study and Conference Center, an Arts International grant, a Yaddo residency and the New York Foundation for the Arts Playwriting Award. She was selected as a 2004–05 Harvard University Clifton Visiting Artist and is currently serving on the New York Foundation for the Arts playwriting advisory board. Shamieh is a screenwriting professor at Marymount Manhattan College and a graduate of Harvard University and the Yale School of Drama. She has been commissioned by Second Stage Theatre and Trinity Repertory. She was selected as the 2005–06 Bunting Fellow at Harvard/Radcliffe. Her life and work have been profiled in *American Theatre* magazine, *Time Out*, *The Washington Post*, *The International Herald Tribune* and *The New York Times*.

SAVIANA STANESCU is a Romanian-born playwright "with roots in Albania, Macedonia, Greece and . . . Long Island, where my grandmother was born. She was three years old when her family took their younger children and emigrated to Romania (yeah, I know, strange idea . . .)." She has published four books of poetry: *Making Love on the Barbed Wire*, *Advice for Housewives and Muses*, *Outcast* (all in Romanian) and *Diary of a Clone* (in English). Stanescu's published dramatic writing includes *The Inflatable Apocalypse* (Best Romanian Play of the Year 1999); *Black Milk* (four plays in Romanian and English) and *Final Countdown/Compte a Rebours* (winner of the Antoine Vitez Center Award, Paris). Her plays have been presented in the US, the UK, France, Austria, Hungary, Macedonia, Montenegro and, of course, Romania. Recent New York productions include *Yokastas* (co-author Richard Schechner) at La MaMa Theater; *Balkan Blues* at the Fringe Festival and *Waxing West* at The Lark Theatre. In Europe, she was Writer-in-Residence at Kultur Kon!takt (2001); co-curator for the Annual British and Romanian Contemporary Writing Seminar (1997–02) and for Theater des Augenblicks' (Vienna, Austria) Performing Arts Festival focused on the Balkans (2002). She has worked as the Interdisciplinary Projects Director for the Museum of Literature, Bucharest and is a theatre/arts critic for Radio Free Europe. Stanescu holds an MA in Performance Studies (2001–02 Fulbright Fellow) and an MFA in Dramatic Writing (John Golden Award in Playwriting), both from Tisch School of the Arts, NYU. Stanescu is currently Associate Artist with The Lark Theatre Company, Playwright-in-Residence of East Coast Artists (director: Richard Schechner) and Adjunct Faculty at NYU, Drama Department.

ZOHAR TZUR graduated with an MFA from the Rita and Burton Goldberg Department of Dramatic Writing at the Tisch School of the Arts, NYU, in May 2004. Her full length play *War and High Heels* won the 2004 Goldberg Playwriting Award, one of the most prestigious playwriting awards for a university student in the country. Tzur was a finalist for the 2003 Heideman Award at Actors' Theatre of Louisville, Kentucky for her play *Border* which was also produced as part of the 2004 American Living Room Festival at HERE Arts Center, New York. She was awarded The Harry Kondoleon Award for Playwriting. Her plays have been mounted as productions and staged readings in New York City including The Goldberg Theatre and The Manhattan Theatre Workshop. *My Political Israeli Play* was chosen for the 2004 Envision retreat for six established women writers, produced by Voice and Vision. The play, developed during the workshop, was part of the Voice and Vision summer play festival at Bard College in Annandale, New York. Thereafter, Tzur received a residency at Voice and Vision and was commissioned to write a new play which was scheduled to receive a staged reading the following summer. Her full-length comic screenplay, *The Birthday Suit*, is the 2005 winner of the CineStory Screenwriting Competition in Los Angeles and is now among the sixteen final scripts for the CineStory Screenwriting competition.

After serving in the military, Zohar graduated with a BFA in film from Tel Aviv University and worked in the television industry in Israel as a writer and director for variety of projects. Her thirty-minute screenplays—*The Underworld* and *Knocked Up*—won the 'Snunit' Award (Israeli Television) two consecutive years in a row. She also collaborated with The Israeli Opera House on a full-length documentary which she wrote and directed. The film had several screenings at the Tel Aviv Cinemateque theatre.

Tzur is currently living in New York and working as a screenwriter and a playwright for a number of projects.